Jossey-Bass Teacher

Jossey-Bass Teacher provides educators with practical knowledge and tools to create a positive and lifelong impact on student learning. We offer classroom-tested and research-based teaching resources for a variety of grade levels and subject areas. Whether you are an aspiring, new, or veteran teacher, we want to help you make every teaching day your best.

From ready-to-use classroom activities to the latest teaching framework, our value-packed books provide insightful, practical, and comprehensive materials on the topics that matter most to K–12 teachers. We hope to become your trusted source for the best ideas from the most experienced and respected experts in the field.

Titles in the Jossey-Bass Teacher Survival Guide Series

Math Teacher's Survival Guide: Practical Strategies, Management Techniques, and Reproducibles for New and Experienced Teachers, Grades 5–12
Judith A. Muschla, Gary Robert Muschla and Erin Muschla   ISBN 978-0-470-40764-6

A Survival Kit for the Elementary School Principal: with Reproducible Forms, Checklists & Letters
Abby Barry Bergman   ISBN 978-0-7879-6639-3

The Reading Teacher's Survival Kit: Ready-To-Use Checklists, Activities and Materials to Help All Students Become Successful Readers
Wilma H. Miller Ed.D.   ISBN 978-0-13-042593-5

Biology Teacher's Survival Guide: Tips, Techniques & Materials for Success in the Classroom
Michael F. Fleming   ISBN 978-0-13-045051-7

The Elementary/Middle School Counselor's Survival Guide, Third Edition
John J. Schmidt Ed.D.   978-0-470-56085-3

The Substitute Teaching Survival Guide, Grades K–5: Emergency Lesson Plans and Essential Advice
John Dellinger   ISBN 978-0-7879-7410-7

The Substitute Teaching Survival Guide, Grades 6–12: Emergency Lesson Plans and Essential Advice
John Dellinger   ISBN 978-0-7879-7411-4

SECOND EDITION

The ENGLISH TEACHER'S SURVIVAL GUIDE

Ready-to-Use Techniques & Materials for Grades 7–12

Mary Lou Brandvik
Katherine S. McKnight

JOSSEY-BASS
A Wiley Imprint
www.josseybass.com

Published by Jossey-Bass
A Wiley Imprint
989 Market Street, San Francisco, CA 94103-1741—www.josseybass.com

Library of Congress Cataloging-in-Publication Data

Brandvik, Mary Lou.
  The English teacher's survival guide: ready-to-use techniques & materials for grades 7-12 / Mary Lou Brandvik, Katherine S. McKnight.
    p. cm.
  Includes bibliographical references and index.
  ISBN 978-0-470-52513-5 (pbk.)
  1. Language arts (Secondary)—United States—Handbooks, manuals, etc. 2. High school teaching—United States—Handbooks, manuals, etc. 3. Classroom management—United States—Handbooks, manuals, etc. 4. English teachers—United States—Handbooks, manuals, etc. I. McKnight, Katherine S. (Katherine Siewert) II. Title.

LB1631.B762 2011
428.0071′2—dc22   2010037985

Printed in the United States of America
FIRST EDITION
PB Printing 10 9 8 7 6 5 4 3 2

Contents

For Olivia, Nora, Ava, Freya, and Esme, whose creativity, enthusiasm,
and love fill my heart with joy every day.

Mary Lou Brandvik

To Jim, Ellie, and Colin, who bring joy to my life, and to the teachers who make a difference
every day in preparing our children to be members of our democratic society.

Katherine S. McKnight

About This Resource

This updated second edition explores successful approaches to teaching English and classroom management. It is a book intended for both new teachers who are looking for solutions to potential problems and for more experienced teachers who may be staggering under an enormous teaching load and conflicting demands.

Most of us have chosen to be teachers of English because we love to read or write—or both—and we want to instill and nurture this same passion in our students. We want to be inspiring and provocative, caring and nurturing—a composite of the best teachers who have taught us. While thoroughly satisfying, the teaching of English is also extraordinarily demanding. The reality of the school day—interruptions, forms to fill out, bell schedules, alphabet grades, tardy slips, admits, PA announcements—drains any teacher's energy, vitality, and creativity. This book will encourage you to look at yourself and your job with a bit of selfishness. To regain or maintain the idealism that caused us to become teachers, we all need to manage and organize our professional lives in such a way that we also have time for ourselves, our families, and our lives outside the classroom.

The English Teacher's Survival Guide, Second Edition will help you do just that. It offers suggestions for beginning the year and managing and planning your classroom efficiently. It will help you organize your teaching units and design your daily lessons. It offers ideas for developing a grading philosophy and will show you ways to involve both parents and students in the evaluation process. This second edition has a new chapter on media literacy and technology and updated resources from the previous edition. It will also help you address controversial issues such as confidentiality and censorship and provides numerous reproducible materials for teaching writing, reading, listening, speaking, and viewing.

All of us have heard the term "excellent school." We are told that in an excellent school, students should be doing authentic work rather than sitting in rows and working on worksheets or activities with little relevance. We are told that subjects should be integrated in order to promote intense, interesting learning activities that are meaningful to students. Instead of filling out workbook exercises to learn the mechanics of language, students should be using writing for a real readership. We are told that schools should promote and encourage collaborative activities as well as competitive ones. And, we are told, excellent schools go far beyond the standardized test routine in the evaluation of students by setting up portfolios—collections that show the progress of student work over time. Most of all, we are told, excellent schools engender an excitement and enthusiasm for learning that students, teachers, and parents share.

An excellent school is everyone's goal. We each want our classroom to resemble this model as closely as possible. But how do we make it happen? Times have changed, we've changed, and our students have changed. Yesterday's lesson plans aren't meeting our needs or those of our students. Along with plenty of suggestions for writing and reading activities, the *Survival Guide* includes specific suggestions for integrating the teaching of speaking, listening, writing, literature, and viewing. It will show you how to introduce cooperative learning activities in your classroom, offer suggestions for portfolio assessment, and provide models for integrating technology. It is intended to help you create an excellent classroom that reflects the excitement for learning that every one of us desires.

About the Authors

Mary Lou Brandvik graduated summa cum laude from Concordia College in Moorhead, Minnesota, with a B.A. in English and art and earned a master's degree in English education from the University of Illinois. She has taught in public schools in Illinois and Minnesota, as well as at Bemidji State University in Minnesota. She has led in-service workshops in Minnesota and was a participant in the Northern Minnesota Writing Project. Brandvik chaired the Bemidji Public Schools' Writing Curriculum Committee and was selected Teacher of the Year in the Bemidji Public Schools in 1988.

In 1991 she received the Lila B. Wallace Teacher-Scholar Award from the National Endowment for the Humanities. During the sabbatical that accompanied the award, she researched the literature of the Ojibwe. She is also the author of *Writing Process Activities Kit: 75 Ready-to-Use Lessons and Worksheets for Grades 7–12.*

Katherine S. McKnight is a former middle and high school teacher who taught in the Chicago Public Schools for ten years and went on to earn her Ph.D. in curriculum and instruction: reading, writing, and literacy from the University of Illinois at Chicago. She is currently associate professor in secondary education at National-Louis University and lives in Chicago. She is also a recipient of the Faculty in Excellence Teaching Award from Northeastern Illinois University. Serving as a consultant for the National Council of Teachers of English, she works in schools all over the United States in many contexts—urban, rural, and suburban—providing professional development in adolescent literacy, curriculum differentiation, arts integration, and strategies for teaching English in the inclusive classroom. She is a regular presenter at local and national conferences, and her recent books include *Teaching Writing in the Inclusive Classroom, Teaching the Classics in the Inclusive Classroom, The Second City Guide to Improve in the Classroom,* and *The Teacher's Big Book of Graphic Organizers.*

chapter 1

BEGINNING *the* SCHOOL YEAR

- Designing a lesson for Day One
- Learning still more about your students
- Helping students to know one another

I'll never forget my first day of teaching. I was so nervous that I reached into my desk for hand lotion and, instead, poured white Elmer's glue all over my hands.

It's the first day of school in your district and it is fraught with capital letters for both you and your students. For the student there are The Outfit, The Supplies, The Bus Route, The Locker Assignment, The Lunch Schedule, The Teachers, The Program Schedule, The Seat Assignments. For teachers there are The Class Lists, The Bell Schedules, The Read-on-the-First-Day Announcements from the Principal's Office, The Add-or-Drop Lists of Student Names from the Counseling Office, The Student Handbook, The Fire-Drill Explanation, The Sign-up Sheet for Audiovisual Materials, The Computer Lab Schedule, and The Library Orientation Schedule. For teachers and students alike, the first day of school is indeed momentous. This is the day students size us up as competent or incompetent, nice or mean, fair or unfair, caring or uncaring.

One of the most important plans we make is the lesson design for the first day of the year. Some teachers spend the entire first class period making seat assignments, handing out books, and reading long lists of classroom and school regulations. If every teacher does this, and many school administrations encourage teachers to do so, a single student may hear a nearly identical set of regulations six or seven times on the first day alone. It is not the tone most schools or classroom teachers wish to set, but it is a tone students perceive and one that's difficult to undo.

Of course, all of us are concerned with discipline. "Be strict in the beginning," they tell us in methods classes and in the teachers' lounge. But what happens when you let up and the students are so intimidated they are afraid to talk? There are guidelines and limits, of course. Your position tells the students you are the teacher in the classroom. How you function will tell them whether you are up to the task, and you will function best if your planning is thorough and organized. Begin setting a classroom tone and atmosphere that is right for you from the very first day of school. If you are required to read school regulations and policies, do it on a subsequent day.

DESIGNING A LESSON FOR DAY ONE

In setting the tone for your classroom, consider the following plan for the first day.

Welcome Your Students to the School and Your Classroom

Take note of what is special for students on this day. If, for example, your students are ninth or tenth graders, this may be their first day in high school. They may have come from several junior highs or middle schools or from other communities. They must form new friendships and solve new problems in the more complex, less sheltered world of the high school. If they are seniors, this is the first day of their last year of high school—a time they've looked forward to with anticipation. There may be transfer students who are unfamiliar with the campus and know few classmates. Some students are raring to get busy; others may not want to be in school at all. View your school and classroom through your students' eyes, and acknowledge and honor the emotions and questions they may have concerning the new school year and your class.

Introduce Yourself

Give information about your own background, jobs you have held, your family, your interests. Explain why you chose teaching English as a career. Show that you are proud to be a teacher and that you value and respect your work.

Introduce Your Subject

Be positive about the class you are teaching. Explain its benefits, and elaborate on these clearly and specifically. What is it the students can expect to learn from you? What new skills will they practice and acquire? What books or novels can they look forward to reading? What units or projects do you have planned? What can they look forward to with eagerness? Be enthusiastic and inclusive as you do so. Don't expect students to understand why they should take a particular class. Many are enrolled only because the course is required. Remember that not every student likes English and not every student hates English. However, each needs to know what he or she will learn in your classroom.

Don't qualify your first-day message by suggesting that some students will succeed while others will fail. Be sure your students understand each is beginning a new year with a clean slate. Let your students know they have a responsibility to attend class regularly, attempt each assignment, and participate in the class. Assure them that if each approaches the class in this manner, each can be a successful student.

Teach a Lesson on the First Day

The first day of school, when motivation is high, is the time for both students and teachers to make a good first impression. Capitalize on this readiness by avoiding a deadly review, and begin with a real lesson that will show off what both you and your students can do. Your goal should be to have your students do something successfully or learn something each can use immediately. The following exercises are a variety of nonthreatening first-day options to foster student success, help set a tone of cooperation and a sense of community in your classroom, and encourage and foster immediate student participation.

Lesson One: Self-Introductions

Have your students write answers to the following directions. Then have them use their answers as a guide while introducing themselves orally to the whole class.

- Write your name.
- Write the name of the city where you were born.
- Write the name of your best subject.
- Write the name of a subject that is difficult for you.
- Do you have a job? If so, where? Please describe it briefly. What are some good parts of the job? Some drawbacks?
- List three things you can do well.
- Tell one thing your best friend doesn't know about you.

Using their answers for notes, ask students to stand and take turns introducing themselves to the class. The teacher might introduce herself or himself first as a model for others. Encourage students to listen carefully because they may be called on to repeat some of the information they have heard. After each person offers his or her sketch, ask the next person to summarize orally what the previous student revealed. When the introductions are complete, call on individuals to identify someone in the class and give one or two details about him or her from memory. By the end of an exercise such as this, your students will no longer be strangers to one another, and you are likely to know each student by name and also by what they are willing to reveal about themselves.

Lesson Two: Partner Introductions

Pair students (preferably stranger-to-stranger to encourage new friendships), and ask them to spend approximately five minutes each interviewing one another. Point out that unusual questions elicit the most interesting information—for example, "What did you learn this summer that you'll remember for the rest of your life?" Encourage students to take notes during the interview. Give them time to write a brief profile emphasizing the two most interesting things they learned about their partner. Allow students to check their information with their partners. Finally, ask each student to read the profile to the entire class. If students resist speaking or seem particularly insecure about speaking and reading in front of the whole class, you might have them form groups of six to eight students to make their introductions.

A more challenging option is to ask students to recast their profiles into another format, such as a poem, lyric, letter, or story. One format that is accessible to all students is the recipe. Brainstorm with the class for a list of cooking terms, such as *bake, broil, mix, whip,* and *simmer.* After you have listed several terms on the blackboard, suggest they write a recipe for the person they interviewed. The following is a sample:

Mike Peter Surprise Delight

To create this exotic senior, combine:

> 1 family of 8 children

Sift out the third youngest son.
Beat rapidly, adding:

> clear, blue eyes
> 1 pinch of shyness
> a heaping love of drums and carpentry

Bake at 350° for 17 years and frost with an application to vocational school.
Serve immediately. Your guests will be sure to ask for more.

Lesson Three: Props with Introductions

Another approach to interviewing is to have the whole class interview you on the first day and move on to interviewing one another on the next day. On Day One, bring to class several meaningful personal objects (mementos, documents, and a piece of clothing, for example) and encourage your students to base their questions on these. (What is it? How was it acquired? Why is it important to you? What plans do you have for its future?) Following the questioning, ask the students to write a brief profile of you either individually or collaboratively in groups to read aloud. Near the end of the period, call on students to identify the questions that produced the most information. Questions that pursue a point, for example, garner the most information.

On the following day, students bring to class three items important to each of them. Stress sentimental value as opposed to material value and the importance of keeping the items stored safely when they are not in use. Students present and explain their items to the class, and class members ask follow-up questions. Additional activities might include student-authored profiles of class members or papers based on the significance of one of the author's possessions. Final polished versions may be read aloud, displayed on a bulletin board, or bound as a class book for everyone to enjoy (Kuehn, 1992).

Lesson Four: Freewriting (or Rush Writing)

Introduce the concept of freewriting or rush writing (writing without stopping or editing for a specific number of minutes). Give your students a topic such as, "The quality I like best about myself is . . ." or "The best class I've ever taken was . . ." Have students write for approximately five minutes. Be sure they understand they will eventually read their writing to the class. Give them a minute or two to edit briefly and then ask each to read aloud. Some teachers let students read these early writings while seated at their desks to keep the activity nonthreatening.

If someone declines to read, suggest that you will come back to him or her after others have had a chance to read, and do so. Don't let this exercise become a showdown between you and a reluctant student. When this student sees that classmates are reading their writings aloud, she will soon contribute too. After everyone has read, ask the class to recall specific answers they particularly liked and explain to the author why they liked the answer. This is an excellent way to give students positive, supportive peer feedback.

Lesson Five: Creative Excuses

Students brainstorm a list of four or five chores they dislike, select one item, and then write a creative excuse directed to a parent, teacher, or some other adult explaining why he or she should no longer be expected to do it. Encourage students to be as wildly imaginative as possible, and discourage responses such as, "I don't have my English paper today, because I had to work late at my part-time job." You may want to read the following sample aloud:

1. Washing the dishes
2. Cleaning the bathroom
3. Cleaning the fireplace
4. Cleaning up after the cat
5. Taking care of my younger sister
6. ?

Mom,

I have a cut on my hand. No, it's not bleeding, but it really hurts. I know it doesn't show, but it throbs and aches. I think it could probably get infected if I stick it into greasy dishwater. And, if that happens, I might even end up in the emergency room. Then I won't be able to help you with the dishes for a long time. So you do them tonight, OK? I'll do them when my hand gets better—really. Just let me rest here and watch TV. Please. It doesn't throb so much in this position.—Eric

Lesson Six: Stretching the Meaning of Words

Write a story that stretches the meaning of one word in every direction. Some possible words to use are:

- Out ~Up~
- Run
- Down
- Side
- Set
- Back

A student's story based on the word *down* might look like this:

When I lost my bookbag I figured that I was down on my luck. Feeling dogeared and down, I decided to go downtown to visit my best friend, Charlie. He is absolutely the best person to talk to when you're feeling down. On the way to Charlie's house, I decided to down a big container of lemonade. I guess it didn't go down well because when I got to Charlie's house, I had to lie down because I wasn't feeling all that well.

Lesson Seven: Lists

Lists of ten is a quick scaffolding idea that helps student find topics to write about. It also provides you with the opportunity to get to know your students. Have the students take out a sheet of paper and create lists of ten for each of the following categories. It is helpful to time the students so that they are able to stay on task and more freely write (Passman & McKnight, 2007).

Here are some suggested categories:

- Ten favorite songs
- Ten favorite foods
- Ten places I'd like to visit
- Ten favorite games
- Ten people I'd like to have dinner with
- Ten important goals for the future
- Ten important things I'd like to learn more about

You may have the students choose one idea from their lists that surprised them or is special in some way, write about it briefly, and then explain it or read it to the class. Encourage students to keep these lists as a resource for later writing projects.

By introducing a first-day lesson such as one of these, you will have achieved a number of objectives: your students will have written and shared their writing with a real audience; you will have begun to establish a positive, cooperative atmosphere; you will have eliminated some of the tension and fear associated with new experiences; and, ideally, you will have shared laughter.

LEARNING STILL MORE ABOUT YOUR STUDENTS

In middle schools, junior high schools, and high schools, we frequently meet 150 students every day even though the schedule breaks them into segments of twenty-five to thirty-five. In addition, we are expected to teach students with diverse ability levels and from varied linguistic backgrounds. To be effective at the secondary level, we need to know our students well and to get to know them as quickly as possible.

Name Tags or Student Name Plates

To take roll and learn student names, teachers have frequently begun the first day of class with assigned seating, and this arrangement frequently remains the same throughout the year. However, if you want your classroom seating plan to be more flexible, if you are also concerned that students learn one another's names, and if you want to begin moving students from large groups to small groups early in the year, consider distributing name tags or having each student design one of his or her own.

Another option is to have students fold a large sheet of notebook paper into thirds and to have them print their names in large letters on the middle section of the folded paper. The paper will sit upright on a desk, and the teacher and the students are able to read one another's names easily. (See Figure 1.1.) Students may keep these name sheets in their notebooks and begin the first few weeks of classes by placing this identification on their desks. This is also a useful and helpful way to identify students when guest speakers are invited into the classroom.

Questionnaires

Some information about your students will be available prior to the first day of school in cumulative records, tests results, and discussions with other teachers (but don't let negative comments color your perspective). You may be able to receive information about a student's health status from the school nurse, but you may have to seek it out. It will also be possible to ask for additional information about students during parent-teacher conferences. However, much of this information will come to you later in the school year. Consequently you may wish to design and distribute student questionnaires or inventories at the beginning of the year and at other appropriate times throughout the school year. Forms 1.1 through 1.4 (which you may duplicate in their entirety or use as a basis for developing your own) are useful in surveying student interests, experiences, spoken languages, favorite subjects, friends, classroom expectations, and ability to study at home. This information will help you know your students more quickly and will be an immediate aid in planning your curriculum and in designing both large- and small-group activities.

FIGURE 1.1 Name Plates

Getting Acquainted

Name _____ Date _____

Some of my friends call me by my nickname, _____.

Right now, I'm _____ years old, and my birthday is _____.

I live with (names, and relation to you) _____

at the following address _____.

My phone number is _____.

My best subject is _____.

My most difficult subject is _____.

One thing that makes me happy is _____

_____, and I am really sad when _____

_____.

Someday I hope to _____.

Getting to Know You

Name _____ Date _____

1. Suppose you are a major character in one of your favorite books. What is your name? _____

2. In what book do you appear?_____

3. Write the names of five people you don't know but would like to.

   _____

   _____

   _____

   _____

   _____

4. Name five things that you can do as well as or better than anyone else.

   _____

   _____

   _____

   _____

   _____

5. Many authors have used pen names to substitute for their own. Invent a pen name for yourself. _____

6. Explain your choice below.

   _____

   _____

Reading Inventory

Name _____ Date _____

Reading is one of the most valuable things we do. As we work to develop our skills, it is helpful to understand how our attitudes are formed. Please answer the following questions about your own reading history.

1. When you were a young child, did your parents or someone else read to you or tell you bedtime stories? _____ If so, what were your favorites?

   _____

   _____

   _____

2. What fairy tales or children's rhymes can you recall by heart?

   _____

   _____

   _____

3. Were there books and magazines in your house? _____

   If so, who read them? _____

   Did you see your parents or other adults reading? _____

4. Did you go to a nursery school, a Head Start center, or a local library where stories were read aloud to you? _____

   Did you like the stories? _____

5. Did you watch TV as a child? _____ If yes, did you watch the reading segments on television shows such as *Sesame Street*? _____
   If so, did you enjoy them? _____

6. If yes, what other kinds of shows did you watch on television? _____

   _____

   _____

   _____

7. Were you given books as presents or rewards? _____ If so, please name a book and explain how you acquired it.

_____

_____

8. What were some of your favorite childhood books? _____

_____

9. Recall the names of some of the teachers who taught you to read in school.

_____

Try to remember how they taught you. Explain:

_____.

_____.

10. Did your teachers read to you? _____ At a certain grade level, did they stop reading to you? _____ Did they ever talk about what they read?_____

11. Did you enjoy reading in school, or did you read just because it was required?

_____

12. Do you recall having to read aloud in front of the class? _____

If so, how did you feel about doing this? _____

_____

13. As you entered middle school, did you enjoy reading? _____

Did you begin to read more or less frequently? _____ Please explain.

_____

_____

_____

14. Did your middle school friends read? _____ Was there peer pressure on you to read or not to read? Please explain. _____

_____

15. What is the best book you've ever read? _____

What makes it the best? _____

_____

_____

16. What is the worst book you have ever read? _____

    Did you finish it? _____

    Who or what made you read it? _____

    _____

17. What magazines or newspapers do you look at regularly?

    _____

    _____

18. What Web sites do you look at regularly?

    _____

    _____

19. Where and when do you like to read?

    _____

20. What book are you reading now?

    _____

    How did you choose it? _____

    _____

21. What books are you considering reading next? _____

22. Do you have friends who enjoy reading and with whom you can talk about books?

    _____

    _____

23. Do you buy books and keep them? _____ If so, where do you keep
    them? _____

    Do you like to read books in a digital format (on a computer screen or
    smartphone)? _____

24. Do you listen to audiobooks?

    _____

25. In general, how do you feel about reading?

    _____

    _____

Writing Inventory

Name _____ Date _____

1. When you begin a writing assignment, how do you approach it?
   Circle one:

   a. I look forward to it.

   b. I don't know where to begin.

   c. I'm sure I will fail.

   d. With a feeling I can do okay.

2. What are your major strengths as a writer?

   _____

   _____

   _____

   _____

3. What weaknesses do you have in your writing?

   _____

   _____

   _____

   _____

4. Describe one of the most interesting writing assignments you've ever been asked to do. Why did you find it so interesting?

   _____

   _____

   _____

   _____

   _____

5. What is the worst writing assignment you can recall?

_____

_____

_____

What made it so terrible? _____

_____

_____

_____

6. Have you ever kept a journal? _____ Do you keep a journal or diary now? _____ If so, explain how you began, and what it means to you.

_____

_____

_____

7. Do you keep a blog? _____ If so, explain how you began and what it means to you. _____

_____

_____

_____

8. Do you text and e-mail your friends? _____

How do you define "good writing"? _____

_____

_____

_____

_____

HELPING STUDENTS KNOW ONE ANOTHER

We often make the assumption that most students in our classes know one another. But they may not, and even if they do, the acquaintance is likely to be superficial. A shy student may sit for months alongside students whose names he or she doesn't know. Short get-acquainted activities at the beginning of a class period are well worth the class time, especially if you wish to promote a feeling of cooperation and trust within the group.

Opening Exercises

Occasionally, as part of the opening exercise, encourage students to move around the room to talk with one another and find out the answers to one or two questions that you've written on the board at the front of the room—for example:

- Who walked to school this morning?
- Who skipped breakfast this morning?
- Whose first language is not English?
- Who has a part-time job he or she really enjoys?
- Who has an unusual job or once had one?
- Who has an exotic pet?
- Who has an unusual hobby?
- Which student in this class gets up the earliest in the morning?
- Which student in this class works the latest hours at night?

Improvisation Activities

Improvisation, a discipline within the larger context of theater and drama, develops our ability to create, develop, and share information. Not only do these activities carry the potential to develop a collaborative classroom context, they also can teach important literacy skills (which will be discussed in a later chapter). Here are some beginning-level improvisation activities that can build community (Passman & McKnight, 2007).

A. Mirror

Group the students into pairs who will face each other and mirror each other's movement. This activity teaches the students focus, concentration, cooperation, and self-awareness and takes only four to five minutes of class time.

B. Who Started the Motion?

This activity teaches the students how to focus as they work together to conceal the identity of the person starting the motion. Ask the students to stand in a circle. Have one student volunteer to leave the room for a few seconds. Select another student in the circle to be the leader. The leader begins a repetitive movement, and the other students in the circle imitate the movements of the leader. Invite the student who left the classroom to return and stand in the middle of the circle and identify the leader. This person is allowed three chances to make the correct choice.

A Get-Acquainted Activity for the Whole Class

A series of sequenced questions that encourage students to take risks, respond honestly, and get positive reinforcement for doing so is helpful for setting a positive class climate. This activity requires a full class period:

1. Seat the group in a large circle. The group leader or the teacher participates as well and answers first. Some students may elect to pass temporarily on any question. Come back to them when all the others have answered.
2. Ask each person his or her first name. The students take turns going around the circle repeating the names of every person in the circle. Students usually do this with ease, but classmates may help one another if someone can't recall a name.
3. Ask each person in turn, "If you were a musical instrument, what instrument would you be, and why?"
4. Ask each person, "If you were an animal, what animal would you be, and why?"
5. Ask each person, "What is one thing of which you are proud?"
6. Ask each person in the group to choose one other person's response to the preceding question and tell that person why he or she especially likes that response. Make sure members address each other directly by name: "Tony, I liked your answer because . . ." rather than, "I liked Tony's response because . . ."

If time is limited, stop here and give students time to respond in writing to this exercise (see item 9). If there is plenty of time, continue:

7. Ask each person, "If you could change one thing about yourself, what would you change, and why?"
8. Repeat activity 6 in response to question 7.
9. Ask students to respond in writing to this activity. How did they feel about doing it? What did they like? Dislike? What did they learn? Collect the papers and, without correcting, read them to learn more about your students and their reactions to this type of activity.

chapter 2

MANAGING YOUR CLASSROOM

- Arranging the room
- Planning for books, paper, and equipment
- Planning an efficient classroom
- Devising a fair grading system

Please, Richard, calm down for just a moment. There are thirty desks in here, and you're the thirty-first student. I'll find somewhere for you to sit as soon as I take roll.

Effective teachers organize their space, materials, auxiliary personnel, and students to create a pleasant and effective environment for learning.

ARRANGING THE ROOM

Spend time planning the layout of desks and materials before students arrive in the fall. Maybe you're one of those lucky teachers with a state-of-the-art classroom—the kind with plenty of storage space, bulletin boards and chalkboards, lots of electronic gadgets, and, best of all, plenty of extra space for specialized learning and activity centers. It's more probable, though, that your classroom is cramped, dingy, and poorly ventilated. You may have gotten into the habit of arranging student desks in rows all year long because nothing else seems possible or as efficient. But every room presents some options, and you should try for a variation from time to time. Figures 2.1 through 2.5 illustrate some options.

In Figure 2.1, students' desks face the middle of the room, and the focus is away from the teacher. This is an ideal configuration when students are reading aloud.

In Figure 2.2, desks are arranged in a large circle so that each student can see every other student in the classroom. The teacher becomes a member of the circle and his or her position as the authority figure is deemphasized. This arrangement is ideal for class discussion and is less threatening for shy students who fear speaking at the front of the room.

In Figure 2.3, desks are arranged in twos, threes, or fours for small group work. Group members face one another and are close enough to communicate effectively. It's best to have plenty of space in order to separate groups, which naturally tend to become louder as everyone actively participates. Have a clear access lane to each group. If classroom space is limited, consider moving one or two groups to the hall or to an empty neighboring classroom for small group activities. If students work in groups in the hall, ask that they move their desks or chairs and a table there as well. Sitting on the floor is not conducive to serious group work.

In Figure 2.4, desks are arranged in a horseshoe, with the teacher's chair or stool at the open end. This arrangement allows students to see one another, and the teacher is able to move easily from student to student as necessary. Some teachers who wish to emphasize the

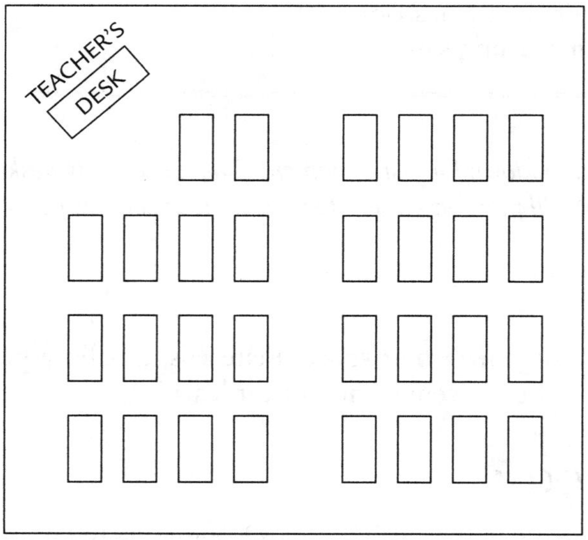

FIGURE 2.1

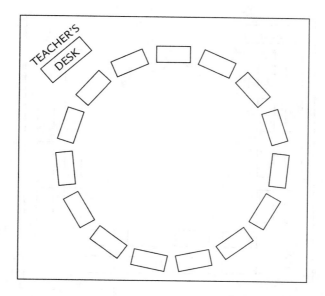

FIGURE 2.2

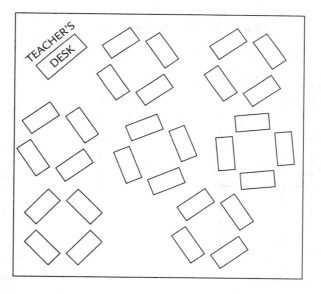

FIGURE 2.3

cooperative nature of their classrooms eliminate a lectern or designated spot from which to speak and turn their desks to a wall to eliminate the suggestion of a barrier between students and themselves.

Finally, in Figure 2.5, desks are arranged in centers. There are student work centers for writing and reading where the students work collaboratively. They consist of four or five

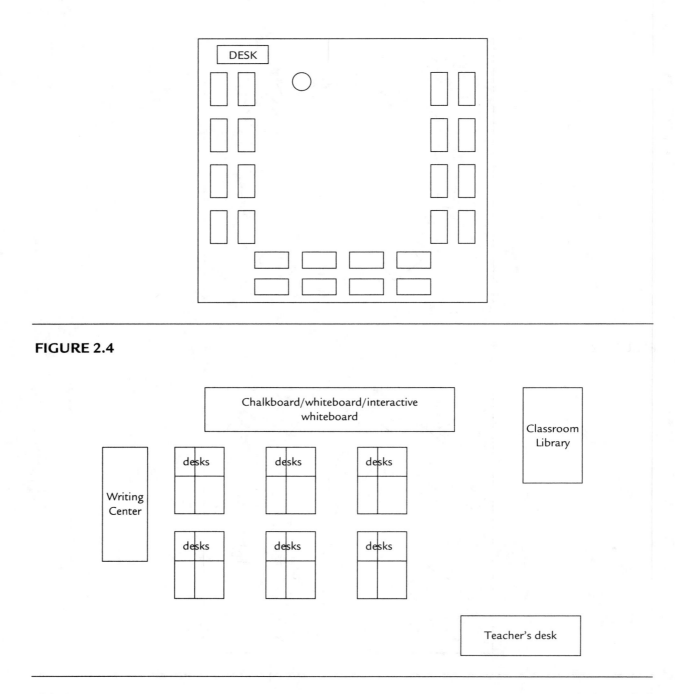

FIGURE 2.4

FIGURE 2.5

desks each or, even better, tables. A computer station is also featured where students can conduct research on the Web or compose writing assignments.

An option you might consider for combating monotony is to move your class to other settings in or near the school from time to time. Is there a lawn, a park, a playground, or an art gallery nearby where your class might write or read poetry or give presentations?

Why not occasionally move to a small auditorium, the library, or an empty classroom or exchange classrooms with another teacher for a period? Students need variety in their lives, and so do teachers.

What Do You Do When You Don't Have Your Own Classroom?

Many teachers never have the luxury of being assigned their own classroom. Some teachers are assigned a desk in a department office and share everything: bookcases, classrooms, bulletin boards, and computers. Katie, one of us, never had her own classroom since she taught in overcrowded schools. She has these suggestions:

- Planning is always important, but it becomes more critical when you don't have your own classroom. You have to carry everything with you all of the time. In this situation, a cart with wheels becomes a valuable tool. You can put books and other materials on your cart and wheel it from class to class.
- Use a file box. Many teachers have a file box with a handle for each class that they teach. Store handouts, graded papers, and homework assignments in the file box.
- If possible, if the classrooms where you teach have file cabinets or built-in cabinets, obtain a key or lock so you can secure materials that you use for nearly every class.
- Request at least one locker. Here you can store books that you use, your personal items, and large posters or other materials.
- Create an effective and efficient storage system at home to help track your materials and have access to them.
- Assign students jobs that help you get your class under way quickly (arrange desks, hand out materials, for example).
- To save time at the beginning of the class, write down the agenda and other pertinent information and post it as soon as you enter the classroom.

If none of your colleagues has an assigned classroom, the school probably has procedures and expectations regarding shared space. Make sure that you communicate with your colleagues in this regard.

PLANNING FOR BOOKS, PAPER, AND EQUIPMENT

Students should know where reading and writing materials are kept in the classroom and what is available for their use.

Equipment and Materials

Designate a specific location for equipment and materials such as the following:

- Pens, pencils, and colored markers
- Lined and unlined paper in a variety of sizes and colors
- Construction paper

- Poster board
- Stationery and envelopes
- Staplers, staples, and staple removers
- Tape
- Glue sticks, glue, or paste
- Scissors
- Paper clips
- Erasers and correction fluid
- Index cards
- Rubber bands
- Paper punch
- Transparent tape
- Rubber cement
- Tape recorder and blank tapes
- Overhead projector, transparencies, and markers
- Television and DVD
- Computers with Internet access and printer

It's good to have all of these materials available in the classroom. Students should be encouraged, however, to have their own paper, pens, and pencils. They should also know where they might find them in the classroom on an emergency basis. Pencils and pens tend to disappear quickly, and some teachers tell their students, "These materials are here for you to use, but once they're gone, I won't replace them. Be thoughtful of others."

Reference Materials

Decide where reference materials such as dictionaries, thesauruses, and style handbooks are to be kept. If you expect to allow students to use these materials outside the classroom, plan a clear checkout procedure.

Ideally your classroom should be equipped with a dictionary (containing etymologies) and a thesaurus for every student. It may be possible to store these on or below each student's desk. However, the books tend to disappear from the room as students gather them with their own books. Keep resource books in easily accessible bookcases and require students to consult them frequently. Students who do not have access to these materials at home should be encouraged to check them out using a sign-out form (Form 2.1) that is kept in a prominent place.

Sign-Out Sheet

Student's Name	Time Checked Out	Material Checked Out (include book title and number)	Date Out	Date In
_____	_____	_____	_____	_____
_____	_____	_____	_____	_____
_____	_____	_____	_____	_____
_____	_____	_____	_____	_____
_____	_____	_____	_____	_____
_____	_____	_____	_____	_____
_____	_____	_____	_____	_____
_____	_____	_____	_____	_____
_____	_____	_____	_____	_____
_____	_____	_____	_____	_____
_____	_____	_____	_____	_____
_____	_____	_____	_____	_____
_____	_____	_____	_____	_____
_____	_____	_____	_____	_____
_____	_____	_____	_____	_____
_____	_____	_____	_____	_____
_____	_____	_____	_____	_____

It's helpful to have an atlas and an almanac nearby, as well as colorful laminated maps of the United States and the rest of the world. Among other books you might want to have available are these:

- Atlas of historical fiction or fantasy
- Rhyming dictionary
- *Guinness Book of World Records*
- *Dictionary of Classical Mythology*
- Collection of single titles of novels, poetry, and short stories
- Magazines such as *The Writer*, *Voice*, *Literary Cavalcade*, and *Merlyn's Pen*
- Booklets of writings by previous students
- Photographs of art works, diagrams of theaters and other sites, videos about authors or settings, recordings of literature, and tapes of music contemporary with literary works

Computers

If you have computers in your classroom with Internet access, list expectations for their use, and include a sign-up sheet when it is appropriate to use this equipment. Most schools and school districts have policies for Internet use. Go over the rules and expectations for the responsible use of the computers and Internet. The Internet and Computer Responsible Use Agreement in Chapter Eight (Form 8.1) is helpful in this regard. If you wish to allow your students to use the computers during lunch periods and after school, have the students sign up in advance.

PLANNING AN EFFICIENT CLASSROOM

Be clear about your expectations and management style. Give students as many responsibilities as possible. Enable them to go about their business of being independent, productive students without interrupting you with unnecessary, time-consuming questions such as, "May I borrow a pencil?" The goal is to create a self-starting classroom filled with students who come into class and begin work immediately.

Students Should Know What to Bring to Class Each Day

It is desirable for every student to have a copy of whatever material is being studied. Students should be expected to bring the appropriate material to class each day. Hand out short-term or unit schedules (see Chapter Three), and make your expectations specific and clear.

Have a Clear Plan for Obtaining Forgotten Materials

If practical, allow students to leave the classroom to retrieve forgotten materials. Encourage them to do so as quickly and with as little commotion as possible. One effective means of discouraging this practice is to be sure students who have to leave the classroom to gather forgotten materials understand your school's policy for unexcused tardies.

Explain the Procedure for Leaving Your Classroom

Do all in your power to discourage the tendency for heavy traffic in and out of your classroom—to the library, the office, or the lavatory, for example. Many teachers tell students they may leave the classroom only at the end of the class period if all other work is completed or when there is an obvious, valid emergency. Many schools expect teachers to issue hall passes for situations like this. Avoid writing passes for each occasion. Some teachers make and laminate a master pass. Others use a block of wood with the word *pass* and the teacher's name and room number on it. The point of the block of wood is that it's too large and cumbersome for students to lose or to inadvertently leave in a pocket. It should be assigned a specific location in the classroom.

Plan for Distributing and Collecting Materials

Consider using one of the following time-saving suggestions for distributing or collecting materials:

- If possible, put materials for the class on students' desks before class begins.
- Designate a few students to distribute materials and collect assignments and place them in a specified location.
- Place a table or desk near the classroom door, and lay out materials for students to collect as they enter the classroom.
- Set up a file folder for each student. When students enter the classroom, they quickly check their folders for the day's materials. This method can also save time in distributing makeup materials to absent students. If you must float from room to room, make arrangements with the teacher whose room you are using for a bit of space of your own—a shelf on a bookcase and a drawer in a file cabinet, for example.
- Distribute materials in packets rather than as separate handouts.

Design an Efficient Means of Taking Roll

If you prefer to take attendance yourself, one time-saving approach is to introduce the day's activity or assignment, and after your students are involved in their work, take a minute or two to complete the attendance form. Many teachers who have their students keep a reading or writing journal regularly set aside the first five minutes or so of each period for writing. During this time, the teacher quickly takes roll and then writes along with the students.

Another approach is to appoint one or two students in each class as attendance takers. The small amount of effort and time necessary at the beginning of the year to explain the procedure will ultimately allow you to move quickly to your teaching objectives. Place a master list or master seating chart and a stack of forms (such as Form 2.2) in a designated location and explain these to the responsible students. Each day one student fills in an attendance sheet. (It's unwise to give students access to your grade book.) Late students entering the classroom are instructed to present their admit passes to the attendance taker rather than to you.

Absence and Tardiness Report

Day _____ Date _____ Month _____

Class _____

Hour _____

Teacher _____

Absent students, excused (please write clearly)

_____   _____

_____   _____

_____   _____

Absent students, unexcused

_____   _____

_____   _____

_____   _____

Tardy students, excused

_____   _____

_____   _____

_____   _____

Tardy students, unexcused

_____   _____

_____   _____

_____   _____

Attendance taker's signature _____

Attach all passes to this sheet and return to the classroom teacher at the end
   of the class period.

Organize and Plan for Makeup Work

Each day write a brief summary of the day's lesson, activities, and assignments on a dated index card. Place the card in a file box in a designated spot in the classroom. When absent students return, they will quickly learn the efficient habit of checking these summaries for makeup assignments. You may prefer a spiral-bound notebook, which ensures that the materials stay together and in order.

Ideally students should take turns writing these summaries. Often we teachers do the work ourselves because it seems expedient. It's well worth your time—and it's a legitimate learning activity—if you organize a dated schedule for your students to follow as they take turns writing the summaries. The following is a sample set of directions for students who are writing daily summaries:

1. Write the date: month, day, and year.
2. List the names of students who are absent.
3. Write a summary of what happened in class on this day.
4. Collect handouts (if there are any) for people who are absent.
5. Write the name of an absent student on each handout.
6. Place the handouts in the appropriate file box.
7. Sign your name.

Call on the writer on the following day to read his or her summary aloud. In assuming this responsibility, students gain experience in summary writing and are immediately aware they are writing for a real audience. The summary itself is a good review of the previous day's work and leads smoothly into the next assignment or activity.

Whenever you hand out materials or give tests, instruct your student helpers or remember yourself to write the names of absent students on a copy of each handout. Then place this material on a shelf devoted to materials for that particular class period. Students seeking makeup work will find it easily, and you'll avoid having to rummage through stacks of old handouts or your filing cabinet. (You'll want to keep makeup tests elsewhere, however.)

Form 2.3 can also be helpful in dealing with students who have serious makeup difficulties. The teacher itemizes the missed assignments on this form, provides handouts and explanations, and sets a due date for the work. Make a duplicate of the completed form so that both student and teacher have a copy. Both student and teacher sign the form, and the student attaches his or her copy to the makeup work when it is handed in.

Student Make-up Work

Student _____

Class _____

Dates missed _____

Make-up work _____

_____

_____

_____

Last date to
submit work _____

Student signature _____

Teacher signature _____

To avoid having assorted papers tossed on your desk just as you are preparing to begin a class, clearly label baskets or boxes for each class period and instruct students where to place daily assignments and makeup work.

Use Student Aides to Perform Routine Tasks

In some schools, students seek out teachers and ask to be designated as student aides. These students usually assist a teacher before or after school or during a free period. Ideally, the student will be available during your preparation time to help you in the following ways:

- Run errands or deliver and collect materials.
- Set up equipment such as filmstrip projectors, tape recorders, DVDs, or digital cameras. You may have to train a student to handle these tasks, but that student will then be able to train others.
- Sort and staple materials.
- Place materials in students' file folders.
- Put up or take down displays of classroom work.
- Water plants, and keep the room neat and organized.
- Correct simple multiple-choice or true-and-false quizzes and tests. Some schools have electronic scanners for correcting these tests. If one is available, instruct your aide in its operation. For the sake of privacy, you may want to assign numbers to students for test taking and posting grades. Some teachers simply assign students the same number as that next to the student's name in the grade book. Record all grades yourself, however. Students should not have access to your grade book.

Involve Students in Decorating the Classroom

You'll want your classroom to be attractive and comfortable. Give students some ownership in the process of creating bulletin boards and displays. Ask them to choose from your collection of posters, and decide where these should be placed. Display as much student work as possible. Add plants, a comfortable old couch or chairs, and even window curtains if space permits and this reflects your personal style.

As you plan your teaching units, suggest bulletin board and display projects to students as part of their individual assignment options. Student-made bulletin boards are not new, of course, but projects such as these are worthwhile learning activities for the students themselves as well as timesavers for you. Displays created by students within the classroom elicit high interest and responses from their peers and offer a legitimate opportunity for students to recast their ideas in a visual manner. Ask students to donate examples of outstanding work to your own classroom collection. These samples can serve as models for subsequent classes, and students enjoy knowing you admire their work enough to save and display it. Don't recycle the same materials over and over, however. If you're short of display space, cover a wall with colored paper for thematic or seasonal murals or string wires or fishing line from wall to wall. Then attach material to be displayed to the line with colorful clothes pins or clips. Older students enjoy the unexpected too.

The way we each use time reflects our individual teaching priorities and teaching methods. When students become an asset to our classroom management style, we provide them with valuable responsibility and experience and free ourselves from some of the tasks that can overwhelm our teaching efforts.

Create a Positive Design for Discipline Within the Classroom

The most effective teachers seem to have fewer problems with discipline, yet no single description applies to them all. Some are charismatic and have great personal warmth, while others are more formal and somewhat aloof. Some exude an exuberant enthusiasm, while others are gentle and congenial. Despite personality and style differences, there seems to be a common thread that characterizes such teachers. Studies suggest that effective teachers (through everything they do) positively communicate to their students, "We want to be here." They believe in the value of their discipline and are committed to it. They care about the students and expect a great deal from them. In addition, their classrooms and teaching plans are so well organized and managed there is frequently little time or opportunity for discipline problems (Wayson, 1981).

We often hear colleagues lament about how students have changed and how difficult it is to teach today. In many ways, this is true. Family structure has changed, society has changed, and discipline can be a tough, complex job. One teacher recalls worrying about squirt guns twenty-five years ago; today, he points out, his school has metal detectors. Nevertheless, the majority of students we meet and teach each day are cooperative and anxious to please. Others will work hard if we give them rules and plenty of structure. A very small percentage have behavior problems and challenge discipline. They are the ones who can "drive a teacher crazy" or into retirement (Kronenberg, 1992).

Researchers suggest that the basic needs (survival, belonging, power, freedom, and fun) of the most defiant students are not being met. Many of these students are barely surviving. They may be abused, hungry, homeless, or unloved. As a classroom teacher, you cannot solve all their problems, but you do need to understand what is happening at their home, and you need to involve the school's support staff. Your classroom, despite their behavior, may be the only safe place these students know. As a teacher, you can provide a setting that is predictable. You can tell them the rules, state the consequences if they break the rules, and provide the structure that is lacking in their lives. These students need to feel they belong someplace to have some power over their lives. Provide opportunities for choices and options for assignments. Like every other person in your class, these students need a chance to succeed, and they need honest, positive recognition when they do. Troublemakers are often students who have too little to do or cannot do what is assigned. In these cases, shorten assignments, try to make the goal of each assignment clearer and more immediately attainable, monitor their progress frequently, and involve them in their own self-evaluation.

In dealing with this type of student, also remember that we cannot control other people, only ourselves. The best classroom teacher is not a boss but a manager who avoids power struggles and gives students the responsibility and the opportunity to succeed (Glasser, 1986). Good managers have few rules, and these are specific and positive. Some teachers solicit their students' ideas and suggestions because they believe students are more likely to implement rules they have helped develop. The following concerns routinely need to be addressed:

- Tardiness
- Late homework assignments
- Disruptive behavior
- Dismissal procedures

These guidelines are helpful as you or you and your students design rules for your classroom:

- Limit the number of rules. Five or six positive rules are best.
- Design rules that encourage student learning.
- State the rules in language students understand.
- Determine in advance the consequences of keeping and breaking rules.
- Print and distribute the rules to each class member (New Teacher's Handbook, 1988).

Some teachers also ask students and their parents to sign a verification form acknowledging that they have read and agreed to the list. Form 2.4 provides an example.

Classroom Regulations

Class _____   Teacher _____

1. **Required materials.** Bring the following materials to class each day:
   - Pencil
   - Pen
   - Notebook paper
   - English folder
   - Book for reading

2. **Tardiness.** You are expected to be in your desk with the required materials and reading book when the bell rings. If you are not there, you will be marked tardy.

3. **Classroom behavior.** Your responsibilities in this class are to:
   - Attend class regularly;
   - Be on time;
   - Be prepared for class;
   - Meet deadlines (all assignments due at the *beginning* of each class on the due date);
   - Use your time wisely;
   - Be actively involved as a member of a group;
   - Have a positive attitude; and
   - Pay attention, listen, and not be disruptive.

4. **Absences and makeup work.** You are expected to make up any work missed because of any absence. Check the card file for a summary of the work you have missed. If anything is unclear, see me about a further explanation. You will be given two days to make up major assignments. After that time, points will be deducted for lateness. However, it will be nearly impossible for you to make up any in-class group activities if you are absent. In some cases, I will give you alternative assignments, and you will need to confer with me about options. If you know beforehand that you will be absent, please inform me so that I can help you plan your makeup work. The quality of your work will be higher if you attend class regularly and meet all deadlines.

5. **Dismissal.** I will dismiss you at the end of each class period.

6. **Graded papers and handouts.** Keep all graded papers and handouts in your English folder for reference. At the end of each quarter, I will point out any unneeded papers that you may discard.

If a student is causing a problem, keep a written, dated log of classroom incidents. Follow your school's procedure in notifying the parents of the behavior. If a conference becomes necessary, you will have an accurate record of what has occurred. The following format is a useful guideline for a conference with a student or students and parents:

Student's Name: _____ Date: _____

Description of behavior:

What are the student's strengths, interests, and goals?

What is the student feeling in my class?

What do I need the student to do in my class?

What specific steps can I try?

What can the student do?

Although some students may present increasing challenges, we can still do many things that successful teachers have been doing for a long time. We can be prepared for class, care about our students, and have fair expectations for them. We can show our enthusiasm for English, use our class time for teaching and learning, balance our goals with the interests of our students, look for the root of behavioral problems, and use fair, positive, and prompt measures to address discipline problems.

Plan for Productive Homework

Many teachers lament that students don't do homework. In assignment homework, it is critical to consider the value and purpose. Here are some suggestions regarding homework assignments:

1. Communicate your expectations for homework to your students and their parents.
2. Avoid skill-and-drill worksheets.
3. Do not use homework as a punishment or a reward.
4. Assign creative homework. If the homework is interesting, the students will be more motivated to complete it. For example, if the students are learning parts of speech, instead of asking them to complete worksheets, have them create their own sentences that demonstrate their knowledge of the parts of speech or develop posters about each part of speech.
5. Give students choice. Offer a variety of homework assignments that are designed for students to extend their understanding of material. Giving students choice is important because it is motivating. For example, if the students have a reading assignment, instead of having them answer teacher-made or textbook-made questions, ask them to bring in questions that they have as a result of their reading.
6. Never assign new material for homework.
7. Emphasize quality over quantity.
8. Avoid grading every assignment. Research supports the practice of not grading every assignment. In one study, two high school teachers were studied. Teacher A

graded every assignment, and teacher B asked the students to bring in questions and comments as a result of the homework. Teacher B gave the students a "satisfactory" or "unsatisfactory" on the assignments and offered the students the opportunity to revise the homework. The result was that more students completed the homework and performed better on summative assessments. Remember that mastery is the important goal (Ames, 1990).

9. For students with special needs, adapt the homework assignment so that they will be successful. Maybe the student needs a deadline adjustment, or instead of assigning twenty vocabulary words, give them ten. Adjusting assignments for students with special needs is critical to their individual success.

10. Consider giving students the homework assignments one week at a time. If they have a homework calendar, they are better able to manage their time between school work, activities, work, and their busy social lives.

DEVISING A FAIR GRADING SYSTEM

Grades are meant to reflect the quality of each student's performance in the classroom. They are intended to be both a means of communicating with students and parents and a method of record keeping. Colleges ask about class rank. Businesses inquire about grades. What makes grading so troublesome for teachers is that an abstract symbol does not adequately express the complexities of a student's growth and says nothing about interest, involvement, cooperation, competency, improvement, or effort, for example. (Later chapters discuss in detail the evaluation and grading of writing, reading, listening, speaking, and cooperative activities.)

Grading Scales

How we handle the whole issue of grading and grades is important. As concerned teachers, we want to arrive at a fair system for computing grades—a system that best reflects the student's work in our classroom. In designing a grading system, many teachers use a grading scale like the following:

95%–100% = A	90%–100% = A
85%–94% = B	80%–89% = B
75%–84% = C	70%–79% = C
70%–74% = D	60%–69% = D
0%–69% = F	0%–59% = F

In some schools teachers choose their own scale. Others have a school or department policy that determines the scale.

Every assigned activity or exercise carries a total number of possible points. Major assignments are allotted a greater number of points than short quizzes or exercises. The actual points accumulated by the student are added, and the student's total is divided by the number of possible points to determine the percentage. This percentage is converted to a letter grade based on whatever scale the teacher is using and becomes the grade the student earns for a grading period. A variation based on such a scale can be achieved by indicating what kinds of effort will affect the final grade in a particular way. For example, you may decide that unit tests will count for 20 percent of the grade, daily grades another 30 percent, writing 30 percent, and group projects 20 percent. This will involve more time in computation, but the advantage is that it will give you more specific information for parent-teacher conferences. Although it gives the appearance of objectivity, this approach is also variable and subjective.

In conjunction with grading scales, many teachers who have access to computers use computer programs for recording and reporting student grades. These programs not only make it possible for you to closely monitor each student's total points and grade percentage, but they also perform a variety of computations, such as final percentages, grades, and class averages. It is possible to print a spreadsheet report for an entire class or for an individual student at any time. The individual reports are especially helpful in conferences with students at midquarter reporting time or as a resource for parent-teacher conferences. If you use or are required to use a computer program for grading, make sure that you back up your files. Nothing is more upsetting than losing important information prior to the submission of grades.

Portfolio Grades

More and more teachers and schools are turning to portfolios, samples of actual school work, to help evaluate student progress. Portfolio grades are generally not used to determine a student's entire grade for a marking period. It is a single grade that is averaged with others earned throughout a grading period to determine a student's final grade. Those who encourage teachers to use portfolios in the classroom do so because they believe we need to look at a student's growth and development over time. In addition, they emphasize that portfolios become a partnership involving students and teachers and teachers and parents. Portfolios can be the focal point of a student-teacher conference or a parent-teacher conference. They are especially effective in fostering parent involvement because parents get a chance to see and understand their child's work instead of just looking at letter grades. Used effectively, a portfolio will help you assess your students, involve them in their own assessment, and, most important, promote their further learning.

There are enormous variations in the way portfolios can be used. It's important to distinguish between writing folders and portfolios. Writing folders generally contain all the writing (including drafts) a student has produced. Portfolios contain representative samples of a student's efforts in several areas. In combination with reading and speaking activities, they may become hefty collections of reading logs, photographs of projects or the projects themselves, video and audio recordings of dramatic responses, as well as self-evaluations by the student, evaluations by peers, and evaluative material by the teacher.

If you plan to use portfolios, avoid making them a collection of all the work a student has done. This can become messy, hard work for you, or just another file of papers you must shuffle and store. The portfolio is a collection assembled by the student, and it is meant to illustrate the student's efforts, progress, or achievements. The best portfolios:

- Have a clear plan for selecting the material to be included
- Involve students in the selection of the pieces to be included
- Encourage self-reflection on the part of students (Paulsen, Paulsen, & Mayer, 1990).

Teachers have created a variety of formats for portfolios. For example, some use the portfolio exclusively for the writing portion of their courses. These teachers have their students assemble several pieces of writing along with a written rationale for why they were selected, sometimes in the form of a letter to the teacher. Portfolios, however, need not be used exclusively for writing. They may also include student samples from a variety of reading, writing, listening, and speaking activities.

Getting Started with Portfolios

Portfolios are easiest to manage if you begin by handing out a file folder to each student and indicating a filing cabinet or location in the room where these are to be kept. Make a rule that the entire portfolio should never leave the classroom (only single papers) to ensure that students do not lose their work. Decide before you begin what you want students to place in their folders, and turn this list into a table of contents. If you wish students to include examples of a variety of activities and assignments, consider the following sample.

Sample Portfolio Table of Contents
1. Writing and reading inventories from the beginning of the year.
2. A writing from early in the quarter (or grading period) with all drafts and prewriting materials attached as well as self-evaluation materials, peer conference notes, and the teacher's conference comments. The number of writings and variety of formats depends on the age and ability of the particular students.
3. A writing from later in the quarter with all additional material.
4. A self-evaluation of journal writing.
5. A brief description of a cooperative group literature project in which you participated.
6. A self-evaluation of your contribution to the group project.
7. A self-evaluation of the group's project. (See Form 2.5.)
8. A self-evaluation of your work for the grading period.
9. A statement of your goals for the next grading period.
10. Your teacher's response to your self-evaluation. (See Form 2.5.)

Remind students to carefully date and label all materials and organize them in the order you indicate on your list.

Plan to assess student portfolios every four weeks or so, and include notes about your observations. Some teachers also attach a grade to these observations.

Additional Suggestions for Involving Students in the Evaluation Process

Evaluation is an ongoing process intended to help students understand their strengths and weaknesses as learners. Previously we teachers assumed the role of sole evaluator in the classroom, and we thought of evaluation as a part of our grading process. Today we are learning to involve students because we've come to understand that self-reflection is a significant component of the learning process.

Plan for a variety of ways to encourage your students to respond to and assess their own work. Form 2.5 is helpful for involving students in self-assessment and may be used in conjunction with a portfolio or in preparation for teacher-student or parent-teacher conferences. The form itself becomes a record of student growth. Ideally you will have several of these in each student's file by the end of the year.

Describe Your Work in This Class

Name _____ Date _____

As this grading period comes to an end, I am required to assign a grade that characterizes the quality of your work. I want you to help me with this process by completing this sheet. I value your input as I make my final determination of grades.

   For items 1 to 5, circle the answer that best fits:

1. I always contribute positively to this class:

   Usually

   Sometimes

   Never

2. My assignments are always handed in on time:

   Usually

   Sometimes

   Never

3. I attend class regularly.

   I am absent occasionally.

   My absences are frequent.

4. My makeup work is always completed:

   Usually

   Seldom

5. I work to the best of my ability in this class.

   I do enough to get by.

   I do as little as possible in this class.

I believe the grade I deserve and have earned is _____

because _____

_____

_____

_____

_____

One important thing I have learned this grading period is _____

_____

_____

_____

My goals for next quarter are _____

_____

_____

_____

Student's signature _____

Teacher's response:

_____

_____

_____

_____

Teacher's signature _____

This type of self-evaluation form will help you gain further insight into a student's self-understanding and is an excellent way in which to help students set personal goals for the next unit or grading period. Used just prior to parent-teacher conferences, it helps cut misunderstandings with parents to a minimum. It is also possible, although less desirable, to mail copies of the student-completed forms to parents or guardians who do not attend a teacher conference.

Suggestions for Your Grade Book

Plan to record at least one grade each week for every student in your grade book. Not every grade needs to reflect a major assignment. Give a variety of weekly quizzes or exercises that can be easily evaluated and graded. Without such a plan, you may arrive at the midquarter (when deficiency notices are due) lacking information to keep parents informed about the progress of their child. It's simply not fair to fail a student at the end of the quarter if you haven't earlier notified him or her and the parents of this possibility. Occasionally a student will receive a passing mark at midquarter, yet do so little work after that that he or she is failing by the time final grades are due. If you realize this is occurring, make an effort to reach a parent or guardian by mail or telephone. If you have 130 to 150 students, it may not be possible to keep track of each student this closely, although computer software is especially helpful in monitoring students' points and percentages regularly. A computer printout listing the student's earned points or a folder of the student's earlier and later work is helpful supporting information when such a situation occurs.

Grade more than just written work. For example, if one student gives an oral presentation, grade the other students on their listening skills. Students might earn points by repeating or writing down one fact they have learned from the report or explaining one detail they like about the report. Devise a variety of ways to give grades, because it is within that variety that you achieve the most fairness (Chapman & King, 2004).

Check assignments at the beginning of a class period, and be sure that students understand they will lose points if the work is not complete. If you use this approach consistently, the percentage of students who arrive in class each day with their homework done will rise significantly.

When students are absent, give them zeroes for short in-class quizzes or assignments and then average in the zeroes. At the same time, allow students to earn extra points for extra-credit work, but be sure the additional work is appropriate and reinforces or expands on what is happening in the class. Although this will take extra time on your part, it is worthwhile because it underscores the importance of good class attendance without penalizing any student unfairly. Good students who are legitimately absent once or twice find this approach fair because they are given the option of making up the points.

The work a student does in the last few weeks of a quarter or semester should probably have a greater impact on the final grade than the work early in the course. If a student's writing has improved, weighing all writing equally isn't a good idea. If points are averaged and sit equally between two grades, choose the higher grade if the student's work has improved over the course of the grading period. Choose the lower grade if the quality of the student's work has declined.

If a student disagrees with the grade you've assigned for a particular test or paper, be willing to talk about it and change the grade if reasonable. Plenty of in-class conferences will help eliminate these kinds of problems, as will plenty of student self-evaluation.

Unless your school has a policy against this, collect and keep all major tests after they've been returned and explained to the students. Preparing tests takes time, and if you are likely to use them again, keep them out of circulation. A student's writing, however, should be his or hers to keep. Students are pleased, however, when you ask for copies as models for other students.

Identify and date each grade you enter in your grade book. Some teachers also leave spaces between students' names in order to record any additional information such as numbers identifying textbooks checked out to students. You might also consider color-coding grades as you enter them, thereby differentiating daily assignments, major tests, writing assignments, and group work.

With the ever expanding technological resources, teacher Web sites are more commonplace. (Many school districts require that teachers create and maintain Web sites.) Teacher Web sites provide a platform for communication among teachers, parents, and students and for the exchange of ideas, materials, and resources. If your school or district doesn't provide a platform for a Web site, there are many free or fee sites for creating your own. Here are some suggestions for your own Web site:

- Consider the design of your Web site. How do you want it to appear?
- Organize it for easy navigation.
- Provide information about yourself, including contact information.
- Use separate tabs for the classes and courses you teach. For each course, include class procedures, expectations, and materials. Post homework assignments and the dates due, and consider posting the handouts that you distribute in class.
- Include links to resources that can support your students' learning.

chapter 3

CREATING *a* MASTER PLAN, INDIVIDUAL UNITS, *and* DAILY LESSONS

- Designing a year-long course
- Planning teaching units
- Creating daily lesson plans
- Team planning and teaching
- Planning for English language learners
- Planning for students with special needs in an inclusive classroom

---

Sara, you may not hand in all your writing assignments at one time. It's the last day of class.

One of our goals as teachers is to chart a sensible year-long course for ourselves and our students. In language arts, this is an enormously complex undertaking because we're responsible for such a variety of facts, concepts, and skills, and students generally come to us with widely differing abilities, interests, and goals. Add to this unscheduled assemblies, fire drills, intercom announcements, yearbook pictures, and class trips, and we begin to wonder if it's even reasonable to envision such a plan. But, of course, it is.

You'll want to begin with a general and basic plan for the entire year. In doing so, you won't be trying to fill up your year. You probably have enough material for several years. Instead, you'll need to decide what your priorities are for the material you need to cover to avoid racing from one topic to another in a frenzied attempt to get through an overstuffed course outline. Some teachers divide their textbooks into as many daily lessons as time allows, and this becomes the course curriculum for the year. Still others designate spelling days, vocabulary days, and book report days—a kind of bits-and-pieces curriculum with little correlation of concepts or integration of reading, writing, speaking, and listening. Neither approach is satisfactory or desirable, yet many of us have organized our year in this way simply to survive.

There are really two key words to keep in mind as you plan for the school year: *organization* and *flexibility*. Both long-term and short-term planning are essential. Yet plans should be neither so rigid nor so detailed that they cannot be adjusted to meet daily circumstances and, more important, the changing needs you and your students have.

DESIGNING A YEAR-LONG COURSE

Create a general plan or master schedule for the year, but think of it only as a guide and be willing to revise and adjust it as you go along:

1. Keep in mind the nature of the community in which you teach, the grade level and probable interests of the incoming students, other areas of the curriculum, and the total program of your school.
2. Study the district curriculum and language arts objectives outlined for your grade level or course.
3. Scan the textbooks and other materials available to you, such as curriculum guides, catalogues and publishers' materials, and lists of materials in the audiovisual department and library or media center.
4. Record the page numbers of the sections of texts that must be included in your plans for the year, and keep a second list of optional choices that might be used to supplement your first choices.
5. Look for opportunities to integrate experiences in reading, speaking, writing, and listening. Why not, for example, integrate the teaching of the library's resources with a speaking and listening project in which students interview the librarian and present their finding to the whole class in a series of oral reports or a panel discussion?
6. Think about what's going on in the world, your state, and your community. If something strikes you, jot it down and consider how this item might contribute to or augment your own curriculum.
7. Plan for variety, and consider themes and activities that best fit your own temperament. If you are a less experienced teacher, it is likely you will initially follow the classroom textbooks fairly closely. As time passes, some of the real fun of teaching comes from trying new approaches, new lessons, better films, new writing projects, and new group

activities. One of the best ways to maintain your enthusiasm and creative energy is to try some new things each year.

8. Use a planning sheet such as Form 3.1 or a calendar to plot a general outline for the year.

9. Note any holidays, teacher in-service days, and parent conference dates. Sketch in the dates of the end of the quarter and semester dates.

10. Plot the probable length of units, and assign testing days. In many schools, attendance drops just prior to a vacation, and you may want to avoid scheduling major projects or tests at these times.

11. Consider the timing of major projects. You won't want all your classes taking tests or turning in major projects on the same day. As you schedule, also keep in mind your home life and personal obligations.

PLANNING TEACHING UNITS

Once you have a general plan or outline for the entire course, you'll begin designing the first weeks and the first unit of the school year. You are likely to spend time with management and get-acquainted activities in the first week or so, but move to a more detailed teaching unit as quickly as possible. It is at this point that you'll begin to plan in earnest by unit (see Form 3.2) or by month.

Keep these points in mind as you plan units:

- *Know your students.* The questionnaires and any writing your students have completed up to this point will be useful for identifying some of their strengths, weaknesses, and interests. Ideally, you should also consult and include students in the planning and goal-setting process.

- *Identify specific goals.* What do you want your students to know or be able to do by the completion of the unit? This is important because you need to communicate these objectives to your students. In addition, you will want to align your curriculum goals with the mandated standards students must meet. The NCTE has coauthored with the International Reading Association twelve overall goals (standards) for the teaching of English Arts, and most states have used these same goals to create more specific skill-based standards. You will want to understand your state level standards to create learner goals for your students.

- *Select your resources.* What books, handouts, films, or other materials and equipment will you need?

- *Design the class activities.* What will you do, and what will the students do? What learning activities will help students accomplish the goals of the unit? Because your students will have a variety of learning styles, vary the types of activities you plan. If possible, use more than one type in each class period. You'll have a great many options to consider—for example:

Reading silently	Interviewing
Discussing	Competing in teams
Listening	Playing games
Role playing	Note taking
Watching and responding to a film or video	Drafting and writing
Brainstorming	Researching
Listing	Answering questions
Mapping	Summarizing
Freewriting	Debating
Revising and editing	Analyzing
Participating in large or small groups	Paraphrasing
Peer teaching	Conferring

Create a Sequenced Plan

Writing your unit plans in general terms on a monthly calendar and distributing copies to each student is a good idea. The calendar should indicate the daily assignments, the materials you expect students to bring to class each day, and the dates for tests and major assignments. By distributing this schedule, you will enable your students to practice good time management and your expectations will always be specific and clear. Many computer programs allow you to produce individualized calendars for class assignments. Form 3.3 is also useful for this purpose.

Plan to Evaluate Both the Students and the Teaching Unit

How are you going to know if the students have learned? How will you know if the unit is successful? Decide on the means of evaluation you will use to determine student learning, and make it part of your basic lesson design.

The sample unit plan on page 51 is a ten-week writing unit, "Writing Autobiographically," designed by a teacher for a ninth-grade English class.

You will find additional unit plans in Appendix A of this book. They are units created by teachers, and there are differences in each format as a result of varying requirements for the schools in which they teach. Despite these differences, there are consistent elements that underscore good planning and lesson design.

CREATING DAILY LESSON PLANS

One of the drawbacks in relying on a single textbook for the course is that as we cover the book, it becomes easy to lose sight of our day-to-day objectives. Many of us have simply noted page numbers as a lesson plan for a particular day. When we do this, we have no clear focus or well-thought-out plan for what we want to accomplish. In addition, we have little useful information for another year: what we did successfully and what didn't work.

Year–Long Planning Sheet

Course _____

August
dates

_____ week 3 _____

_____ week 4 _____

_____

September
dates

_____ week 1 _____

_____ week 2 _____

_____ week 3 _____

_____ week 4 _____

_____

October
dates

_____ week 1 _____

_____ week 2 _____

_____ week 3 _____

_____ week 4 _____

_____

November
dates

_____ week 1 _____

_____ week 2 _____

_____ week 3 _____

_____ week 4 _____

_____

December
dates

_____ week 1 _____

_____ week 2 _____

_____ week 3 _____

_____ week 4 _____

_____

January
dates

_____ week 1 _____

_____ week 2 _____

January
dates

_____ week 3 _____

_____ week 4 _____

_____

February
dates

_____ week 1 _____

_____ week 2 _____

_____ week 3 _____

_____ week 4 _____

_____

March
dates

_____ week 1 _____

_____ week 2 _____

_____ week 3 _____

_____ week 4 _____

_____

April
dates

_____ week 1 _____

_____ week 2 _____

_____ week 3 _____

_____ week 4 _____

_____

May
dates

_____ week 1 _____

_____ week 2 _____

_____ week 3 _____

_____ week 4 _____

_____

June
dates

_____ week 1 _____

_____ week 2 _____

_____ week 3 _____

_____ week 4 _____

_____

Unit Planning Sheet

Teacher _____   Class _____

Quarter _____   Semester _____

Week _____   Month _____

Day	Date	Activity
Monday	_____	_____
		_____
Tuesday	_____	_____
		_____
Wednesday	_____	_____
		_____
Thursday	_____	_____
		_____
Friday	_____	_____
		_____

Week _____   Month _____

Day	Date	Activity
Monday	_____	_____
		_____
Tuesday	_____	_____
		_____
Wednesday	_____	_____
		_____
Thursday	_____	_____
		_____
Friday	_____	_____
		_____

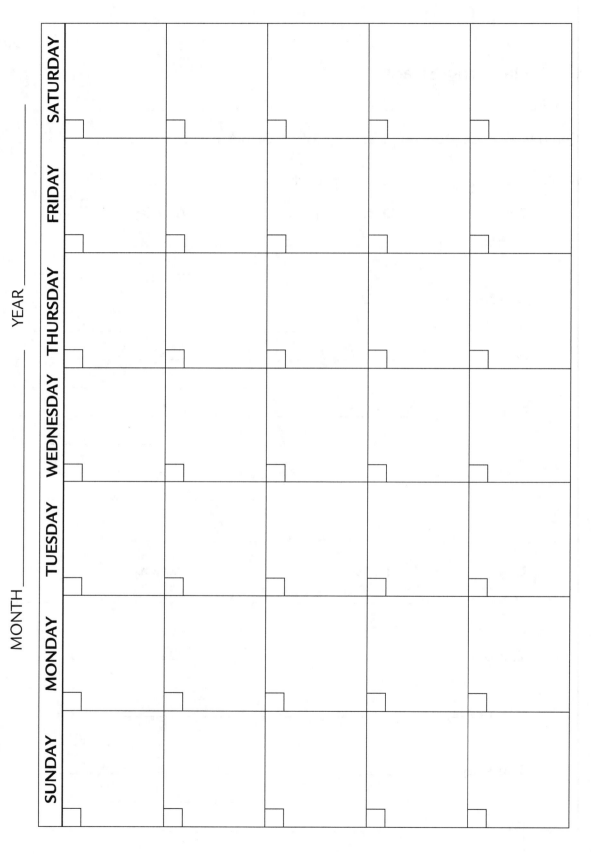

Planning Calendar

FORM 3.3

MONTH _____

YEAR _____

SUNDAY	MONDAY	TUESDAY	WEDNESDAY	THURSDAY	FRIDAY	SATURDAY

Writing Autobiographically: Unit Plan

Know Your Students

These students are still a little frightened by this new world—the high school. They are gregarious and social. Two are extremely quiet and shy. There seems to be a strong sense of group loyalty and a big need for peer approval. All students are reading at grade level or above. (Four are at twelfth grade.) When these students write, they have little concern for editing (especially spelling), and they all seem to write in one long paragraph. Experts say students this age should be showing a growing capacity for critical thinking.

Identify Goals

I want to have these students begin writing and using the writing process early in this course to prepare them for the subsequent writing activities. I want to emphasize prewriting, revising, and editing as separate activities. The students will work in small groups for peer editing, using listening and speaking skills and practicing critical thinking. I also want to structure the lessons to encourage students to write several drafts before they polish and edit the final one. Some of the elements of writing I want to emphasize are appeals to the senses, direct dialogue, metaphor, simile, interesting beginnings, and effective endings. I want to emphasize spelling, punctuation, and paragraphing as editing skills.

Resources

I have lots of samples of student writing that can be used as good models. Dictionaries and thesauruses are available for each student. I use Dandelion Wine by Ray Bradbury and Growing Up by Russell Baker as literary examples of autobiography. There is an audio version of Garrison Keillor reading from Growing Up in AV. Gary Paulsen, who wrote Tracker, lives in our community. It would be good to have these students meet a published author. We can refer to and study any classroom set of novels when the students begin writing dialogue and when I begin emphasizing paragraphing. I can also bring some stuffed toys from home along with The Velveteen Rabbit by Margery Williams when I ask them to write about one of their own childhood toys. The boys may think this topic is too babyish at first, so I want to head that off.

(Continued)

Activities

The students will practice many prewriting activities throughout the ten weeks: listing, brainstorming, mapping, freewriting. I can include a brainstorming game, writing, reading aloud, and working cooperatively in large and small groups to edit and revise their writing to produce a finished, polished draft.

Plan and Sequence

I plan to have these students write five autobiographical papers in the next ten weeks, which will ultimately be collected and bound as their own book. With each writing, I will introduce one or two new elements of strong writing and show students how to incorporate that element into their own writing. This is the sequence of elements I will introduce in each writing assignment:

Writing 1—A Childhood Toy
· Prewriting activities such as brainstorming and listing
· Peer editing and revising
· Editing for spelling, punctuation, and paragraphing

Writing 2—A Childhood Memory
· Appealing to the senses

Writing 3—A Childhood Friendship
· Direct dialogue
· Metaphor
· Simile

Writing 4—An Adult from My Childhood
· An interesting beginning

Writing 5—A Time I Grew Up Quickly
· An effective ending
· Editing for economy

Evaluation

I will design a checklist for small groups to use to respond to one another's writings, and I will use the same checklist when I respond to and grade final drafts. Students will need to know their books should have a cover, title page, table of contents, and a section about the author. We should complete these books for parent-teacher conferences, and I will need student permission to display or share their books.

It is well worth your time to use a consistent format in planning for each day. Begin by deciding on a design that appeals to you or fits your teaching style (Chalmers, 1992). (see Form 3.4). Duplicate enough copies of this or a similar design for each teaching day. On that day, your plan will become a helpful teaching guide. At the end of the day, analyze the plan, and fill in the evaluation section. What worked and what didn't? Some teachers color-code these forms, and write their evaluations in different color ink as a helpful reminder when they use or refer to the plans another time. Place each in a binder or folder, and by the end of the course or the year, you'll have a complete and invaluable record of the year-long course, individual units, and daily lessons.

Sample Daily Lessons

The sample lessons on pages 55–56 are for days 2 and 3 of the Writing Autobiographically unit. On day 1, the teacher talked about and showed some of her own childhood toys, read excerpts from *The Velveteen Rabbit, Growing Up,* and *Dandelion Wine,* and encouraged students to think about some of their own childhood memories. She explained that they too would be writing autobiographically in the coming weeks. (A sample response sheet for evaluating the final draft of the writing is included in Chapter Five, Form 5.6. Because objectives are focused, evaluation is simplified.)

TEAM PLANNING AND TEACHING

There are many possibilities for teachers to plan and teach together. For example:

- *If your classroom is near others whose teachers are teaching similar subject matter, consider planning or teaching (or both) a unit together.* Collaborate and tap one another's strengths, ideas, and resources. You might join forces for a research project. An auditorium or library can be used for bringing students together in large groups, and each of your classrooms could become shared learning centers or spaces for separate group activities.
- *Team up with a teacher in another discipline,* and base the writing assignments in your class on the content in the other area.
- *Create collaborative projects* with a teacher in the visual arts, or become involved in a visiting artist program.
- *Create a new class entirely.* For example, an American studies class might include American history, literature, and composition and involve teachers from the English and social studies departments. It might also involve collaboration with the school's art and music teachers.

Daily Lesson Design

Name _____

Class _____

Unit _____ Lesson _____

Date _____

Objectives _____

_____

_____

_____

Materials _____

_____

_____

_____

Procedure _____

_____

_____

_____

Evaluation of students _____

_____

_____

_____

Evaluation of lesson _____

_____

_____

_____

Writing Autobiographically: Lessons 2 and 3

Lesson 2

Daily Lesson Design Name *M. Jones*

Class: 9th-grade English

Unit Autobiography Lesson 2

Objectives

1. Students will practice brainstorming for writing ideas.
2. Students will focus on one idea and brainstorm for more ideas concerning their focus topic.
3. Students will freewrite about one idea.

Materials

Newsprint

Colored markers—enough for 1 for each group of three students

Tootsie Rolls or peanuts or popcorn or any pieces of small candy, enough for each student

Procedure

1. Explain brainstorming.
2. Organize groups of three.
3. Distribute the candy, one sheet of newsprint, and one marker to each group.
4. Have each group compete for the number of ideas they can list about their candy in five minutes.
5. Individuals brainstorm a long list of their childhood toys.
6. Individuals choose one toy on their list and brainstorm a list of details.
7. Using the brainstormed list, individuals freewrite about the toy for five to six minutes.

Evaluation of Students

Give students time to edit briefly. Have as many as possible read their drafts to the class. Comment on good details to the whole class following each reading.

(Continued)

Evaluation of Lesson

This lesson worked well. Students had fun and came up with many ideas. Because everyone read from his or her own desk, no one seemed threatened by reading aloud.

Lesson 3

Daily Lesson Design Name *M. Jones*

Class: 9th-grade English

Unit Autobiography Lesson 3

Objectives

1. Students will add new detail to their writing about a childhood toy.
2. Students will write a second draft.

Materials

Lost-and-found section of the newspaper

Procedure

1. Read sample lost-and-found announcements.
2. Have students write a pretend lost announcement for each toy, emphasizing specific detail.
3. When finished, read around room; point out good detail.
4. Have students brainstorm a list of words they could use to describe toy to someone who is blind.
5. Have students insert new detail into first draft.

Evaluation of Students

Confer with students, asking each to point out new details he or she has added to the original draft.

Evaluation of Lesson

Students have difficulty inserting new material into an earlier draft. Plan to spend plenty of time working one-to-one with students at this point.

PLANNING FOR ENGLISH LANGUAGE LEARNERS

Many English teachers express concern that they lack training and knowledge for teaching English language arts to nonnative speakers. If you are teaching writing holistically, using student-centered practices for teaching literature, and exposing your students to a wide variety of texts, then you are already relying on strategies that are beneficial and effective for teaching English language learners (ELLs). And if you have an understanding of second language acquisition, you will be far more effective in teaching the English language arts to English language learners.

We acquire a second language in much the same way that we mastered our first language. Language acquisition is a developmental process, and as teachers, we need to be supportive of our students as they work toward greater proficiency in English. The following useful strategies, from *The ESL/ELL Teacher's Book of Lists, 2nd ed.* (Kress, 2008), will help you as you work with English language learners:*

- Welcome students every day with a smile, a greeting, and their given names.
- Speak clearly and slowly, and use short, simple sentences.
- Face students when speaking to them; communicate with facial expressions and gestures.
- Watch students' body language and facial expressions for signs of comprehension.
- Pause between sentences to give students processing time.
- Praise students' efforts and successes appropriately.
- Use the same language for repeated tasks and routines.
- Demonstrate or pantomime responses to directions until all students understand and can perform them.
- Introduce yes/no active response cards immediately to enable active participation; frame questions for yes/no responses.
- Use choral response and whole-group active response cards to limit individual students' anxiety.
- Use labels and pictures to name objects and show actions.
- Establish routines for attendance, calendar review, assignments, and homework review.
- Read to students daily using high-interest controlled vocabulary materials with lots of pictures.
- Present information in more than one modality: words and graphics plus spoken language.
- Provide computer-aided practice for individual students to give them opportunities for self-paced work, including self-selected topics.
- Construct word walls to prompt students' memories and help them to be independent.

---

* Adapted from *The ESL/ELL Teacher's Book of Lists, Second Edition*, pp. 1–2. Jacqueline Kress © 2008 by John Wiley & Sons, Inc. Reprinted with permission of John Wiley & Sons, Inc.

- Provide bilingual dictionaries at appropriate grade levels and encourage students to use them.
- Plan nonverbal ways for students to show they have understood stories and directions. For example, have them select appropriate pictures or draw diagrams.
- Write page numbers and other information on the board after giving directions to "turn to page . . ." or "underline the answer . . ."
- Post homework assignments in the same place every day.
- Establish assessment systems that enable students to record and monitor their own progress in at least one or two areas.
- Have students keep word books and journals and add to them frequently.
- Post a world map (or regional map as needed) and have students identify their countries of origin.
- Provide opportunities for students to share cultural and linguistic information; for example, have them label a family tree with family relationships in both English and their first language; or have them list each language's greeting or its words for excellence, student, learning, and so on.
- Plan music and art exhibits to showcase cultures represented in the class.
- Remember that students know much more than they can say—don't water down content; do simplify the language.
- Gather content reading materials on several grade levels.
- Use cognates to help connect new learning with prior knowledge.
- Establish class rules with brief commands and gestures: *Sit. No talking. Show me the answer. Go to page x.*
- Post the names of students in groups and point to each group's list of names when calling students to a learning station or table. Seeing and hearing group members' names helps ELLs learn the names and eases communication within the group.
- Start portfolios of students' work at the beginning of the term and add to them as they progress throughout the year.

Appendix C in this book provides additional suggestions.

The teaching of grammar and vocabulary is examined in later chapters. Current practice and research indicate that the most effective instructional models for teaching language-based skills and content are best learned through contextually rich and authentic experiences. This is true of English language learners, but it is important to note that we will also need to break down concepts and give students ample practice as they develop proficiency in a new language.

PLANNING FOR STUDENTS WITH SPECIAL NEEDS IN AN INCLUSIVE CLASSROOM

As more students with special needs are placed in our rooms, the need for team planning is even more evident. This involves working with the special education teacher as well as a school psychologist, social worker, parents, other teachers, and possibly a recreational therapist. Through team planning, you will have help, support, and encouragement from professionals who have the records, information, and expertise to design individual learning plans based on what each student can do. In addition, this team will include a case manager who will help you think in terms of possibilities, make adaptations in your expectations and materials, and provide follow-up support.

Although we can expect that more and more students with special needs will be mainstreamed, classrooms already contain many students with learning disabilities. *Learning disabilities* is a broad term for students of average and above-average ability who have difficulty learning in the usual or normal way. These may be students who are mildly disabled, students who have previously received special services, or students whose disabilities have not been identified. Many have been mislabeled as "difficult" or "discipline problems," and they sometimes arrive in our classrooms filled with frustration, anxiety, and low self-esteem. Unfortunately, they are often perceived by some adults as lazy and unmotivated. With older students, it may be difficult to differentiate between what they can do and what they can't or won't do. Having experienced so much failure themselves, they are frequently the first to call attention to the errors of others.

Pacing and Risk Taking

Students with learning disabilities have a difficult time processing language. As a teacher asks a question, most of the students will already be processing an answer. Students with learning disabilities, however, may still be processing the question. These students have twice the processing load to do as opposed to the rest of the class. In addition, many have difficulty focusing anything out because everything grabs their attention. They are not risk takers and do not like surprises. One approach is to control and slow the pace of your classroom and give honest praise for a good response. One teacher makes a pact with his students with learning disabilities. Because he understands that anxiety affects performance, he tells them, "I will never call on you unless I am standing in front of your desk during a class discussion." He is careful to ask only questions the student can answer. Over time the student with learning disabilities becomes confident enough to volunteer (Lavoie, 1989).

Motivation

We frequently believe that students with learning disabilities are unmotivated and the key to overcoming their disability is to improve their motivation. However, motivation only enables any of us to do to the best of our ability what we are capable of doing. We're in error if we believe that if we push these students hard enough, they can learn along with everyone else. The experience of many students with learning disabilities is of being the only student in a classroom who can't do something. Many have difficulty with reading comprehension, motor coordination, and oral expression.

Here are some suggested adaptations for students with special needs who are mainstreamed into the regular education classroom:

- With the special education teacher, complete a plan that addresses the specific educational needs and necessary adaptations for the mainstreamed students with special needs in your class. These adaptations must be communicated with the parents. When an adaptation is no longer needed, it should be gradually removed.

- Clearly articulate the goals and expectations for mainstreamed students with special needs just as you do with regular education students.
- Incorporate Howard Gardner's theory of multiple intelligences in all learning activities (Gardner, 2005). Not only does it support learning for students with special needs, the regular education students benefit as well.

It is also important that you:

- Provide a classroom environment where reading is encouraged for all students: regular education and mainstreamed students with special needs.
- Present instructions in modalities other than orally.
- Give students multiple opportunities to demonstrate what they have learned.
- Clearly articulate consistent expectations for all students.

Reading Comprehension and Class Performance

Many teachers believe that vocabulary building is the key to teaching comprehension. They reason that if readers understand every word in a passage, they will understand the passage. However, comprehension is a complex task requiring much more than the simple decoding of material (Beers, 2002; Fountas & Pinnell, 2008). Because students with learning disabilities must put so much energy into decoding what they have read, the content is frequently lost to them. The following suggestions are useful in helping these students with reading:

- *Individualize reading assignments.* It's especially important to give these students the freedom to choose what they want to read. If they are reading what interests them, they are more likely to gain meaning from their reading.
- *Include plenty of prereading discussion.* Comprehension has more to do with background than it does with vocabulary.
- *Model what you do as a reader for your students.* Use the think-aloud strategy so that all of your students can witness what good readers do as they are exploring and reading a text (Wilhelm, 2001).
- *Encourage students to guess words they don't know and then move on.*
- *Allow students with learning disabilities to stop reading something they are not enjoying or to skip parts of a book that are too difficult for them.*
- *When you assign a section of reading to a class, begin by surveying the material.* Preview major concepts. Raise one or two questions and encourage students to read to answer the questions. Color-coding important information in textbooks helps students with reading disabilities know what is important and what is not.
- *Encourage students to glance back to pick up what they've missed or to skim ahead to prepare for what's coming.*

- *Provide extra information whenever possible.* Pictures and illustrations support and confirm what a reader sees in print (Wilhelm, 2004).
- *Provide auditory support.* Make a practice of reading all directions out loud or calling on another student to do so. Many students with learning disabilities cannot understand a set of directions when they read them, but they will understand when they hear them because they need auditory input for comprehension. That's why it is important that some students hear books. They can get their information through their ears and understand it, but they frequently can't understand if they are forced to rely entirely on their eyes.
- *Give these students plenty of time to complete their oral or written responses.* Many suffer from dysnomia, a word-finding problem similar to the feeling of having a word on the tip of your tongue but not being able to say it. Most of us are capable of both associative and cognitive tasks. Associative tasks are those in which we can do more than one thing at the same time—walking and talking, for example. Cognitive tasks are those we can do only one at a time—a mathematical computation, for example. Some students with learning disabilities are capable of only cognitive responses. They can concentrate on only one task at a time. Some may not be able to take class notes because listening is a cognitive experience for them, and they cannot write and listen at the same time. For these students, ask another student who can take notes to make a duplicate. For students with dysnomia, speaking is a cognitive process. For this student, begin a class discussion by asking everyone to write down several ideas in response to an opening question. After allowing plenty of writing time, call on the student with learning disabilities first because his or her list is likely to be the shortest.
- *Because cursive handwriting may be difficult to read for students with reading problems, type out assignments and handouts.* If this is not possible, especially as it pertains to information on the blackboard, print legibly.

MECHANICS

As you prepare handouts and tests for English language learners and students with special needs, keep the following in mind:

- Leave plenty of white space between sections and items.
- Avoid crowding too much information on one page.
- Include clear and concise directions.
- Use familiar terms.
- Use simple sentence structure.
- Call for one operation at a time.
- Provide examples.
- Limit the types of questions or activities.

The following are suggestions for meeting the needs of ELLs, students with special needs, and all other types of learners:[†]

- Match the modality of instruction to the student (for example, large print, Braille, or audiotaped versions for low-vision students).
- Observe students in individual, paired, small group, and whole class activities, and note which environment maximizes their engagement and success.
- Help students track their success using different strategies to accomplish a frequent task or assignment (such as learning new spelling words) and discuss which strategy worked best.
- Review students' individualized education programs to identify areas of strength, and develop instructional activities that use them to advantage.
- Use error analysis as a basis for planning instruction and practice activities.
- Maximize time on task by simplifying and creating standardized procedures so that time is spent on the learning activity, not on giving and interpreting directions.
- Make connections explicit, or ask leading questions to help students make links and transfer learning to similar but new situations.
- Provide ample response time, and let students know it's okay to take time to think in order to decide on an answer; discourage guessing.
- Focus first on accuracy, then on speed and fluency.
- Use direct instruction and modeling to demonstrate desired learning behavior.
- Provide immediate and clear feedback with an informing, neutral tone.
- Pace instruction so that learning is achieved and skills are practiced, and move on before students become bored.
- Use task analysis with students to show how to break down complex tasks into smaller components that allow students to focus their attention, recognize important sequences, learn subskills, and then reconstitute the tasks.
- Use structured, guided practice, gradually moving students from fully supported to fully independent work.
- Use echo or choral reading to help students pace reading, and use inflection to support understanding.
- Use group response methods (such as having students hold up a response card marked yes or no to answer questions) to keep the active learning level high for all students and to enable scanning of the responses to track individual students' learning.
- Give both oral and written directions. Post the directions on the board or in another prominent location. Keep the language simple, number the steps, and use rebuses or flowcharts to show steps graphically.
- Use cues or prompts to guide students' work. For example, underline or color-code the key element or elements or provide a template for organizing the task.

[†] Adapted from *The ESL/ELL Teacher's Book of Lists, Second Edition*, pp. 290–292. Jacqueline Kress © 2008 by John Wiley & Sons, Inc. Reprinted with permission of John Wiley & Sons, Inc.

- Use a visual thesaurus to show how the meanings of words are related.
- Use concept mapping to help students organize what they know about a concept.
- Use tables and other graphic organizers to show similarities and differences.
- Use KWL charts to help students plan and evaluate their learning. Before reading, have students identify what they already know about the topic, and list this information under the K heading. Next, have students identify what they want to learn from the reading selection, and list this information as questions or topics under the W heading. Later, after reading, have students list what they learned under the L heading and compare their learning to their want-to-learn goals.
- Extend the amount of time provided or reduce the amount of work (number of pages, examples, items, words), to do or both, to reduce stress and focus attention on positive outcomes.
- Provide informative feedback for correct answers to reinforce the use of an effective strategy, as well as for incorrect answers to show how the answer could have been found.
- Permit students to draw or tape a narrative, instead of writing a response, if spelling and writing are challenges.
- Provide advanced organizers, including questions for students to "read and find out." Teach decoding skills, high-frequency words, and frequently used word parts (prefixes, suffixes, and root words) directly. Research shows that a code-and-skill approach is more successful than literature or whole language approaches with students who have learning difficulties.
- Use computer-based programs for individualized practice and reinforcement.
- Use interest inventories and book circles to encourage independent reading.
- Provide texts at different readability levels on the same subject so all students can study and contribute to a themed interdisciplinary unit.
- Use different types of art to respond to a piece of literature or word study.
- Engage students in word play daily. There is no limit to the number of puns, jokes, puzzles, games, odd phrases, and interesting words and idioms that can be used.
- Read to the class every day if possible. Not only is it enjoyable for students (and you!), but you can model fluent reading and interest.
- Incorporate research into each week's lessons. Introduce and teach related skills (key words, indexing, alphabetical order, types of resources, evaluating sources, note taking, and so on) as part of the process.
- Create a language-rich classroom where books, magazines, newspapers, the Internet, craft directions, journals, word walls, favorite authors, and other language artifacts engage students' interests and imaginations as well as help them become proficient readers and independent learners.

Being a successful teacher in an inclusive classroom is rooted in the seamless integration of strategies that reach a wide variety of learners. It is important not to dwell on what students cannot do; rather, look at what they can do—and then work to help them do it even better. Your students need you to have realistic expectations for them and a chance to succeed on these terms.

DESIGNING, MONITORING, *and* GRADING COOPERATIVE LEARNING ACTIVITIES

- Designing group activities
- Monitoring and evaluating cooperative group work
- Grading cooperative group projects

My dad says group activities are unfair. The smart kids do all the work, and everyone gets the same grade.

Some students learn best through competition. Others learn best through cooperation. Still others prefer to work independently toward a goal. Consequently, you will want to keep a fair balance of cooperative, competitive, and independent activities for students in your classroom. Researchers who encourage teachers to use group work in classrooms point out that cooperative learning promotes greater achievement in more students, allows students to participate under less threatening conditions than in whole class discussions and competitive activities, and encourages them to take greater risks. In addition, students working in groups gain self-esteem, exhibit increased motivation, and regularly practice higher-order critical thinking skills (Jacobs, 2002).

DESIGNING GROUP ACTIVITIES

How often you use cooperative groups depends on how comfortable you are with the concept. Simply placing students in groups and telling them to work together does not mean they know how to cooperate or that they will do so even if they know how. Cooperative learning is not assigning a report to a group of students where one student does all the work and the others write their names on the paper. Cooperative learning occurs when each member's efforts are required for the whole group's success.

If you expect to include group work as part of your year-long teaching design, introduce cooperative activities early in the year, and provide plenty of practice for students as they learn to work as part of a team. You will have to make a number of decisions as you plan for cooperative group learning in your classroom.

How Many Students Should Be in Each Group?

The number of students you assign to each group should be determined by the task you want each to accomplish. Large groups, small groups, and pairs are all appropriate at various times. In the beginning, you will be teaching students basic social skills for group work. At this point it's best to begin with small groups of two or three students. As students become more skillful in working together, an optimum number is generally four and no more than five students. Larger groups may represent a greater range of abilities, but they also require more skill on the part of individual members to ensure active participation by each member. Initially very few students have these skills. The size of groups may also be determined by the materials available to you, as well as the time you wish to devote to each group activity. The shorter the period of time available, the smaller a group should be. Larger groups consume more time.

How Will Group Membership Be Determined?

There is no single approach to grouping students for cooperative activities. The easiest way to begin, even before you know your students' strengths and weaknesses, is simply to assign them randomly to groups in one of the following ways:

- Have students count off, and then place the ones together, the twos together, the threes together, and so forth.
- When possible place students in groups of three or five. In groups of four, students tend to work in two separate pairs, and any group larger than five is not ideal for group work. In larger groups, students tend to break off and create subgroups.
- Write a specific number of authors' names or the names of literary characters on the board. Students call off the names, and those with the same names become members of a group.
- Distribute colored strips of paper. If you want students to form groups of four, choose eight colors for a class of thirty-two students. Cut each color into four pieces. Students draw slips of paper and join others with the same color.

Some teachers group students of similar abilities. Others devise groups of high, average, and low abilities. Many researchers recommend heterogeneous groups if possible, because they believe this results in more elaborative thinking and greater perspective in discussing material (Gillies, 2007). The least desirable approach is to allow students to select their own group membership. Self-selected groups tend to be homogeneous based on ability, race, and gender. Teachers who believe rapport contributes to the effectiveness of the group occasionally allow students the option of selecting their own groups. One variation of the select-your-own-group method is to have students list the names of people with whom they would like to work and then place each in a learning group with one person they have chosen plus others selected by the teacher. Still another option is to offer a variety of suggestions for group projects and ask students to indicate the topics in which they are most interested. Students are then assigned to groups according to their topic choice.

How Long Should Groups Stay Together?

Some teachers keep cooperative groups together for an entire year or grading period. Others change membership frequently so that by the end of the course, every student has had the opportunity to work with every other student in the class. Ideally you should plan to allow groups to remain together at least long enough for them to be successful—until they complete a task or a project, for example. If at all possible, avoid breaking up groups that are having trouble functioning effectively. One of the objectives of group work is to enable students to resolve their problems collaboratively.

What Is the Teacher's Role in Cooperative Learning?

As you plan for cooperative projects in your classroom, your role as teacher is complex. No longer will you be the expert at the front of the classroom. Instead you will serve as a consultant, guide, and facilitator. You will also take a less directive role as your students prove their ability to take the initiative. In addition to identifying the objectives of a lesson and making decisions about placing students in groups, you will do the following:

- Be specific about what you expect each group to do:
  - Talk and work quietly.
  - Be considerate of one another.
  - Share equally in the work.
  - Determine a strategy or plan for completing the assigned task.
  - Determine what roles (such as recorder, reporter) are needed to accomplish the task and take turns assuming these roles. Over a period of time, each student should have an opportunity to make an oral report to the class as a whole, for example. For a more complex project, a group may decide to keep a log to record its progress. Will one student do this, or will the members take turns?
- Ensure that all members of the group learn the assigned material.

- Define what you expect of each member:
  - Attend class regularly.
  - Stay with the group.
  - Take turns.
  - Interact with others in the group.
  - Share ideas and materials.
  - Give others feedback, reinforcement, and support.
  - Criticize ideas, not people.
  - Be responsible for their own learning and the learning of others in the group.
  - Meet deadlines.
  - Fulfill designated group roles.
  - Explain and elaborate on the concepts being learned.
- Explain what each group is to produce, the time to be devoted to the work, and the criteria for evaluation:
  - Is the group to produce a list, a written summary, or an oral report, for example?
  - Do you expect the work to be completed in fifteen minutes, one class period, several class periods, or several weeks?
  - How will the group's work be evaluated?

MONITORING COOPERATIVE GROUP WORK

The role of both teacher and students changes dramatically in a cooperative setting.

The Teacher's Role

Although it may be tempting to correct a set of papers at your desk while students work in groups, it's imperative for you to monitor the operation of each group. Your role is to teach collaborative skills and provide assistance when needed. You should plan to observe groups at work and give them feedback based on your observations and notes—for example:

- Do group members smile?
- Do they nod in agreement?
- Do they gesture?
- Do they make eye contact?
- Does one person speak at a time?
- Do they follow directions?
- Do they ask questions?
- Do they acknowledge the good ideas of others?
- Do they disagree in a pleasant way?
- Is everyone involved and on task?
- Have they shared responsibilities?
- Do they check to see that everyone understands?
- Do they take turns acting as recorder or reporter, for example?
- Have they made an effort to include everyone?

Point out what you've observed each group do well. Use the preceding list as an observation sheet, and tally the number of times you observe some of these behaviors; then tell each group what you have observed. If you see possibilities for improvement, ask for suggestions from group members or offer your own solutions, at least in the beginning. Although you may be hesitant to do this with older students, you will find that they too will benefit from this kind of positive feedback. Many teachers omit this opportunity to guide students in their cooperative work, and it is a serious omission. Although we may take these social skills for granted, students who have spent a majority of their classroom time working competitively or independently will have had little opportunity to develop in this manner. The time spent processing (discussing and evaluating) the functioning of groups is essential because you not only want each group to accomplish a task successfully, but you also want the students to maintain these skills and relationships for the next group project.

In addition to making the processing of social skills a component of every cooperative activity, you'll want to ensure individual accountability. As groups complete their work, call on one member to explain how his or her group got an answer, reached a conclusion, or produced a report. At another time, check to make sure everyone in the group understands the material and agrees with the answer the group has produced.

The Students' Role

As you evaluate a group's performance, it's also important that you involve students in self-evaluation. The following reflective questions encourage groups to evaluate their own work:

- What are two things you did well as a group, and what is one thing you need to do better?
- Could you describe a problem your group encountered and explain how your group solved it?
- What is something each member did that was helpful to the group?
- What is something each member could do to make the group function better tomorrow?

Questionnaires (followed by a whole class discussion) at the end of a longer group activity also help students to evaluate their individual performance and the group performance and to encourage growth and more skillful participation in subsequent group work. Form 4.1 is a model questionnaire for group evaluation, and students may complete it either individually or cooperatively.

Group Evaluation

Name _____

Group name or number _____

Names of members in the group:

_____

_____

_____

Who was the group recorder? _____

Who was the reporter? _____

Were there other roles members assumed? _____ If so, who and
    what were they? _____

_____

What were your group's objectives? What were you expected to do?

_____

_____

_____

_____

_____

What procedure did your group follow? _____

_____

_____

_____

_____

What objectives did your group accomplish? What did you do well?

_____

_____

_____

_____

_____

_____

What problems did your group encounter as you worked together?

_____

_____

_____

_____

_____

_____

What might your group do to improve its performance in another such activity?

_____

_____

_____

_____

_____

_____

Sample Unit Plan for Introducing Cooperative Learning

Because most students have little experience with cooperative work, it is essential that you teach cooperative skills. The sample lesson plan outlined here is designed to introduce students to collaborative group work and the social skills necessary for them to function effectively. The beginning exercises are simple activities intended to acquaint students with one another, as well as to help them begin building a group identity. Each exercise leads to a somewhat more complex group problem. This is an ideal beginning unit because it creates a positive classroom atmosphere and climate of cooperation that is essential if you intend to include group work in your year-long curriculum.

Introducing Students to Cooperative Group Work: Sample Unit Plan

Day 1

1. Direct each student to write his or her answers to the following directions:

   · Write your name.
   · Write the name of the city where you were born.
   · Write the name of your best subject.
   · Write the name of a subject that is difficult for you.
   · Do you have a job now, or have you had a job? If so, describe it briefly. What are some good parts of the job? Some drawbacks?
   · List three things you do well.
   · Name one thing your best friend doesn't know about you.

2. Ask students to use their answers as guides while introducing themselves orally to the whole class.
3. Assign students to form pairs (numbering off is quickest), and have the pairs spend approximately five minutes each interviewing one another and taking notes. (If there is an uneven number of students, you should become a student's partner because this is primarily a get-acquainted activity.) Explain that each student is to write a brief profile (based on his or her notes) that emphasizes the two most interesting facts they learned about their partners. Students should also understand they will read these profiles to the whole class on day 2.

Day 2

1. Direct the pairs from day 1 to move their desks next to one another. Then call on everyone in the class to take turns reading his or her profile to the whole class.

---

2. Instruct each pair to draw a line down the center of the page of a single sheet of paper and at the top of both columns, write "I Remember" or "I Wish" or "I Wonder" (choose only one). Have one student begin by writing an "I Remember" (or an "I Wish" or "I Wonder") statement about any memory or idea that comes to mind. The partner reads this statement and then writes one of his or her own.

3. Ask each pair to continue to add to its list. After five or six minutes, call on the pairs to read their responses aloud. After the pairs have read their lists, point out examples of positive interaction that you have observed between students and also remind students that their lists are filled with unexpected twists and pleasant surprises because they worked and wrote together.

Day 3

1. Ask individual students to draw a line down the center of a sheet of paper to form two columns and label one column "Likes" and other "Dislikes." Instruct students to use about three minutes to complete their list.

2. Direct the students to rejoin their partners from the preceding day. (If some students are absent, have single students form new partnerships or have them join another pair.) Ask the pairs or triads to compare their individual lists, note anything they have in common, and produce a new list of likes and dislikes the members of the group hold in common. Allocate four or five minutes for this activity.

3. Have each pair or triad join another pair or triad. At this point, it's best if you decide which pairs should be joined. Early observation will have given you some indication of student attitudes and personalities and an intuitive sense of which students might work well together. You will also combine pairs so that there is a mix of boys and girls and ethnic backgrounds in each group.

4. Instruct the newly formed group of four or five students to complete the following projects. Indicate they will have approximately fifteen minutes to complete their work before presenting it to the whole class during the last fifteen to twenty minutes of the class period.

   a. Using the previous brainstorming material and any new ideas, make a complete list of your group's likes and dislikes.
   b. Calculate the average height and weight of your group.
   c. Think of an appropriate name for your group, and explain its significance.
   d. Choose a reporter to present your material to the class.

5. Following each group's presentation, ask students to evaluate the way their group functioned: "What did you do well?" Point out that their group lists of

likes and dislikes are extensive and often contain surprising details because of their cooperative effort.

6. Explain to the students that they will be members of this newly formed and named group for the next project or for the next several weeks (depending, of course, on what plans you have in mind for them).

Day 4

1. Ask the whole class to brainstorm a list of possible problems they might encounter as they work in their groups. A list might resemble the following:

   · Someone doesn't get along with someone else in the group.
   · Not everyone in the group takes the assignment seriously.
   · Not everyone in the group does his or her share.
   · Some people in the group are frequently absent.
   · Someone in the group hates to work in groups.
   · Someone would rather be with another group.
   · Someone feels too shy to contribute to the group.
   · The group cannot complete a major assignment by the due date.

2. Direct the groups formed on day 3 to move their desks together to brainstorm for additional ideas they might add to the whole class list, and then design a set of positive rules for their group to follow as they work together. (It's best to have only a few rules.) Be sure the groups understand they will present their lists to the class before the end of the class period. If time allows, suggest a bonus topic, such as brainstorming a list of song titles that incorporate a theme of cooperation, such as "Whistle While You Work" or "Together."

3. Call on a reporter from each group to present its set of rules (and list of song titles) to the entire class and to explain the rationale for their decisions. The following is a model set of rules and could be reproduced and distributed to all students on day 5:

   "Happy Together"
   · Keep all comments positive.
   · Encourage one another.
   · Listen to one another.
   · Include everyone.
   · Do your share.
   · Stay on track.
   · Meet deadlines.

4. Conclude with a whole class discussion of the social skills necessary to function well in a group.

Additional Group Activities

You may plan any number of additional lessons to follow these beginning activities. Keep in mind that the best assignments require students to develop their own ideas and thoughts rather than simply memorize ideas or concepts from a textbook (Marzano, 2001):

1. Each group creates a collage that represents the group, being sure it reflects the strengths, interests, goals, and heritage of each member equitably. On completing the collage, the members present and explain it to the whole class. Alternative activities include creating a group flag, a motto or slogan, or a time line featuring the important dates in each member's life.

2. One student in each group begins a story by writing a few sentences. He or she covers all but the last sentence with a piece of paper, and another student continues the story, again covering all but the last sentence before the next students add to the story. Finally, one member of each group reads the group's writing to the entire class.

3. Members share with the group a scary moment in their lives. The group chooses one story and writes and edits it to read to the entire class.

4. Groups brainstorm a list of fairy tales. After selecting one, the members write a new version from another point of view—for example, the witch retells "Hansel and Gretel" or the stepmother retells "Cinderella." The reporter reads the final version to the whole class. As a long-term, more complex group assignment, this project could become a choral reading or a radio play that involves every member in an oral presentation.

5. Groups brainstorm a list of questions in response to a piece of literature. Each chooses one or two of its best questions to use as the basis for their own group discussion or to submit to the teacher for a whole class discussion. If small group discussion is used, one member summarizes the group's ideas in a report to the entire class.

6. Groups write a summary of the important ideas in a paragraph, several pages, or a chapter. For example, if all the students in the class are reading the same novel, each group might be responsible for writing a summary of one chapter or section of the book. A student from each group reports to the class as a whole. This becomes a more valuable assignment if each group is asked to relate summarized ideas about the book's major themes or motifs.

7. Groups write a set of directions for a specific process (how to check out a book from the library, for example). Humorous topics might include how to fail a test, how to irritate parents, how to say the wrong thing, how to waste money, how to break a promise, how to procrastinate, and how to lose a girlfriend or boyfriend.

8. The members of a group research a topic. Each person is responsible for checking at least one different source and writing four or five note cards. The group writes the report together, and each member is responsible for seeing that his or her information is included. For oral reports, each member takes a part, and all members help one another rehearse until they all feel at ease for the class presentation.

9. A group collaborates to complete a guided response sheet. For example, after a class has read "The Gift" by John Steinbeck, the teacher designs and distributes a single response sheet to each group (see Form 4.2). By distributing one sheet to a group, you will encourage cooperation and also reduce your correcting load.

Group Assignment for Steinbeck's "The Gift"

Your group may earn a total of 25 points for this assignment.

The name of your group is _____

Names of group members present. Use both first and last names.

_____   _____

_____   _____

_____   _____

_____

1. Brainstorm a list of words that describe Jody. (5 points)

_____

_____

_____

_____

_____

2. Brainstorm a list of words that describe Carl Tiflin. (5 points)

_____

_____

_____

_____

_____

3. Brainstorm a list of words that describe Billy Buck. (5 points)

_____

_____

_____

_____

_____

4. Who is the protagonist in the story? (2 points)

_____

_____

5. What is the protagonist's problem and how is it solved? (2 points)

_____

_____

6. What event is the climax of the story? (1 point)

_____

7. Diagram the various crises that lead to the climax of the story. Include the exact day and details of each. (5 points)

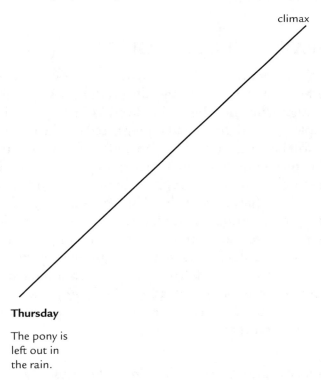

climax

Thursday

The pony is
left out in
the rain.

This activity is worth up to 25 points.

Your group's total _____

10. To ensure individual accountability, require each student to complete an assignment independently. Group members discuss and compare the work of each before submitting a single master copy for evaluation. For example, in working with Harper Lee's *To Kill a Mockingbird*, you might ask each student to draw a map of the book's setting: the main street, the school, the business district, the courthouse, the residences of the Finches, the Radleys, Rachel Haverford, Mrs. Dubose, and Miss Maudie, and so forth. After individual maps have been completed, direct students to compare and discuss the maps in groups. Finally, ask each group to produce a master map and submit it for evaluation. This is an ideal exercise because it promotes both individual responsibility and cooperation. It also prepares students for a more complex group project, such as the dramatization of a neighborhood tour (suggested in Form 4.3). Chapters Five through Seven present additional ideas for cooperative projects involving writing, reading, speaking, and listening.

It is essential that you give your students plenty of practice in learning to work cooperatively. Early practice with simple problems will allow them to gain skills such as developing brainstorming techniques, assuming positive group roles, and making group decisions—skills that will help prepare them for more complex problems later in the year. Not every effort will go smoothly, but over time, students can and will improve their ability to work as a part of a team.

GRADING COOPERATIVE GROUP PROJECTS

One advantage of cooperative work is that the teacher's paper load for evaluating and grading decreases because each group generally produces a single product, report, or paper. Although group assignments may be as simple as, "List five questions you have about this poem," or as complex as, "Produce a radio play based on the theme of this novel," grading such assignments will be much easier if you include a plan for evaluating and grading along with each assignment you design. For some, simply completing the assignment may be enough. If, for example, you ask a group to brainstorm and write five questions about a poem and report their questions to the class, the group's grade might be based on the number and quality of questions it produces. Major group projects that extend over a longer period of time take much more careful planning in execution, evaluation, and grading. It's best to set up rules for grading major group projects early in the year. Because student absences can disrupt scheduled presentations, criteria such as those that follow are helpful in both planning and evaluating group projects. In addition, clearly stated guidelines will promote better attendance in your classroom as students learn they are accountable to other members of their group.

Criteria for Grading Major Cooperative Group Projects
1. Each member of a group will receive the same number of points for each group assignment. Therefore, it is important that you encourage and help one another to contribute equally and to work cooperatively.

2. To receive the points you must:

   • Participate in planning the project
   • Participate in your group's presentation at the scheduled time. You will be given options for the dates for major assignments and presentations, and it is important that you plan ahead.

3. Anyone who is absent on the day of a major oral presentation loses all points. If the remainder of the group has the material and is able to make a presentation, it will be evaluated and graded accordingly. If a presentation cannot be given because a group is unprepared or students are absent, all members will lose the points. If a problem arises, consult with your group and the teacher before the due date to find a positive solution.

Form 4.3 is a sample assignment for a major cooperative project in conjunction with the entire class reading *To Kill a Mockingbird.* (See also Forms 4.4 and 4.5.)

Group Response Project

Name _____ Date _____

Each of you is to work in a group to plan and present a response to this novel. Your presentations are each worth up to 50 points and will be due on the following dates:

_____

Choose from the following options:

1. Each group member is to become one of the major characters in the novel. Each person writes and delivers a five-minute monologue for his or her character. Work together on writing and rehearsing the monologues to make the presentation a collaborative effort. You are encouraged to use props and costumes in your presentation.

2. Write a script for a tour conductor showing people the town in which this book is set. Describe the homes of the characters and the places where important events take place. Plan to include brief chats with the novel's characters along the way. You are encouraged to include a musical background and sound effects. This project may be taped or presented live. Each group member should contribute to the script as well as to the taped material and to the class presentation.

3. Suppose the major characters in this book are guests on a radio or television talk show. Write and deliver an interview with the major characters. One member of the group will become the talk show host. Other members will each become one of the major characters. All members should participate in writing and producing the script.

4. Design and produce an issue of a Maycomb newspaper following a major event in the novel. For example, you may choose to publish on the day following the trial of Tom Robinson or on the first day of November (following the events of Halloween). Each group member should contribute at least one signed story or article to the publication. Plan ahead because you may want to make enough copies of your publication for each member of the class. Involve everyone in your class presentation, and be prepared to explain the steps you followed in producing the newspaper, the roles each of you assumed, and your editorial decisions.

5. Design your own group project, plan it, and have it approved by the teacher.

Group Performance Self-Evaluation

Name of project _____ Date _____

Group name _____

Names of people in group:

_____   _____

_____   _____

_____   _____

A. List the steps you followed in planning and completing your project:

1. _____
2. _____
3. _____
4. _____
5. _____
6. _____
7. _____
8. _____
9. _____
10. _____
11. _____
12. _____
13. _____
14. _____
15. _____

B. Groups of students working together are expected to encounter a variety of problems. Describe the major problems you encountered in completing your project.

_____

_____

_____

_____

_____

_____

C. Problem solving is a skill that can improve with practice. Explain how your group solved its problems.

_____

_____

_____

_____

_____

_____

D. List the names of people in your group who were absent for at least one day of class preparation time. _____

_____

_____

_____

_____

_____

E. Explain how the group and the absent individual(s) solved this problem.

_____

_____

_____

_____

_____

_____

F. Did you have enough class time to complete your work? _____

If not, explain how you solved this problem. _____

_____

_____

_____

_____

_____

G. List the contributions made by each member of the group:

Name   Contribution(s)

_____   _____

                                 _____

_____   _____

                                 _____

_____   _____

                                 _____

_____   _____

H. List the names of the people in your group who made the greatest or best contributions to your project, and explain what each did.

_____

_____

_____

_____

_____

_____

I. On a scale of 1 (low) to 10 (high), rate both your work as a group and the quality of your presentation to the class: _____
Explain your answer.

_____

_____

_____

_____

_____

J. What changes would you make if you were to do this project again?

_____

_____

_____

_____

_____

_____

K. What did you learn from this project?

_____

_____

_____

_____

_____

_____

L. If this assignment were to be given to another class, what changes or improvements would you recommend?

_____

_____

_____

_____

_____

_____

Evaluation of Group Project and Presentation: 50 Points

Group name _____

Name of presentation _____ Date _____

Names of students in group:

_____   _____

_____   _____

_____   _____

1. Presentation of project to the class as a whole   (10) _____
Does the whole class understand clearly what is
being presented?
Is each group member involved in the presentation?

2. Completeness of project   (10) _____
Has the group developed its project as completely
as possible?
Has each member contributed to the final project?

3. Originality of final project   (10) _____
Does the group's presentation exhibit independent
and original thinking?

4. Mastery of project   (10) _____
Is the group in control of its project or does the
presentation appear to be an indifferent attempt
to complete an assignment?
Has the group solved its major problems?

5. Group self-evaluation   (10) _____
Has the group evaluated its work carefully and
thoroughly?

Total (50) _____

Additional Suggestions for Evaluating and Grading Cooperative Work

- For some projects, consider giving two grades—one for achievement and one for cooperative skills. In addition to grading a group's project, you might also give each group a total number of points for its group work. Have the group decide how the points will be distributed. It must be a team decision on who earns what points.
- Provide group awards. Suppose a group works together during the week in preparation for taking individual tests. Award bonus points if every member of a group achieves a specified number of correct answers. If everyone scores 75 percent or above, for example, give five bonus points to each team members. You may want to evaluate academically handicapped students according to specialized criteria so that other group members are not penalized. This option is perfectly acceptable, and students will welcome and support this decision.
- Have students work independently to complete a study sheet or to answer a set of questions. Then have the members work in a group to certify that each person's work is correct. Pick one paper at random, grade it, and award all group members the same score.
- If at all possible, don't allow cooperative work to lower a student's class average. Offer alternative independent assignments for students who are absent.
- Group work in conjunction with long-term reading assignments can be particularly frustrating if some students are unprepared. One approach is to tell students they cannot work in a group if they have not completed the necessary preparatory work. Without being judgmental or punitive, suggest they read or work quietly in a corner while the students who are prepared to work in groups do so. Assure everyone you will provide the same or alternative assignments to individuals when they are sufficiently prepared to complete them. (This isn't as much work for the teacher as it sounds, because in most cases, individual students can be given the same assignment as that given to a group.) This is a fair approach, and students view it as reasonable. Students who do the assigned work either cooperatively or independently are rewarded. The progress of the class is not impeded by its least prepared member. Most important, over time, you will see more students completing assignments promptly because they come to view cooperative work as both productive and enjoyable. They will also understand that their work in groups is often better than that completed independently.

Grading students in their cooperative efforts often raises concern among teachers and parents, especially in relation to students who are gifted. The fear is that one student's academic progress is being sacrificed so a slower student can learn. Of course, you will want to balance your curriculum so every student has plenty of opportunity to work independently, competitively, and cooperatively. However, the bright student who excels academically but cannot work with others in a social setting is equally deprived. The real world values negotiation and cooperation: health care personnel consult one another, advertising executives brainstorm and coordinate sales campaigns, and the automotive industry promotes team effort. Every student will benefit by learning, practicing, and using cooperative skills.

chapter 5

TEACHING WRITING

- Teaching the writing process
- Managing your writing classroom
- Using mini-lessons
- Sharing student writing: Presenting and publishing
- Evaluating and grading student writing
- Designing assignments for a variety of formats

I thought I'd write about the galaxy for this report. Is that okay? I'm really interested in astrology.

The teaching of writing has undergone a quiet revolution in the past decade. Students are encouraged to choose topics that interest them, develop and edit their work through several drafts, share their work with others in a workshop setting, and deliver the final draft to a real audience. Today the expectation is that English teachers use the process approach for the instruction of writing and this chapter is designed to help you introduce it into your own classroom. If you have already adopted the writing process approach, you will find many ideas and suggestions for refining your teaching. This chapter also includes information about structured writing activities that are helpful for classroom instruction.

There are a variety of successful approaches to the teaching of writing, and the suggestions offered here are intended to help every teacher be an effective teacher of writing, to help you reduce your paper load, and to help you encourage your students to become active participants in their own writing and learning as well as the writing and learning of their classmates.

TEACHING THE WRITING PROCESS

The process approach to teaching writing views writing as a recursive process with many steps: prewriting, drafting, revising and editing, and sharing the results (presenting and publishing).

- *Prewriting.* This is a time of preparation before writing the first draft. It helps writers generate and explore ideas and is critical to the success of the entire writing process. By introducing a variety of prewriting activities, you can help your students discover many ideas for their own writing topics. (Options for a variety of prewriting activities are discussed later in this chapter.)
- *Drafting.* A completed writing usually has gone through several drafts. In the earliest draft, the student begins by quickly jotting down ideas in rough form. It is a time to gather, explore, and discover ideas without worrying about neatness or correctness. Not every draft will be taken through the entire writing process. Those that are undergo further revision and refinement in subsequent drafts.
- *Revision and editing.* Revision is the re-seeing of a piece of writing. Once a first draft is completed, the writer becomes concerned with the effect of the writing. Early changes may address ideas and their sequence. The writer deletes material that doesn't belong and adds to or keeps what is strong. Later drafts are concerned with rearranging, reforming, and unifying the piece as a whole. Sentences may be combined and paragraphs adjusted. A final revision involves proofreading, polishing, and editing. Not all writers work in the same way, but by emphasizing writing as a several-stage process, you can help your students become successful writers.
- *Presenting and publishing.* This is the stage frequently omitted from school writing. Students have generally written only for the teacher. Today we encourage them to write for and deliver their writing to a variety of audiences. This may include reading aloud in class, in a group, or in another public forum; turning in a piece of writing for evaluation to you; delivering it to someone outside the classroom; displaying it; or submitting it for publication.

Encourage your students to work as nearly like professional writers as possible. Although you may suggest subjects, help them discover their own topics and expect them to write in a variety of forms for a variety of readers. Confer often with your students, and encourage collaboration in small and large groups. Your students will revise and edit their work when it counts most—before submitting it to you as a final draft for a grade.

A number of concerns about teaching the writing process are common:

- *What about teaching the basics? Shouldn't my students complete the grammar book before moving on to writing?* Students do need to master certain skills. These are best taught, however, in the context of writing, primarily during the revising and editing stages, rather than through isolated exercises. The revision stage is the time when the most learning about writing occurs, and it's important that you elicit several drafts from students when you expect them to carry their writing through the entire process. Rather than teaching the grammar book from cover to cover, use it as a helpful resource for mini-lessons as your students revise and edit their own writing. (Mini-lessons are discussed later in this chapter, and some sample grammar mini-lessons are included.)
- *Will my students be prepared for competency tests—the SAT, for example?* More and more of these tests require students to prepare a writing sample. Because your students will write frequently and produce many kinds of writing, they are likely to be more versatile and fluent than students who have not done so. In addition, their experience with revision and proofreading prepares them for objective questions that require them to detect and correct errors. If you teach writing in this way, your students will be well prepared for writing assessments found on a standardized test.
- *Having my students write more will take time. How can I possibly do all this and still teach literature, speaking, and listening?* Current research encourages us to view both reading and writing as naturally compatible processes. Although some writing may be taught independently, writing may also be a prereading activity, an activity during reading, and one of many possible responses following reading. (See Chapter Six for a discussion of a variety of responses to literature.)
- Researchers point out that students who write about what they read remember more and read more critically. Their reading scores improve, and their vocabularies expand. In addition, collaborative group work with both reading and writing encourages students to practice listening and speaking skills. Your planning and successful classroom management will allow you to create a classroom that combines reading, writing, listening, and speaking. It is possible for you to teach all the elements of language arts effectively and well (Beach, 2006).

MANAGING YOUR WRITING CLASSROOM

There is no single approach to teaching writing, but planning is essential. At times you will plan for whole class activities. At other times, your students will work independently or in small groups. Use whole class instruction when you:

- Introduce a new prewriting activity
- Discover the whole class needs a particular lesson in mechanics
- Want to give everyone essential information
- Want to involve students in solving problems or setting up procedures
- Want the whole class to listen to students' writing

If you want to keep the entire class together through an entire writing process, try the following schedule:

Day 1: Introduce a prewriting activity to help students discover a variety of possible topics; then narrow these options to a more focused topic and generate additional ideas concerning the topic.

Day 2: Plan to have students use the entire class period for writing a first draft based on their ideas from day 1. (Although most writing happens in the classroom, students may continue to work on their drafts outside class.)

Day 3: Students rework their drafts in any way necessary to share with classmates on day 4.

Day 4: Students meet in peer groups to share their writings with classmates and respond to the writing of others.

Day 5: Introduce a mini-lesson. The type of lesson will depend on the element of writing you wish to emphasize. It's best to concentrate on only one or two concerns rather than trying to cover everything.

Day 6: Students revise and produce a more polished draft. Student-teacher conferences occur at any time throughout these days, especially as students move to more polished drafts. (Student-teacher conferences are discussed later in this chapter.)

Day 7: Students proofread individually or in pairs and begin a final draft.

Day 8: Students complete final versions to present to a particular reader.

You may plan for a single writing or a unit project that includes a series of related writings. Introduce or emphasize one or two new elements with each new assignment. The following sample plan is an autobiographical unit, previously mentioned in Chapter Three, designed by a teacher for ninth-grade students (it could be used with other age groups as well). This teacher plans for a variety of prewriting activities based on broad, general themes. Instead of trying to teach everything about writing in every assignment, she will introduce and focus on one element at a time (such as appealing to the senses or using direct dialogue). Earlier get-acquainted writings have indicated that her students have difficulty with paragraphing and that they need help in editing for spelling and punctuation. These elements become the focus for editing in each paper in the series. Finally, she plans to have the students collect and bind their five final polished writings as personal booklets at the end of the unit.

Writing Autobiographically: A Sample Writing Unit

· *Writing 1: A Childhood Toy.* The students will be introduced to brainstorming, listing, and freewriting. They will produce several early drafts to fuse into a single, more polished writing. Finally, they will work in peer groups to edit for spelling, punctuation, and paragraphing.

- *Writing 2: A Childhood Memory.* This writing will focus on appealing to all five senses. The emphasis on editing will continue to be spelling, punctuation, and paragraphing.
- *Writing 3: A Childhood Friendship.* The emphasis will be on direct dialogue, as well as spelling, punctuation, and paragraphing.
- *Writing 4: An Adult from My Childhood.* This paper will be concerned with an effective beginning as well as spelling, punctuation, and paragraphing.
- *Writing 5: A Time I Grew Up Quickly.* An effective ending will be the focus of this writing. In addition to spelling, punctuation, and paragraphing, the students will edit for economy.

Planning for Many Types of Writing

Although we encourage students to choose their own topics and formats, it's unrealistic to think they will try all kinds of writing without guidance. Most students prefer expressive writing and personal narrative, and you won't want to discourage this because this type of writing builds fluency in young writers and underlies all other kinds of writing. You may want to begin with expressive writing early in the year, but you'll also want your students to write in a wider variety of forms as the year goes on.

The terminology used to classify writing can be confusing. Sometimes writing is classified according to purpose, sometimes according to form and style. The four modes of discourse are often called narration, description, exposition (also referred to as explanatory), and persuasion, and these terms are found in many textbooks today. Another classification, based on both purpose and audience, can be helpful as you plan for a variety of writing formats:

- *Expressive writing* is loosely structured and exploratory. Journals, diaries, logs, informal personal essays, informal letters, brainstorming, freewriting, short reaction papers, personal narratives, reminiscences, and memoirs encourage this kind of writing.
- *Structure writing* conforms to standardized forms such as letters of appreciation, sympathy, congratulations, and application; business communication; invitations; résumés; and jokes, riddles, and fables.
- *Imaginative writing* is intended to delight and entertain and places its emphasis on language and plot. Students writing in this way produce songs, tales, poems, myths, jokes, riddles, stories, anecdotes, essays, or letters.
- *Informative writing* emphasizes subject matter and is intended to explain or clarify some content to a reader. Reports, reviews, letters, advertisements, research papers, examinations, essays, newspaper articles, profiles, and observations encourage this kind of writing.
- *Persuasive writing* is intended to influence the reader's point of view. Students writing persuasively may produce reports, editorials, letters, research papers, advertisements, or essays.

Prewriting Activities

Ideally students will choose their own topics and define their purpose and audience. We teachers have commonly used class discussion, listening, observation, research, or field trips as activities prior to writing. Other highly effective prewriting techniques will also help students generate writing ideas.

Not every student needs prewriting activities such as those that follow, but some will find them useful. Most important, avoid an inflexible approach that leaves little room for individual learning styles or modes of expression. Give students many options, and allow them to recognize and use what works best for them.

Brainstorming

This technique is intended to generate as many ideas as possible about a subject. Although students may brainstorm independently, interaction in groups is an especially effective way to gather many ideas and to view a subject from a variety of viewpoints. Generally the teacher leads such a session, but you may also want to encourage students to be leaders. Begin with a stimulus—a word, a phrase, a picture, or an object. Some teachers use the (volunteered) contents of students' pockets as stimuli for a brainstorming session. For example, the collection may contain coins, a red pen, two keys, a note, and some mints. What are all the words and ideas that might be generated by observing this collection? No answer is wrong and unexpected observations are welcomed. The leader asks open-ended questions, probes for more complete responses, and then asks more open-ended questions. In brainstorming there are no wrong ideas or suggestions. Record every answer or appoint a student to record them.

Listing

A variation of brainstorming is listing. The leader encourages students either independently or in a group to make long lists of ideas about possible topics. This often revolves around a common theme such as, "List as many of your childhood toys as you can recall." Once students complete their lists, they choose one item on the list that interests them and seems to have possibilities as a writing topic. Then they make a second extended list of details and ideas concerning that single item: for example, "How to . . . ," "Things I Know," or "Things I Would Like to Know."

Listing in Response to Questions

Students list in response to questions designed by the teacher. Questions for a prewriting exercise in preparation for writing a memoir might resemble the following:

1. Make a list of people who have been important in your life.
2. From this list, choose someone who would be a good subject for a writing—someone you'd like to write about. Write that person's name below your original list.
3. How would you describe this person to someone who does not know him or her?
4. List several places you remember being with this person.
5. List several things (pictures, songs, clothing) you associate with this person.

6. What feelings do you have when you think of this person?
7. List several incidents involving this person.
8. Look over your list of incidents, and underline the most interesting, memorable incident.
9. Look over all the ideas you have jotted down, and circle material that pertains to the incident you have underlined.
10. Using the underlined and circled material as a reference, begin writing a memoir of your special person. Focus on a single incident involving the two of you (Daniels & Zemelman, 1985).

Clustering or Webbing

Clustering is a nonlinear brainstorming activity that generates ideas, images, and feelings around a stimulus word such as the example in Figure 5.1 based on the word *toy*.

In listing, the writer usually connects ideas to a preceding word in the list. Clustering allows connections to be observed and recognized in a variety of directions across the page. Introduce clustering to students by first modeling it on the blackboard. Circle a single word or phrase and ask students to contribute as many ideas as possible. Write down all the student responses (radiating outward). Next, have students work independently, choosing their own nucleus word. Encourage the students to cluster as long as possible. Some researchers encourage writers to cluster until they experience a sense of direction—a conviction that they "have this to write about" (Gere, 2005). Successive clusters can

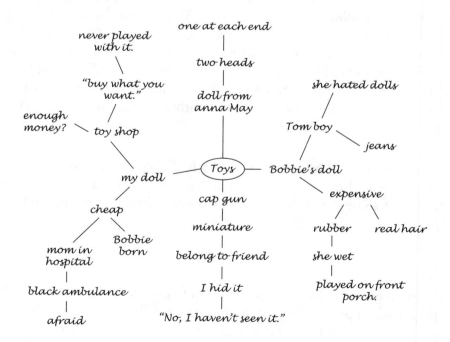

FIGURE 5.1   Clustering Example

help writers narrow a topic that is too general. *Mind mapping* is a term often associated with clustering or webbing. It is used more often to organize material that students have brainstormed earlier. For example:

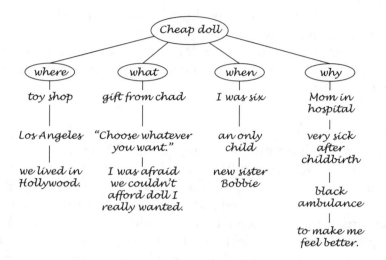

Freewriting and Focused Freewriting

Freewriting (sometimes called rushwriting) is stream-of-consciousness writing. The writer begins by putting down whatever comes to mind as quickly and impressionistically as possible without rereading, pausing, or editing. When writers slow down or get stuck, they keep their pens or pencils moving across the page, writing the same words or phrases over and over until something else comes to mind—and it will. The goal is to generate a variety of ideas. Freewritings are typically short and intense and usually timed from three to ten minutes. Focused freewritings are written in response to a general idea or topic, but it's perfectly acceptable for the writer to move in other directions. The following is a sample prompt for a focused freewriting:

Accidents can be good or bad, and we've all had them. Think of an accident you have had. Have you ever broken a bone, been hurt in a car, met someone unexpectedly, accidentally? List some possibilities on your paper. Choose one idea, and freewrite about this accident.

Rehearsing

After students have completed a prewriting activity and have found possible topics for writing, they work in pairs, taking turns discussing their ideas and clarifying the plan each has for a writing. The student's partner listens carefully so he or she can paraphrase what was said. You may have the students explain their plans a second time to another partner or to the class as a whole. Talking about writing prior to the actual drafting helps students focus and clarify the topic and purpose of their writing.

Drawing

This technique is frequently used with young writers, but it is equally effective with older students. Students may simply be asked to draw a picture before writing. This could be a response to an idea, a depiction of a locale, a sketch of a still life, or a single object. Some teachers give students objects from a desk drawer and ask them to draw the objects before writing about them. This is an ideal prewriting activity for a poem, for example. In drawing, the writer must really look at the object, and the sketch may serve later as an illustration to accompany the final draft.

In a variation of this activity and as preparation for writing a short story, one teacher asks each student to find a picture in a magazine of an interesting face. The students are instructed to attach their pictures to a sheet of blank paper and place these inside a school locker door or on a dresser mirror. Mentally the students are to take their characters with them wherever they go—to the mall, to an after-school job, to a basketball game. What would this character buy? What would he or she say? Whenever an idea occurs to the writer, he or she jots it down in the blank space surrounding the picture. In this way, the student begins to create the protagonist for a story. Students may also be asked to draw a floor plan for the character's house or a map of the character's neighborhood, or clip out a wardrobe for the character from a magazine. From here, students may have their characters "meet" in letters, telephone conversations, or face-to-face encounters. Student writers create an antagonist in the same way. Later, students brainstorm for a setting and conflict, and finally they write their short stories (Brewster, 1988).

Mapping

Mapping as a prewriting activity can be used in a variety of ways. Students might be directed to draw a map of a neighborhood, a classroom, or a trip, for example. Here is a sample set of directions for mapping a childhood room:

1. Take out two sheets of paper. On the first, draw an outline of the room you slept in when you were young.
2. Pretend you can look down on your room. Label eight or nine things in that room. If you can't remember, make some up.
3. Write a 1 on your map where there is a window. On your second sheet of paper, write the number 1, and tell me what you see from the window.
4. Suppose you're playing a game with someone in the room. Write a 2 on your map where this is happening. On your second sheet of paper, write the 2 and describe a game you played.
5. Write a 3 on your map where some scary sounds are. On your second sheet, tell about them.
6. Write a 4 on your map where something you loved the most (an object or a feeling) would be. On the second sheet of paper, tell me what it is like and why you care about it so much.
7. You're being punished (you may be innocent). Write a 5 on your map where you would go in the room. On the second sheet of paper, tell what you are accused of and how you feel about it.

At this point, the teacher asks for suggestions from students about what other details might be added to the map. Additional ideas include:

- Something under the bed
- A pet in the room
- Objects on a shelf or a favorite book
- Someone in the doorway saying something important

Then the students are instructed to continue with their map:

8. Mark two places on the map that seem most interesting.
9. Find a group, no smaller than three, no larger than four, and explain your two items to the rest of the group. The group members may ask you questions about your ideas.
10. Pick one idea to write about, and begin a draft (Dunning & Stafford, 1992).

This activity helps writers generate many ideas. It also encourages them to focus and choose their best option and requires them to try out these ideas on an audience.

Visualization (Guided Imagery)

Visualization encourages writers to travel mentally to another time or place—to an imaginary locale or to a real memory—to discover specific details and sensory images. You act as a guide to help students create pictures in their minds. The following is a sample set of directions for a memory exercise:

Today we're going to do a visualization exercise. As I turn off the lights, I'd like you to relax at your desks and close your eyes. Now I'd like you to pretend you are looking at a movie of your life. Let the images flow as you look for moments in your life that appeal to you as a writer. [Pause.] Recall a time that is important to you. Perhaps it's a time when you are unbelievably happy or a time when you are sad or afraid. Pick one memory, and replay the images. See the memory again. [Pause.] Look at the scene carefully. Where are you? What is happening? Examine the details of your surroundings. Find a detail you have forgotten. Now move on. What do you look like? What are you feeling? What are you doing that shows this? Are there other people in your memory? If so, what are they doing? Look at them carefully. Listen carefully. What are the sounds you hear? What do you smell? Watch this movie in your mind for as long as you want, and when you are ready, pick up your pen or pencil and begin writing.

Idea Starters or Prompts

Students may find ideas for writing in films, field trips, poetry, and guest speakers or from set prompts—for example:

- Show students a picture or a series of pictures, and have them create a story based on what they see.
- Give students a short vocabulary list, and have them work in groups to use each word in a story.

- Distribute copies of a poem (or have students choose one) and "translate" it into a newspaper article, a personal letter, or a television news report. You might also bring in short, quirky news stories from magazines or newspapers and ask students to rewrite them in a different format.
- Read the opening lines of a story, and ask students to create their own version from that point on: "Tonight I'd like to dream about ... ," "Tonight I'd be afraid to dream about ... ," "Be quiet, the whole neighborhood will hear ... ," or "Turning the corner ..." Or supply concluding sentences, such as, "We just smiled at each other," "I did it," or "Suddenly everything went black."
- Bring a collection of interesting "junk" to class (old eyeglasses, an empty aspirin bottle, a few coins, a torn ticket stub, for example), and ask students to create a character who might own this junk. Use the collection as a basis for writing a character sketch or inventing a story. If students are to work in groups, each group may be given a separate collection. Reading a story in which an article of clothing has special significance is a good follow-up activity (the fur piece in Katherine Mansfield's "Miss Brill," for example.)
- Gather several travel posters, and write haiku in response to the poster.
- Examine the travel section from several newspapers, and ask students to write about their own neighborhoods as a tourist attraction.
- Read newspaper weather reports, and write a script for a TV weather person or read the "letters to the editor" section and write a letter in reply to one.
- Study a dog training manual or driver's license handbook, and rewrite a rule as a poem.
- Select several pages from a popular teenage novel, and adapt them as a screenplay or radio play.
- Examine a copy of *Who's Who in America,* and write an entry for a friend or someone the students have interviewed.
- Use set prompts such as the following:

  "Not all inventions or discoveries have been good for the world. Write about one the world would be better off without, explaining why."

  "Some people feel high school students should not work at after-school jobs. Take a position on this issue, and state the advantages or disadvantages of working after school. What effects do these jobs and the long hours have on students? Give supporting reasons (The NWEA Direct Assessment Prompt Collection, 1989).

Interviews

Give students plenty of classroom practice in interviewing:

- Practice interviewing one another.
- Write and distribute a short biography of yourself, and ask students to write interview questions based on it. Then let them interview you.
- Bring someone into the classroom for a whole class interview, and have students collaborate in writing a paper based on the interview.

- Expect your students to write on a topic that will require them to acquire information from other students, teachers, parents, or community people. For example, a student might interview other students and a counselor about the difficulties of having divorced parents. Another might interview a doctor and students about an eating disorder. Still others might interview their parents and teachers concerning the changes in their school in the past fifteen years. When students have completed a writing project, ask them to interview one another about their papers, and include the interviews as well as the writings in a class publication.

Journals

Many teachers ask students to write in a journal notebook several times a week. (This may be coordinated with a reading journal. See Chapter Six.) Some expect students to discover their own topics. Others provide suggestions, such as the following:

- What is the quietest sound you know?
- What is the noisiest racket you've ever heard?
- Write a note that is going to be put in a bottle and dropped into the sea.
- Describe yourself as a friend would describe you.
- Write about a simple pleasure in your life.

The journal provides a risk-free setting for writing practice and for experimenting with and exploring language and ideas. In addition to Anne Frank's *The Diary of a Young Girl* and Henry David Thoreau's *Walden*, display other published books based on the journal format. Students enjoy the following, for example:

Phillip Hoose, *Claudette Colvin: Twice Toward Justice*
Francisco Jiminez, *Breaking Through*
Adeline Yen Mah, *Chinese Cinderella*
Walter Dean Myers, *Bad Boy: A Memoir*

Journals have become so popular with teachers there is a danger of their being overused. If this is the case in your school, consider requiring students to keep a more focused journal for a shorter period of time. For example, ask students who work before or after school to keep a journal of their work experience. Then expect them to develop at least one entry into a more polished writing. (A work journal might extend to research concerning nutrition and fast food.) An assignment such as this helps students see the value of a journal in discovering and developing their own topics.

Still another option is to assign a travel journal for students who are away from school for a family vacation (Borax, 1992). They can use Form 5.1 for this purpose.

A Travel Journal

Name _____ Date _____

You're making plans for travel. While you're away, we'll be thinking of you and looking forward to hearing about your journey. Complete this travel journal, and plan to share it with your teacher and classmates when you return.

Background

1. Where are you going?

2. What is the reason for this trip?

3. When did you begin making preparations?

4. Who will accompany you?

5. How will you travel (car, airplane, boat)?

6. What is your itinerary? List it here:

7. Have you been to this location before? Explain.

8. Make a list of the clothes you plan to pack.

9. In addition to clothes, what else do you plan to take with you?

10. Don't forget a good book! List the titles of books you expect to take along.

11. Have you encountered any problems so far? If so, describe one, and explain how you solved it.

12. What are you most looking forward to during the time ahead?

13. Draw or trace a map of your trip. Plot your route in red.

Day 1

Day _____ Date _____

Weather: _____

1. Schedule of activities:

    a. _____

    b. _____

    c. _____

    d. _____

    e. _____

    f. _____

2. In a paragraph, describe some of the features of this location: land, plants, animals, climate, for example.

3. Write a poem focusing on the sights and sounds around you.

Day 2

Day _____ Date _____

Weather: _____

1. Write a paragraph describing as completely as possible your room at this location. Include a rough sketch—for example, the size of the room, color of walls, floor covering, windows, beds, closet, ceiling fan, air-conditioner, phone, television, or radio. You might also include a description of the view from a window.

2. What are the best-known towns or cities in the area you are visiting?

3. What are the best-known historical sites in the area? What makes them notable?

4. Include a postcard or pictures cut from a travel brochure. Explain each in a sentence or two. Attach this to an additional sheet.

Day 3

Day _____ Date _____

Weather: _____

1. Compare and contrast this location with home. Begin with a brainstorming chart:

Home		Vacation spot
1.	1. language	1.
2.	2. food	2.
3.	3. clothing style	3.
4.	4. recreational activities	4.
5.	5. people	5.
6.	6. sounds	6.
7.	7. smells	7.
8.	8.	8.
9.	9.	9.

Write your paragraph here:

2. On an additional sheet of paper, sketch something you did or saw today. Include a sentence or two explaining your sketch.

Day 4

Day _____ Date _____

Weather: _____

1. People watching is always fun. Describe at least three people who have caught your attention. Include both a physical description and an explanation of what they were doing.

   a.

   b.

   c.

Day 5

Day _____ Date _____

Weather: _____

1. Make a list of the unusual or exotic foods you have eaten.

2. Make a list of the most memorable events so far.

3. Choose one item from the list above and write a letter on the back of this sheet to a friend at home, describing this event in detail.

Day 6

Day _____ Date _____

Weather: _____

1. Schedule of activities:

   a. _____

   b. _____

   c. _____

   d. _____

   e. _____

   f. _____

   g. _____

2. In a paragraph, describe the best or worst part of this day.

3. Time is slipping away. What will you miss most about this spot when you return home?

4. What will you miss least?

Day 7

Day _____ Date _____

Weather: _____

You have decided to develop your travel adventure into a major motion picture. You will be the producer as well as the author, so you'll have to begin making plans. Complete the form below:

1. List the cast of characters needed for this film.

2. Decide which well-known actors you will hire to play these roles. Write their names alongside the cast of characters above.

3. Where do you plan to make this movie?

4. List the major scenes to be included in your movie. These should be based on real events.

   a. _____

   b. _____

   c. _____

   d. _____

   e. _____

5. List five possible titles for this film. Circle your first choice.

   a. _____

   b. _____

   c. _____

   d. _____

   e. _____

6. What rating would you give your movie?

7. On an additional page, sketch a poster advertising your movie.

Day 8

1. You've returned home. Think about all you've done and seen on your travels. What advice would you give someone planning to visit the same location?

2. Evaluate your travel journal.

3. Would you recommend a journal for anyone else who is planning to travel? Explain.

4. Which entry might you use as the basis for a more formal, polished writing?

5. What changes and revisions would you make to your entry to polish it?

Helping Individual Students Get Started

Despite a variety of excellent prewriting activities, some students may still have trouble initially in getting anything down on paper. Try asking questions about what they are considering. Then repeat their answers and ask for amplification. Echoing a student's words builds confidence and gives him or her the first lines to begin writing.

Handling Painful Topics

If your students write often, sooner or later you will encounter a paper about a painful topic. If the paper recounts physical or sexual abuse, the law is clear: you must report it. It's important, however, that you decide beforehand how you will handle such an occurrence. Many teachers explain to their students that if a particular writing makes the teacher fear for their safety, the teacher must do something about it. Most students who write in this manner are signaling for help and are usually willing to seek a counselor or proper agency if encouraged to do so. If at all possible, avoid using a student's writing as evidence; at the very least, seek permission to do so.

There are many painful subjects students write about that need not be reported. You must be prepared to respond to these in a healthy way as well. It's important to understand that the act of writing out something that has caused pain is itself a therapeutic act (Dittberner-Jax, 1992). Students who write personally about painful topics are dealing with these problems in a healthy way. Respond with empathy, but don't try to become the student's therapist. If the writing is submitted for your eyes only, maintain the student's privacy and confidentiality. Nevertheless, painful topics shared aloud with the whole class can have an enormous effect on an audience. Some students are willing to do a presentation, although, of course, you must never require it. Again, it's important that you keep your response in perspective. If you spend an inordinate amount of time reacting to inflammatory topics and less time with more ordinary topics, other students will feel the need to write in a confessional mode. No student should feel pressured to do so, but those who do should feel that freedom as well. Balance is important.

Student-Teacher Writing Conferences

Student-teacher conferences, that is, one-to-one discussions, may happen at any time in the student's writing process. They may be informal and impromptu as you move around the room from student to student pointing to strengths in a writing, giving honest, specific praise, and answering questions. Ideally, you should respond as a reader, not as a teacher (or expert, or judge, or literary critic). This is called an "I-referenced response." Each time you make a comment, precede it (at least mentally) with the phrase, "When I read this, I . . ." for example, "When I read this part, I feel . . . ," "When I read this part, I see," "When I read this, I get confused about _____." Researchers tell us a reader's response is more useful and less threatening for students than any other kind we can make. I-referenced responses help students pay attention to the elements in their writing in ways that help them develop their writing further (Caddy, 1989).

Student-teacher conferences may also be formal and planned. Some teachers schedule formal conferences before or after school, during lunch periods, or during prep periods and have students fill out sign-up sheets or appointment cards. However, there is only so much time in a teacher's day. It's preferable to hold these meetings during class time in a quiet corner of the room when the other students are at work. You may schedule a block of days for formal conferences or fit them in as your students' needs and the schedule allow.

For writing that is to be carried through the entire process, plan to meet briefly with a student several times through a series of drafts. At the prewriting stage, conferences may simply consist of offering suggestions for a focus or helping a student discover more details or information. Ideally conferences will be concerned with only one or two features of a writing at a time. Comments concerning editing and proofreading are reserved for later drafts. Formal conferences are most successful when they follow a predictable routine, even to the extent of asking the same questions to begin each conference (Atwell, 1998). The following questions provide a useful format for a formal conference:

"What would you like me to listen for [or read for] and react to?" If time allows, students should read aloud because confusion about meaning and syntax often disappears when they do so.

"What part of your draft do you like the best?"

"What part gave you the most trouble?"

"What would you like to change in the next draft?"

"What have you learned from writing this draft?"

Questions such as these will allow you to see the writing through your students' eyes and keep them responsible for it.

Unfortunately, the tendency for many of us is to assume the initiative in a conference to the point of becoming active collaborators in a student's writing. One of our goals as teachers is to help students become independent writers. It's important to remember that during these conferences, the student should be doing most of the talking and we should be listening. Write on students' papers as little as possible. Show them how to solve problems, but do not do it for them.

Formal conferences with student writers may appear to be difficult and time-consuming. However, once these are an established and practiced routine, your students will become more articulate about their own writing. In addition, your response will be immediate and meaningful and far more helpful and effective than red-penciling a final draft when the student believes his or her work is completed.

Keeping Track of What Each Student Is Doing

Some teachers keep a set of index cards in a file box to record formal conferences with students. A separate card is kept for each student and is available to students at any time. As you confer, write a brief summary on the front of the card, such as, "Working on setting—planning to add sensory words." At the next conference, review the card with the student, and then go on to discuss the student's progress. You can reserve the back of the card to note skills the student is working on. When one card is filled, staple another to it. The card will serve as a good record of the student's progress. Other teachers keep a record of formal conferences with students by using a notebook with a page for each student. The page has columns for the date, the title of the writing in progress, conference notes, and skills to be worked on and resembles the sample in Form 5.2.

Student Record of Writing

Date	Writing Assignment	Plans for Revision
1.		
2.		
3.		
4.		
5.		

Teachers whose students keep writing folders use separate sheets of paper to record the same information. The sheets are stapled to the inside of the folder or the drafts of the writing itself. Keeping the notes on a student's progress with each writing saves time. Your students will see evidence of their progress and will be reminded of their goals; you will be able to quickly identify the needs of each student and groups of students as you plan for mini-lessons. Form 5.3 is also helpful as a means of charting a student's overall progress.

Student Writing Profile

Student's Name _____

Enter a check if the student has any of the problems listed.

Writing	1	2	3	4	5	6	7
Date							
Ideas							
Organization							
Sentence variety							
Voice							
Grammar, usage, mechanics							
Many misspellings							
Errors in punctuation							
Errors in use of verbs							
Errors in use of pronouns							
Errors in use of modifiers							
Errors in word usage/vocabulary							

Small Group Conferences

Peer conferences can occur with two students, small groups, or an entire class. They require a good deal of initial effort on your part to make them succeed. (Chapter Four provides a detailed discussion of cooperative learning.) Despite this, peer conferences are well worth your effort in saved time and student learning and involvement. Peer groups expand a writer's audience and provide an opportunity for students to analyze and evaluate the writing of others—the kinds of thinking we teachers too often reserve for ourselves. Students must learn how to respond to the writing of others in a positive, constructive manner. In addition, working together is not a skill that most students have had practice with. Plan with other teachers to demonstrate a peer conference for several classes at one time or rehearse small groups of students to demonstrate for the whole class. Peer conferences are most successful when you establish a consistent routine. Form 5.4 is a helpful format for peer conferences.

Directions for Students Working in Small Groups

Name _____ Date _____

Directions for the author:

1. Don't apologize for the writing.
2. Read your draft out loud just as it's written on your paper.
3. Ask question 1: "What do you like about my writing?"
4. Listen to the responses of every person in the group.
5. Ask question 2: "What questions do you have about my writing?" Wait for everyone to respond.
6. Ask question 3: "What suggestions do you have for making this writing better?"
7. Ask to have anything you don't understand clarified.
8. Thank the members of your group.

Directions for small groups:

1. Bring a draft of your paper to class on the due date.
2. After being assigned to a group, move your desks together quietly.
3. Quickly decide who will read first.
4. Listen carefully as a draft is being read. When an author is reading, no one else should be talking.
5. When asked, respond to the author's questions out loud. Do not interrupt others.
6. Remember to be kind and helpful in your responses.
7. Go on to the next author and repeat the process.
8. After every person in your group has read, work quietly and independently on your own revisions.

Remember that the purpose of writing groups is not to attack, criticize, find mistakes, or concentrate on surface errors. It is a time to be supportive and kind, to let the writer know that you hear what he or she is saying. Tell the writer what you like, and offer suggestions for making the next draft better.

As students meet in peer conferences, encourage them to jot down their ideas as the writer reads. Some teachers have students write out complete answers before responding orally. The written response is then given to the author, who refers to it when revising. Ideally group membership remains the same as a paper is taken through the entire process. New groupings may be planned for subsequent writings. The preceding response format is based on three questions:

1. What do you like about the writing?
2. What questions do you have about the writing?
3. What suggestions do you have for making the writing better?

Some teachers use the same response format for every writing. Others design focus questions to reflect the basic characteristics of specific kinds of writing. For example, the focus questions for a fable might be:

1. Are the main characters animals or inanimate things in nature?
2. Are the personalities of the characters appropriate for what happens in the story?
3. Does the moral grow out of the story?

The focus questions for a memoir might be:

1. What is good about this writing?
2. What is the relationship between the writer and the subject of the memoir?
3. On what incident does this writing focus?
4. Could the reader point out the subject of the memoir in a roomful of people?
5. What needs to be added to this writing?

As a writing nears completion, students also help one another edit for mechanical concerns. Checklists such as Form 5.5 are helpful.

Editing a Final Draft

Author _____ Date _____

Editor _____

Editor
Author

_____ 1. Are all the words spelled correctly? _____

_____ 2. Is all end punctuation correct? _____

_____ 3. Are words capitalized correctly? _____

_____ 4. Are commas where they belong? _____

_____ 5. Do all the verbs agree with the subjects? _____

_____ 6. Are the paragraph indentions where they should be? _____

Editor's comments:

_____

_____

_____

_____

_____

_____

_____

There are likely to be several students in each class whose mechanical errors are beyond the help of another student. On editing days, place these students in a group to work with you.

Be prepared for some "failed" conferences, but don't give up on them. At first some students may be reluctant to participate in responding to one another's work. Collaborative work requires practice and patience and encouragement from you. In time, students can learn to work well together, and successful conferences will evolve.

USING MINI-LESSONS

We need to be involved with our students at every stage of their writing. Students need to learn to master certain skills if they are going to become proficient writers. These are best taught in the context of their writing rather than in isolation. At this point students have a reason for learning, and they are able to apply this learning immediately. Many teachers design mini-lessons to help students along the way, being selective rather than overwhelming students with too many activities. Mini-lessons can involve small groups of students or whole class activities. This section provides examples of the kinds of short lessons you can plan for your own classroom. We begin with some tips for developing effective mini-lessons:

- *Determine content need.* As writing teachers, we see patterns in student writing. Use these observations to develop mini-lessons for your students.
- *Keep them short.* Mini-lessons are generally five to fifteen minutes long.
- *Make them simple.* Mini-lessons should be broken down to the barest components so that students can focus on the critical contents of the lesson. For example, instead of teaching your students all seven comma rules, maybe one or two would be sufficient for a mini-lesson.
- *Engage students, and provide interaction.* Worksheets and exercises do not support students' learning and retention of grammar and writing skills. Build on what students already know about language in mini-lessons.
- *Provide practice time.* Once the students have learned a new skill or grammar point, they will be more actively engaged.
- *Consider what's next.* Once a mini-lesson is completed, consider what should be taught next.

Mini-Lessons for Prewriting and Drafting

Use large sheets of paper or the chalkboard to model a prewriting process such as listing or clustering. Talk as you write, and explain your ideas to students. Tell about each possible topic and why it matters to you. Plan your list so you can reject one because you can't think of enough to say about it, another because it's too personal to share, or another because you don't like thinking about it right now. Explain which topic you will choose, and invite students to ask you questions about it. Demonstrate another list or cluster based on the more focused topic.

On another day, model your own drafting process. Demonstrate that early drafts are hurried and chaotic as a writer hurries to capture as many ideas as quickly as possible. Invite students to make comments and observations and to ask questions.

Mini-Lessons for Revision

Don't expect students to revise every writing draft. Instead, spend more time on some pieces, and teach your students how to revise. Many don't see the possibilities for change. Others are satisfied with neat drafts and are reluctant to make changes. Some teachers counter this by asking students to write early drafts on only one side of a sheet so that they might cut them apart and move sentences or paragraphs around. One teacher rewards revision efforts by offering a "messiest draft of the week" award. It's important that students understand that revision is separate from drafting. Students should write on one day and revise on another if possible. Consider using one of the following mini-lessons to acquaint your students with revision and give them practice in responding to one another's writing.

Introducing Revision

1. Display on bulletin boards drafts and revisions of student papers. Include the messy first drafts as well as the final copy. Read papers written by former students as models, and make plenty of student writing, bound in handmade booklets and anthologies, available for students to read. Let them see and read the result of thoughtful revision. Show how much pride you take in the polished work of previous students.

2. Use the overhead projector, LCD projector, or interactive white board to demonstrate as you revise one of your own papers or show the changes a former student has made in several drafts of a writing piece.

3. Practice with the whole class in responding to writings. Find copies of several drafts of a single writing by a previous student. Duplicate copies for everyone. Hand out the first draft, and ask students to read and respond to it using the same format they will use in their peer groups. ("What do you like about this draft?" "What questions do you have?" "What suggestions do you have for making it better?") Unfortunately, students often feel they are expected to find only what is wrong with a writing. Dispel this notion. Help them look for the strengths first. Teach students how to make helpful responses to writing. Force them to be specific and to explain why they answer as they do. "It's a good story" isn't a helpful response, but explaining what makes it "good" is—for example, "The verb *clattered* helps me hear the sound." Students need to be encouraged to examine texts carefully. After the class has arrived at suggestions for making the draft better, hand out the second draft and go through a similar response ("What is still strong?" "What has improved?" "What could make it still better?"). Lessons such as this early in the year will help your students better understand how they should respond to writing in their peer groups and will also help them begin to form their own definition of effective writing.

4. After students have worked in peer groups for a time, ask them to write a paragraph about a particular response or the kind of peer response that is most helpful to them personally. Ask them to analyze and explain the changes they have made from one draft to the next.

5. Display a student paper on the overhead, LCD projector, or interactive white board. Ask the students to respond in writing to the following or similar questions:

- What did the writer write about?
- What is strong about this writing?
- What sensory details help you imagine the incident?
- Where is dialogue used, or where could it be used?
- What word choices do you admire?
- What changes might make the writing stronger?

Writing prior to a class discussion involves everyone, focuses thinking, and guarantees a stronger whole class discussion. Consider asking students to give the model paper a grade, and explain why they gave the grade they did. Grades will of course vary. Discuss how this can happen and why.

Revision is a highly complex process. It varies according to the type of writing as well as the age and ability of the writer. To make revising more manageable for students, some teachers break the process into several stages: adding, cutting, substituting, and rearranging. The following suggestions for mini-lessons are arranged according to these categories and the options suggested here simplify it even further. Don't expect your students to do all of these. Use them only when you see a need. Even then, one or two mini-lessons per final draft may be plenty.

Revising by Adding

Encourage students to expand portions of their writing. Direct them to examine their drafts and note places that lack detail or are underdeveloped. They can then brainstorm, list, or cluster for ideas to expand that section. Finally, on a separate sheet of paper, they write a new version of the section to insert in a later draft:

1. If your students have access to computers, ask them to type two consecutive sentences from their drafts onto the computer screen. Next, have them place the cursor between the two sentences (for example, between "The telephone rang" and "She answered it") and start typing here until the screen is entirely filled with additional ideas and details that could logically fit at that point in the original draft. If computers are not available, ask students to write the first sentence at the top of a sheet of paper and the second at the bottom of the page and add details between the two to fill the page.

2. Encourage students to include sensory detail by reading through their drafts and adding information about how something looks, sounds, feels, smells, or tastes.

3. Enable students to include specific information and sensory detail by suggesting they write additional short drafts in a new format or for a new audience. For example, the students' first drafts might be descriptions of an object such as a toy. After the original drafts are completed, students write a lost-and-found notice for the same object. Next, they write a paragraph describing the object to someone who is blind. Finally, they underline the specific detail in all three versions and incorporate the best details into a new draft.

4. Ask students to add surprises and comparisons. Are descriptions fairly ordinary? Is the snow always white, the sky always blue, the night always scary? Have groups brainstorm for surprising ways to describe snow ("scarred by a North Dakota wind"), the sky ("green as mold"), and the night ("shivering in northern lights"). Finally, ask students to examine their own drafts to add surprises or comparisons.

5. Suggest the addition of direct dialogue. Examine an author's use of direct dialogue in a familiar novel or short story:

- How does it differ from indirect dialogue? ("She said that she was happy."/"She said, 'I am happy.'")
- What do quotation marks tell the reader?
- What are dialogue tags (such as "she said" or "he explained"), and does the author use them?
- How do we know when the speaker changes?
- What rules has the author followed in using quotation marks?

Next, ask students to study their own drafts and mark one or more places where direct dialogue might occur. Finally, on a separate piece of paper, they write a scene of dialogue that might be inserted into the original draft. When the dialogues have been completed, students exchange papers and check one another's writing for accurate use of quotation marks.

Sometimes it's useful to ask students to write a piece completely in dialogue. After such an exercise, they will use direct dialogue more frequently in other pieces of writing. Suggest scenes such as the following:

- You are at a bank and witness an attempted robbery. The teller is hard of hearing.
- You overhear a "funeral service" that two children are conducting for a dead pet.
- Two canoers encounter stormy weather.
- You have driven your parents' car to the mall. When you return to the lot, you discover the car has been sideswiped. You drive the car home, and your parents meet you at the door.

6. Rewrite a draft from a new point of view. (The description of a toy might be rewritten from the toy's point of view, for example.) Students compare and add the best new material to the earlier draft. A similar activity requires students to write in a new verb tense—from past to present, for example—or to change the level of language from formal to informal to slang. How might a justice of the Supreme Court describe his or her memory of a toy as opposed to a description by a professional thief?

7. Change point of view and audience. In preparation for this, review the events of the story "The Three Bears" or a similar familiar tale. Ask students to retell the story from another point of view and to a different audience. Papa or Mama Bear might retell the incident at work or to a next-door neighbor, Baby Bear relates his version to a playmate, or Goldilocks explains to the police what happened. If students are writing in groups, each group works with a different story.

A logical extension of this activity is to ask students to write three versions in addition to their original piece: one for a close friend, another for a stranger, a third for a parent.

Students also enjoy reading children's literature based on this concept, and you may want to share samples with them to demonstrate how changes in point of view, characterization, and setting can alter the outcome of a story—for example:

Prince Cinders, by Babette Cole
Snow White in New York, by Fiona French
Terrible Tales: The Absolutely, Positively, 100 Percent TRUE Stories of Cinderella, Little Red Riding Hood, Those Three Greedy Pigs, Hairy Rapunzel, . . . and Gretel as Told at the Beginning of Time, by Felicitatus Miserius
The True Story of the 3 Little Pigs! by A. Wolf, by Jon Scieszka

8. In a second draft, the writer adopts a new mode. A narrative might become a persuasive piece, or a description of one place might become a comparison of two. The new details this produces may be added to the earlier draft. The new mode may be a stronger writing. Perhaps it should be the next draft.

Revising by Substituting

It isn't the number of words an author uses but the best word choices that lead to strong writing.

1. Consider word choices by having students use correction fluid or erase every fifth word in a paragraph or paper, number the blanks consecutively, and then exchange these papers with a partner. On a separate sheet, have a partner supply words in the blanks based on the context of the paper. This will help an author look at the writing in a new way.

2. If your students aren't already using a thesaurus, encourage them to do so. Explain the format thoroughly, and then write several lines from a familiar story on the chalkboard: "There was an old woman who lived in a shoe. She had so many children she didn't know what to do." Students rewrite these lines using no words with the letter *o*. If they can't think of new words or phrases, they consult a thesaurus. Students have fun with this exercise, and although the resulting sentences may be awkward, the exercise forces them to become familiar with this resource. Next, students study their own drafts and underline words they think are imprecise and search for better choices. If your students are using word computers, be sure they understand and use the thesaurus feature as well as the spell checker.

3. Help your students to use specific, active verbs. Consider the sentence, "The girl walked down the hall." Discuss how many changes a writer can effect in the reader's perception of the girl by changing the verb *walked*. What verb could make her young? Old? Tired? Angry? Afraid? Beautiful? Sneaky? Also consider the sentence, "The boy cut the leather." Think of as many verbs as possible that would be more precise than the verb *cut*. Finally, have students examine the verbs in their own drafts and substitute active, precise verbs for any that are weak.

4. Substitute precise adjectives. Consider sentences such as the following: "His shoes were unusual." "She wore strange glasses." "The cat was ugly." "The day was unpleasant." "The road was dangerous." Then have groups brainstorm for better descriptions to share with the whole class: "He wore red and pink high-tops." "Her glasses were rhinestone-studded half-moons." "The scrawny, one-eyed cat." "The temperature was forty below,

and the wind howled all night." "The road was filled with unmarked potholes and strewn with fallen branches." Finally, students make similar additions in their own drafts.

5. Direct an author or peer editor to circle repeated words lightly in pencil and connect the circles. Students will realize they need to find context-appropriate synonyms for the repeated words.

6. Help students avoid monotonous sentence patterns by underlining the first four words in each sentence in a rough draft. Study the patterns. Does every sentence begin the same way? If so, can some of them be varied to provide greater interest? Another option is to count the words in every sentence. Then on a second sheet of paper, students draw lines equivalent to the number of words (as in a bar graph). Are all the sentences the same length? Which ones can be changed or combined?

Revising by Rearranging

A writing rarely begins in its final arrangement. The beginning is the most important part of a piece because it has to hook the reader's attention. The ending is the next most important part because it must leave the reader with something to remember. The middle of the piece should tell more about the beginning and be filled with good details and examples. Sentences sometimes need rearranging too.

Begin by reading and discussing interesting introductions or opening sentences by published authors—for example:

"When he was nearly thirteen, my brother Jem got his arm badly broken at the elbow."—
    Harper Lee, *To Kill a Mockingbird*, (1960).
"The Herdmans were absolutely the worst kids in the history of the world. They lied
    and stole and smoked cigars (even the girls) and talked dirty and hit little kids and
    cussed their teachers and took the name of the Lord in vain and set fire to Fred
    Shoemaker's old broken-down toolhouse."—Barbara Robinson, *The Best Christmas
    Pageant Ever* (1973)
"'Where's Pap going with that ax?' said Fern to her mother as they were setting the table
    for breakfast. 'Out to the hoghouse,' replied Mrs. Arable. 'Some pigs were born last
    night.'"—E. B. White, *Charlotte's Web* (1952)

Suggest that a good introduction might open in a variety of ways:

- *A question:* "Have you ever wondered how you'd survive without a cent?"
- *An announcement:* "This is not a story for the timid!"
- *A bold and challenging statement:* "Contrary to what some people think, most learning
  takes place outside the school."
- *A quotation:* "'You'll be sorry you ever asked,' he whispered."
- *A personal experience:* "I'm glad I didn't cry in front of Mom."
- *How the writer felt:* "My chest hurt, my legs ached, and I itched all over."

Ask students to work to improve the beginning of their own drafts.

Changing the chronology is another choice. Recall the story of Cinderella and then write this line on the chalkboard: "The prince slipped the glass slipper on my foot." Then ask groups or the whole class to collaborate in retelling the story with the new beginning.

After this, students turn to their own draft. They underline an important detail in their own draft and move at least a mention of the detail to the beginning of the draft. Finally, they write a new draft based on the restructured chronology.

Revising by Cutting

When students write their early drafts, they are working for quantity. Before a draft is completed, they should get rid of anything that doesn't really add to the writing. You'll have to convince them that length does not necessarily determine the quality of a writing. They are used to being told to "write a five-hundred-word essay."

Here are two hints for them on how to go about this:

1. Examine the first and last sentences of a draft. Can these sentences (or more) be omitted?
2. Write sentences similar to the following on the chalkboard. Students revise them for economy before examining their own drafts or the drafts of their peers.

> *Original:* He heard it make a sound of scratching.
> *Revised:* He heard a scratching sound.
> *Original:* The girls were runaways, and they took a bus to go downtown.
> *Revised:* The runaway girls took a downtown bus.
> *Original:* The flowers were picked by a man who was growing flowers for a living.
> *Revised:* The florist picked the roses.

Mini-Lessons for Editing

Editing for spelling, punctuation, and grammatical errors should be saved for the end of the process, but it is important, too, especially if the final draft is to be shared with a particular audience.

- Each day select a sentence containing common errors and write it on the board. Ask students to discuss and explain corrections orally.
- Present a lesson dealing with a critical editing skill, such as comma splices. Use a grammar book or worksheets if necessary, and then ask students to examine and edit their own writing. This may be a whole class exercise or a small group exercise for students who share the same problem.
- Involve all students in a class practice. Duplicate a sample paper with numerous mistakes in spelling, capitalization, punctuation, and usage. Students work independently or in groups to improve their editing skills.
- Have students read their drafts backward, from end to beginning, from right to left to check for spelling errors.

What do you do if you're required to cover the grammar book? One option is to assign each group of students a single concept—a part of speech or a rule for capitalization or punctuation or usage. Expect the group to learn the concept, study a handbook or grammar book, prepare it for presentation, develop worksheets or an assignment, and administer a test. Exercises such as this might be repeated several times throughout the year in order to cover the required grammar material. A plan such as this is an effective approach because it involves much more than the mastery of isolated skills. Your students will be reading, listening, speaking, writing, editing, and evaluating in the course of their learning.

Mini-Lessons for Teaching Grammar

Mini-lessons need to be developed as a result of student need and should be developmental. For example, if the students are making frequent errors in subject and verb agreement in their writing, then mini-lessons that focus on types of nouns (common, proper, and plural, for example) and verb tense should be covered in a series of mini-lessons. The following examples of grammar mini-lessons are from Passman and McKnight, *Teaching Writing in the Inclusive Classroom* (2007).

Sample Mini-Lessons

Postcards from the Past

Postcards from the Past is a mini-lesson designed to develop students' understanding of time in their writing. This lesson builds on their innate understanding of verbs in determining time. Verbs are not only action words; they are also time determiners. In this case, they describe past actions.

This activity takes about fifteen to twenty minutes.

Materials

You will need postcards with pictures of various tourist destinations, poster paper, and markers.

Procedure

Step 1. Begin a discussion about postcards. Ask the students why people send postcards. What do people write on postcards? Model a postcard that you have written to someone. Then distribute postcards and invite the students to think about the picture on theirs. Ask the students to pretend they've visited the site on the picture and ask them to describe what they did there to a friend at home.

(Continued)

Step 2. Give the students about five minutes to write their postcards.

Step 3. Collect the postcards so you can read some aloud, or read them together in class. Once you have read three or so postcards, ask the students to write down the verbs—or action words—or time determiners. Then read a few more postcards.

Step 4. Ask the students to share their list of verbs and compile a class list. A pattern will form that will be dominated by verbs in the past tense.

Step 5. Conduct a whole group discussion about past tense verbs and how these words are time determiners.

NCTE/IRA Standards

5. Students employ a wide range of strategies as they write and use different writing process elements appropriately to communicate with different audiences for a variety of purposes.
6. Students apply knowledge of language structure, language conventions (e.g., spelling and punctuation), media techniques, figurative language, and genre to create, critique, and discuss print and nonprint texts.

Knowing Nouns and Venturing About Verbs

This is an exercise designed to develop students' innate understanding of nouns and verbs. Katie developed this lesson and often uses it to determine what her students already know about grammar and, more specifically, the parts of speech. Definitions such as, "A noun is a person, place, or thing," are not very helpful for student writers. Far better is when the students can articulate how nouns, verbs, and other parts of speech work in the language. This hands-on lesson actively engages the students as they build on their understanding of nouns.

In this lesson, students articulate their reasons for identifying nouns as nouns. For example, they may develop rules such as the following: *Most nouns can be turned into plurals by adding "s" or "es" at the end. A noun can have "a," "an," or "the" in front of it.* (The latter definition can be an introduction to articles in addition to determining noun rules.) Usually, through class discussion, we come up with five or six rules like these by the end of the lesson. Thus, we prompt the students to examine the ways in which language works and how we use it to express ideas. This gives them a far more specific understanding than when they merely regurgitate the familiar definitions. Student writers can tell us a ton about language if we provide them with opportunities to do so, and from there, they can build on their previous knowledge about language.

This activity takes about ten minutes.

Materials

You will need poster paper or large sticky notes, markers, and envelopes. Before you begin, make photocopies of this list.

Knowing Nouns and Venturing About Verbs Handout

book	birthday cake	answered
walking	ran	flower
computer	music	drove
sings	cutting	oregano
pencil	sandwich	sent
played	growing	paper clip
video game	homework	wrote
cooking	cleaning	box
map	envelope	listening
prepared	painted	refrigerator
studied	compact disk	hears
sports car	questioned	house
leaped	concert	jumped
milkshake		

Cut the words contained in the exhibit into individual strips and put them in envelopes. There should be one envelope for every group of three to five students, and each envelope should include all of the words contained in the exhibit. Write the following directions on the outside of each envelope: *Dump the contents of this envelope onto a desk, and based on what you already know about the parts of speech, divide these words into two separate groups: nouns and verbs.*

Procedure

Step 1. Divide the students into groups of three to five. Give each group one envelope.

Step 2. Direct the students to read and follow the directions on the outside of the envelope.

Step 3. Repeat the directions orally. Tell the students to divide the words into two groups: nouns and verbs.

Step 4. Circulate among the groups and monitor the students' progress. Ask students, "How did you divide the words?" Encourage the students to articulate why they divided the words as they did. Ask them to label each list. The students may develop labels like: "nouns and verbs," "nonaction words and action words," or "things and

(Continued)

moving words." All of these are fine, because they will trigger a discussion about what makes a noun a noun and what makes a verb a verb.

Step 5. Once the students have divided their words, distribute poster paper and markers. Instruct the students to write down the group's reasons for dividing the words as they chose. This should take about five minutes.

Step 6. Conduct a whole group discussion about the students' lists, and create a combined class list that identifies the characteristics of nouns and verbs.

NCTE/IRA Standard

6. Students apply knowledge of language structure, language conventions (e.g., spelling and punctuation), media techniques, figurative language, and genre to create, critique, and discuss print and nonprint texts.

Capitalizing Capitalization

In Capitalizing Capitalization, students identify the instances where capitalization is needed for proper nouns and create a list of rules for doing so.

   This activity takes about ten minutes.

Materials

You will need a blindfold, a large box or bag, and items that can spark discussion about capitalization. Here's a list of possible items:

· Map with a city or location circled
· Newspaper or magazine
· Soup label with the name of the kind of soup (not the brand name) circled
· Soup label with the brand name (not the type of soup) circled
· Book with the title circled
· Spiral notebook
· Compact disc with the artist's name circled
· Stapler
· Compass, with the directions North, South, East, and West capitalized
· DVD
· Picture of a famous person
· CD
· Pencil with the brand name circled
· Notebook with the brand name circled
· Calendar or date book

   For fun, label the box "To Capitalize or Not! That Is the Question."

Procedure

Step 1. Blindfold a student and instruct him or her to remove an item from the box.

Step 2. After retrieving an item, have the student remove the blindfold and determine whether the name of the item should be capitalized. The student must also explain why the item should be capitalized or not.

Step 3. Have another student record the item and the capitalization on chart paper or the chalkboard.

Step 4. Repeat steps 1 to 3, with the remaining students taking turns being blindfolded while the observing student records their choices and explanations for why they capitalized the item or not.

NCTE/IRA Standard

6. Students apply knowledge of language structure, language conventions (e.g., spelling and punctuation), media techniques, figurative language, and genre to create, critique, and discuss print and nonprint texts.

Source: Passman, R., & McKnight, K. (2007). *Teaching writing in the inclusive classroom: Strategies and skills for all students.* San Francisco: Jossey-Bass.

Effective and Supportive Writing Instruction for Students with Special Needs

Here are some general tips for writing workshop adaptations for students with special needs who are included in a regular education classroom from Passman and McKnight's *Teaching Writing in the Inclusive Classroom* (2007):

1. The regular education and special education teacher needs to complete a plan that will address the specific educational needs and necessary adaptations for the mainstreamed students with special needs. They should be sure to communicate these adaptations to the parents, and when the adaptation is no longer needed, slowly remove it.
2. As with their regular education students, they should clearly articulate goals and expectations for the students.
3. When creating mini-lessons, teachers should incorporate Howard Gardner's *Theory of Multiple Intelligences* (Gardner, 2005). This volume offers many examples when more than one type of intelligence is included in the mini-lesson design. It's important to do this for regular education students, but it's even more critical for students with special needs.
4. Teachers can model their process in writing through think-alouds.
5. They can teach specific writing skills through mini-lessons.

6. They can provide a motivating environment for writing for *all* students, including mainstreamed students with special needs.
7. They can develop adaptations that encourage students to be independent learners.
8. Teachers should make sure that instructions are detailed and presented in additional modalities, other than orally. Directions must be clear and explicit.
9. They should provide multiple opportunities for students to demonstrate what they have learned.
10. Finally, it's important to be consistent in expectations for all students and support them in reaching those expectations.*

SHARING STUDENT WRITING: PRESENTING AND PUBLISHING

Your students may share or publish their writing in a variety of ways:

1. Students read their completed work to the whole class.
2. The students meet with another class and read to one another. Older students write stories, fairy tales, legends, and myths to share with younger students. Bind these writings in booklets, and donate them to the elementary library.
3. Plan a formal reading occasion (an author's tea, for example). Send invitations to guests: parents, principals and other administrators, school board members, students and teachers from other classes, and a reporter from the school newspaper or the community newspaper.
4. Read to interested community groups.
5. Post writing on a bulletin board or in a display case outside your classroom, in the hallways, in the school's offices, in public libraries, or in waiting areas of a hospital or doctors' or dentists' offices.
6. Feature a "writer of the week" in a display case. Include samples of the student's writing, a picture, an autobiographical sketch, and questions and answers from an interview or a complete interview written by a classmate.
7. Students send messages, letters, or notes to other students, administrators, school board members, family members, sports figures, political figures, businesspeople, media figures, or civic groups.
8. Present copies of final drafts as gifts to adults outside the classroom: parents, grandparents, former teachers, or anyone else the author admires.
9. Students produce a final copy of their best writing on computer. Add a title page, bind all copies or laminate them, and deliver them to the school librarian. Be sure the copies are catalogued and featured as new acquisitions. Send an unbound copy of this writing along with a supportive note to the parents of each student. Explain to the students beforehand that you plan to do this.
10. Publish each student's best writing in a handmade book, or collect the writing of all students in handmade class anthologies. Include a table of contents and title page. Add

---

*From *Teaching Writing in the Inclusive Classroom: Strategies and Skills for All Students,* R. Passman and K. McKnight. ©2007 by John Wiley & Sons, Inc. Reprinted with permission of John Wiley, Inc.

sections such as "About the Author" and "Advice to Writers." Make copies for your classroom, for gifts, for the media center, for nursing homes, or for waiting rooms and offices.

11. Produce a class newsletter or magazine with samples of student writing, and mail these to parents, administrators, and school board members. You may want to include an editorial in which you comment on what you have been teaching or are going to teach next.

12. Write articles for and submit student writing to a schoolwide newsletter that is sent to all parents in the school district.

13. Collaborate with students and teachers in another discipline. For example, write poetry in language class in conjunction with a science unit on insects. Publish this collection, and share it with students in other classrooms.

14. Submit final drafts to the school newspaper, the yearbook, a school literary magazine, or a local newspaper.

15. Produce a class magazine or newsletter featuring a theme of local community interest ("ecology in our community" or "the future of our community," for example). Seek out a variety of resources, including interviews with members of the community. Involve the local media, and distribute the completed publication or arrange to have it published within a community newspaper.

16. Collaborate with other English faculty members to select and publish exemplary student writing produced in response to English class assignments by students at every ability level. This might also be expanded to feature outstanding samples of assigned writing from all the disciplines.

17. Submit student writing to publications that accept manuscripts from young writers—for example:

    - *American Poetry Review,* www.aprweb.org
    - *Merlyn's Pen,* www.merlynspen.org
    - Poetry Society of America, www.poetrysociety.org
    - *New Voices,* www.newvoices.org
    - *Scholastic Magazine,* www.scholastic.com/browse/scholasticNews
    - *Writer's Digest,* www.writersdigest.com

EVALUATING AND GRADING STUDENT WRITING

You will want your students to write frequently, but you are no doubt concerned about time. How can you possibly read and grade everything your students write?

Assignment Design

The key to easing the burden of grading student writing (especially if you expect to grade individual papers) may be found in carefully designed writing assignments. As you plan an assignment, begin with a clear idea of what you want your students to learn and what the students must do to achieve this goal. An assignment such as, "Write a short paper that is related to this week's reading," is ambiguous. A better choice provides a student with a definite route through the assignment: "Write a haiku reflecting your understanding of the theme in the book *Night* to share with your classmates at the beginning of class tomorrow."

If possible, all major writing assignments should be given in writing. Ideally each will be duplicated and distributed to every student. You might also write these assignments on a chalkboard and expect the students to copy them in assignments notebooks. It's best to give these assignments in a consistent format such as the following:

- The topic
- The speaker/writer
- The purpose
- The audience/readers
- The format (or options)

All major assignments should include deadlines and final dates as well as an explanation about how the writing will be evaluated. The following is a sample assignment based on the personal essay about a childhood toy mentioned earlier.

Assignment for a Personal Essay: "A Childhood Toy"

1. *Assignment:* Write a personal essay about a childhood toy.
2. *Speaker:* You will be the speaker describing a toy you once owned and loved.
3. *Purpose:* Make your audience "see" this object and understand why it was special.
4. *Audience:* Your classmates.
5. *Format:* Three- to five-paragraph personal essay.

Important Dates:
· We will spend _____ with prewriting (listing), drafting, and revising activities (combining several drafts).
· Your rough draft is due for peer evaluation on _____.
· Your final draft is due _____.
· Your final draft will become a chapter in your end-of-the-unit autobiography. Give your essay a title and write (or type) neatly on one side of your paper in blue or black ink. This assignment is worth _____ points and will be graded for:

  · Specific detail
  · Appeal to the senses (sight, sound, touch, taste, smell)
  · Paragraph development
  · Correct punctuation
  · Correct spelling

A clearly written assignment such as this sample not only lets students know what is expected of them but also helps parents understand what is happening in the classroom.

Be clear about your expectations for final drafts from the beginning of the year. Form 5.6 can be posted in the classroom or distributed to each student.

Instructions for Final Drafts

Name _____ Date _____

1. Head each paper in the following manner:

Title (on first line, centered on page)
(blank space)

The first word of each paragraph should be indented and the second line should begin at the margin line.

2. Capitalize the first and final word of the title and all other words in the title except articles, conjunctions, and prepositions with fewer than five letters.

3. Use only regulation-sized paper, 8½ inches by 11 inches.

4. All final drafts should be written neatly in blue or black ink or completed on a word processor.

5. Write on only one side of the paper.

6. If your paper does not have the left-hand margin marked, establish a margin of about 1 inch and adhere to it closely. On the right side, leave a margin of about 1 inch and keep it as even as possible.

7. Indent the first word of all paragraphs uniformly.

8. Do not use the sign "&" or the abbreviation *etc.* Remember, *a lot* is two words.

9. Divide a word only at the end of a syllable. Words of one syllable may not be divided.

10. Always reread your final draft, and correct errors in punctuation and spelling (with correction fluid if necessary) before handing it in. If using a word processor be sure to use the spell-check feature.

11. Your name should be included on your draft.

Student Self-Evaluation

As part of your lesson design, involve students in self-evaluation. One way to do this is to ask them to evaluate their writing by responding to a checklist. An ideal checklist has two characteristics: it is designed for a specific writing assignment, and it distinguishes between revising and proofreading. The following is a sample student checklist designed to accompany the preceding assignment.

"A Childhood Toy": Student Checklist for Personal Essay

Revision
1. Do I include specific detail in several well-developed paragraphs?
2. Do I appeal to several senses (sight, sound, touch, smell, taste)?

Proofreading
1. Does my writing have several paragraphs, and is the beginning of each indented?
2. Is my punctuation correct?
3. Is my spelling correct?
4. Is my copy neatly written on one side of the paper (in blue or black ink) or carefully typed?
5. Did I include a title at the top of the first page?

A checklist such as this encourages students to become part of the evaluation process and can be used for peer evaluation as well.

Teacher's Scoring Guides

The information in a well-designed assignment sheet is easily converted to a teacher's scoring guide or analytical scale. Rather than undertaking the enormous task of responding to everything about a writing, you will be able to concentrate on those skills that are the focus of the assignment quickly, efficiently, and fairly. Form 5.7 is a sample scoring guide.

Sample Scoring Guide

Student's Name _____ Date _____

Assignment: Personal Essay: "A Childhood Toy"

Revision

A. The writing includes specific detail in several well-developed paragraphs.

   2   4   6   8   10

B. The writing appeals to several senses.

   2   4   6   8   10

Proofreading

C. The writing has several paragraphs and the beginning of each is indented uniformly.

   1   2   3   4   5

D. The spelling is correct.

   1   2   3   4   5

E. The punctuation is correct.

   1   2   3   4   5

F. The final draft is neatly written in blue or black ink (or typed neatly) on one side of the paper.

   1   2   3   4   5

G. The writing has a title.

   1   2   3   4   5

TOTAL POINTS (45)

Additional comments:

_____

_____

_____

An analytical scale designed for each kind of writing according to its own terms is also effective as a teaching tool and will help your students better understand the characteristics of these types of writing. A description (such as that of the toy) is graded according to its clarity and focus (Does the writing reveal what the writer sees, hears, smells, feels, and tastes?) and its use of language (Does the writer use exact words and language that show rather than tell?). Or a letter could be graded by rating its voice (Does it sound as if a person is talking?) and its form (Does the letter use the correct heading, greeting, and closing?).

It is also possible, although less desirable, to use one self-evaluation sheet (and grading scale) for most student writings. Such a scale emphasizes general features such as content, order, style, punctuation, grammar, and spelling and might resemble Form 5.8.

Self-Evaluation Sheet

Name _____ Date _____

Content

1. My paper has a clear purpose or makes a point.
2. I use specific details and examples to help my reader understand what I am saying.
3. I omit details that are not important to my main ideas.
4. I have thought about my topic carefully, and I know what I am talking about.

Order

5. I've started my paper in an effective way. The reader will want to keep reading.
6. I've told things in an order that makes sense, and it is easy for the reader to follow what I am saying.
7. All the details in my paper fit together and contribute to my main point.
8. My paper ends well. It doesn't stop suddenly or drag on too long.

Style

9. This writing sounds like me.
10. This paper shows how I feel and think about this topic.
11. It's easy to picture what I'm talking about. My words show the reader what to see.
12. I've tried saying some things in a new way. I've had fun with the language.
13. My sentences are clear, and no words are left out.
14. My sentences have variety. Some are longer than others, and they do not all begin the same way.

Editing

15. I've read my paper over. It's smooth and easy to read.
16. I've proofread my paper and corrected spelling, punctuation, and capitalization.
17. My paragraphs begin in the right spots, and I've indented them correctly.

If you plan to grade individual papers, do not grade everything a student writes. Grade only finished papers that have been carefully revised and presented to you as final. Sometimes students hand in anything to meet a deadline, and we have often graded these papers too soon. Don't hesitate to return a paper to a student and ask that a revision be completed before assigning a grade. You may reduce your grading load even further by having students choose one final draft from among several for a formal grade.

Holistic Grading of Student Writing

If it is necessary for you to grade the final draft of each major writing assignment, holistic grading is another valid time-saving approach to consider. In holistic grading, a procedure for sorting or ranking the content and form of written pieces is considered, but the tallying and marking of errors is not required. Holistic grading is helpful in assigning grades fairly quickly, but it is not useful in showing a student or parent the strengths or weaknesses of a piece of writing.

In the simplest form, the teacher reads the first paper, then reads the next and decides whether it is better or worse than the first. If it is better, it is placed on top of the first. If it is worse, it is placed underneath. The scoring or placing occurs quickly and impressionistically. The reader continues until all papers are arranged from most successful to least successful. A grade is assigned after the ordering is completed.

Another approach to holistic grading is to match papers with another piece in a graded series or to score a paper for the prominence of certain features. Again the scoring is done quickly and is usually guided by a rubric that describes particular features of writing such as content, wording, organization, flavor, and mechanics.

Grading Contracts

Another time-saving approach many teachers use in classrooms where students are expected to do a great deal of writing is a contract system for determining grades (England, 1986). Students agree to fulfill certain obligations in order to earn a particular writing grade. The writing grade is then averaged with points earned for other class assignments to determine the final marking period grade. Form 5.9 primarily reflects the quantity of writing a student chooses to do rather than the quality of his or her work. However, students aren't expected to work and write entirely on their own. The teacher works individually with students, reads and responds to early drafts, and devotes most of his or her time to students when it really counts: when they are in the process of writing rather than after their writing is completed. One of the best features of this sample is the variety of audiences called for. We used to believe that the "threat" of grades caused students to edit and polish final drafts. In this contract, the revision for publication, the expectations of an adult outside the classroom, and the quality of editing demanded by a contest are all highly effective in promoting higher standards in final copies. A contract should also indicate due dates for final drafts in order to prevent students from turning everything in at the last minute.

Writing Contract

Name _____ Date _____

One of the goals of this class is to help you become a better writer. You will be asked to write frequently. You will also read and share your writing with other class members as well as the teacher. Finally, you will polish and revise some of your writing for other audiences.

To earn a grade of C in writing for this grading period, you must:

1. Write and place three writings in your folder.
2. Revise two of these writings, and attach each revision to the earlier draft.
3. Confer with the teacher, and revise one of these revisions to include in the class booklet.
4. Confer with the teacher and revise the other writing to deliver to an adult outside this class.
5. Meet the following due dates:

   Final draft for the class booklet: _____

   Final draft for an adult outside the class: _____

To earn a grade of B in writing for this grading period, you must:

1. Write and place four writings in your folder.
2. Revise three of these writings, and attach each revision to the earlier draft.
3. Confer with the teacher and revise one of these writings to include in the class booklet.
4. Confer with the teacher and revise one of these writings to deliver to an adult outside this class.
5. Confer with the teacher and revise another of these writings to submit as a display piece for a class exhibition.
6. Meet the following due dates:

   Final draft for the class booklet: _____

   Final draft for an adult outside the class: _____

   Final draft for the display piece: _____

To earn a grade of A in writing for this grading period, you must:

1. Write and place five writings in your folder.
2. Revise four of these writings, and attach each revision to the earlier draft.
3. Confer with the teacher and revise one of these writings to include in the class booklet.
4. Confer with the teacher and revise another of these writings to deliver to an adult outside this class.
5. Confer with the teacher and revise another of these writings to submit as a display piece for a class exhibition.
6. Confer with the teacher and revise another of these writings and submit a final draft to a local or national contest or for possible publication.
7. Meet the following due dates:

   Final draft for the class booklet: _____

   Final draft for an adult outside the class: _____

   Final draft for the display piece: _____

   Final draft for contest or publication: _____

Please sign and return

I, _____, understand that in order to earn the

grade of _____, I must and will do the following:

   Date _____

   Signature _____

There are many options for writing contracts. It is also possible to specify and require a variety of formats: a personal essay, a poem, a letter to the editor, a memo, an analytical piece.

If you intend to use a grading contract in your classroom, you must help parents understand your approach. They are accustomed to seeing grades and comments on most of what their child writes for class, and they will need to know that you will place less emphasis on grading early in a course, that you will grade fewer papers, if any, but that you will also respond to more writing in a variety of ways. (See Chapter Nine for additional suggestions for working with parents.)

Portfolio Grades

More and more teachers and schools are turning to portfolios—samples of actual school work—to help evaluate student progress. Portfolios are not the same as writing folders, which generally contain all of the writing a student has done. A portfolio may be used in conjunction with reading and speaking activities or may be used exclusively for writing. It is assembled by students and is a collection that illustrates their efforts, progress, or achievements. If you plan to use portfolio assessment, decide before you begin what you want students to place in their folders and turn this list into a table of contents. The following model table of contents is one you might consider if you plan to limit the portfolio to writing samples:

1. The first writing of the semester.
2. The beginning-of-the-year writing inventory.
3. A writing from early in the quarter with all drafts and prewriting materials attached, as well as self-evaluation materials, peer conference notes, and teacher's conference comments. The number of writings and variety of formats will depend on the age and ability of the particular students.
4. A writing from later in the quarter with all additional material.
5. A student-selected best writing with an explanation for this choice.
6. A self-evaluation.

Student Self-Evaluation

Because self-reflection is such an important concept in portfolio assessment, you'll want to plan for a variety of ways to encourage your students to assess their own writing. Form 5.10 provides a helpful format to use in conjunction with portfolios.

Student Self-Evaluation

Name _____ Date _____

Writing Assignment _____

1. How much time did you spend on this paper? _____

2. Describe the process you went through to create this paper.

   a. Where did you get the idea for the paper or what prewriting activity did you use to help you explore your subject and get words down on paper? _____

   _____

   _____

   _____

   b. What problems did you have with an early draft? _____

   _____

   _____

   c. What kind of revision strategies did you use to shape and to refine your draft?

   _____

   _____

   _____

3. Analyze two suggestions that members of your group gave you. First, list the point, and then respond to the comment. Did you agree or disagree with what they said? What did you do as a result of their feedback?

   a. Group comment: _____

   _____

   b. Your response: _____

   _____

   c. Group comment: _____

   _____

   d. Your response: _____

   _____

4. What are the strengths of your paper? What points still cause you trouble?

_____

_____

_____

_____

_____

_____

_____

_____

5. What do you want me to look for when I evaluate this paper? What questions do you have for me? _____

_____

_____

_____

_____

_____

6. If you were to grade this paper, what grade would you give it and why?

_____

_____

_____

_____

_____

_____

Additional Options for Self-Evaluation

- Consider having students respond to questions such as these:

  - Why did you choose this format (essay, short story, for example)?
  - What pleases you the most about this writing?
  - What strategies were most effective for you as a writer as you worked on this piece?
  - What new strategies did you try? How successful was this attempt with a new technique?
  - What problems did you encounter, and how did you solve them?
  - Who gave you helpful suggestions? What were they?
  - What could your peer response group do to give you even better feedback about your writing?
  - What additional changes would you make in this writing if you had the opportunity?
  - How does this writing compare to other writing you have done?
  - What did you learn in the process of completing this writing?

- Ask students to write a description of the phrase "best writing." Then have them pick one of their writings and show how their own best writing reflects their standards.
- Instruct students to rank their papers from most to least effective and give a rationale for their ranking.

Plan to assess portfolios periodically, every four weeks or so, and include notes about your observations. Some teachers attach a grade to these observations or formally grade an early writing as well as a later one.

DESIGNING ASSIGNMENTS FOR A VARIETY OF FORMATS

Writing Assignments That Require Little Teacher Time

Sometimes teachers make too much work for themselves by assigning long papers that require time and weekends of "correcting" and grading. Mini-writing assignments encourage students to write often without creating unmanageable work for the teacher.

- *"I learned" statements.* Each student writes three to five sentences stating what he or she learned during a class hour or during an experience such as a film, a presentation, or a field trip. A writing assignment such as this helps students practice making notes and summarizing. While you are putting materials away following a film, for example, students write. On the following day, call on several students to read from their lists to recall and review the previous class material. These summaries increase long-term retention and may become an ongoing journal or learning log assignment.
- *Memos.* Students write a brief explanation to a specified reader of something they have learned to do or have done. For example, students write a memo about a class activity for someone who has been absent, or they write a memo to you explaining what they know about a topic (either before or after studying it).

• *Microthemes.* Students write short essay answers or summaries on index cards or half-sheets of paper to a question you have posed. (Some teachers also require a one-sentence summary of the response as a heading.) Microthemes provide good practice in preparation for writing essay answers on exams. They are fast and easy for you to respond to, and the limited space forces students to focus their thinking and write precisely and economically. Asking students to read these aloud reinforces their learning, makes them aware of a broader audience, and calls for an immediate response.

Essay Answers

Students are frequently unsuccessful in writing essay answers because they too often overlook prewriting activities and begin drafting immediately. Teach them to approach an essay answer in a series of steps:

1. Analyze the question.

   a. Circle all direction words such as *list, compare, trace.*
   b. Underline key words.
   c. Determine the number of parts to a question.

2. Develop ideas.

   a. Brainstorm, list, or cluster.
   b. Number or jot a brief outline.
   c. Reread the question.

3. Write the answer.

   a. Restate the question as the first sentence.
   b. Write a draft using the brief outline as a guide.
   c. Reread and make all changes legible and clear, if necessary, but do not recopy.

The following sample exercise is designed to help students practice writing such answers:

A Practice Essay Answer

1. Hand out two lemon drops to each student. (One is to eat immediately.)
2. Explain that they will practice writing an essay answer based on the following directions: "Define and describe a lemon drop. Be sure to appeal to all five senses in your answer."

(Continued)

---

3. Ask students to identify the instruction words and circle them (*Define, describe,* and *appeal*).
4. Identify and underline other key words (*lemon drop* and *five senses*).
5. Identify the number of parts to the question (*two*).
6. Brainstorm for ideas. A sample brainstorming list for "lemon drop" might look like the following:

definition candy		description senses		
sight	**sound**	**touch**	**taste**	**smell**
yellow oval	pings on desk crunches	coarse gritty	sour sweet tart	lemon

7. Number or letter the ideas in the order to be considered in the answer.
8. Reread the question. Then write an answer using the lettered brainstorming sheet or brief outline as a guide and restate the question as the first sentence of the answer. ("A lemon drop is a piece of candy that may be described according to the five senses.")
9. After the writing is completed, students read and edit their original drafts, making neat and legible changes if necessary, but they do not recopy.
10. Call on volunteers to read their trial answers aloud and comment on what makes them successful.
11. On the following day, students write an answer to an authentic question based on material they have been studying.

Research Reports

We have long asked students to write formal research reports because we believe it is essential that they learn to gather, organize, and interpret information. They need to synthesize sources with their own thinking and handle quotations and cite references. Formal research papers require a great deal of instruction and class time and long hours on the part of the teacher in grading final drafts. Despite our best effort, the writing produced by this kind of assignment is frequently dull and voiceless.

Teachers have begun to design a variety of research projects around the concept of the "I-search." As opposed to the standard research paper in which the writer usually assumes a detached and objective stance, the I-search paper allows students to personalize their search for facts and ideas. Students choose topics they care a great deal about. The final draft is a first-person step-by-step narrative of their own discovery process.

Section 1 is "what I assume or imagine or already know about this topic." Before conducting any formal research, students write a section to explain to the reader what they think they know, what they assume, or what they imagine about their topic as well as why they have chosen it. For example, a student writing about teenage alcoholism might estimate the severity of the problem, create a profile of a typical teenage drinker, and explain why he or she is interested in the topic.

Section 2 is about the search. Students consult books, magazines, newspapers, film, tapes, and other sources for information. Whenever possible, they interview people who are authorities or are familiar with the topic. A student whose topic is teenage alcoholism would read several books on the subject, as well as pertinent articles in a variety of recent magazines, visit a rehabilitation center for alcoholics, attend a meeting of Al-Anon or Alcoholics Anonymous, and consult an alcoholism counselor. He or she would write about the search in narrative form (usually chronologically), documenting all sources of information and using formal footnotes or endnotes when appropriate.

Section 3 is about what the writer discovered. Writers compare what they thought, assumed, or imagined with what was actually discovered. They include some personal commentary and draw conclusions. For instance, the writer on teenage alcoholism might learn that the problem is far more severe and often begins at an earlier age than he or she believed. He or she may have assumed that parental neglect was a major cause of the problem but may find that peer pressure is the prime factor contributing to teenage alcoholism.

At the end of the report, the writer attaches a formal bibliography listing the sources consulted during the search.

Variations of the I-Search Report

- Students work collaboratively in a group investigation and present their findings orally as well as in a short paper with a bibliography.
- Students research an author or a well-known person, but the final response format is multigenre—a poem, a news article, a dialogue, a story, a journal entry, and a letter, for example.
- Students research a career. The final format consists of four main sections: (1) a library research section describing the career, (2) an interview section with a person working in the career field, (3) a personal experience section about spending a full day observing and working with a professional from that career field, and (4) a summary of the writer's findings.
- Students research a particular time in history and then write their own historical fiction, such as a narrative, drama, or exchange of letters reflecting the same era.
- Each student chooses a year in history, researches it, and produces a newspaper with important news items of a particular day in that year.

Letter Writing

Pen pals have been used extensively to help students write for a real audience. An alternative approach is to pair students in two different classes. Without using their names (or identifying them only by number), they write back and forth to one another. No attempt is made to bring them together, and they rely only on a written exchange. Teachers of remedial reading students often ask teachers and counselors to become pen pals with their students. The replies are immediate, and students realize that their writing matters. You can also pair students with residents of a convalescent center or members of a senior citizens center.

Comparison and Contrast Writing

There are a number of organizers that are helpful when students are asked to write comparison and contrast papers:

1. Circles within circles (Figure 5.2) are useful for helping students see relationships and categories. The largest circle contains all members of the class; smaller circles within the large circle contain species or individual examples.
2. Venn diagrams feature overlapping circles (Figure 5.3). In the outer areas, points of contrast are written; in the area of overlap, points of similarity are noted.
3. Ladder notes are graphic organizers that help students look at the differences between two things (Figure 5.4). The points of consideration are listed on the rungs in the middle. On one side they note the attributes of one subject, and on the other side, those of the second.

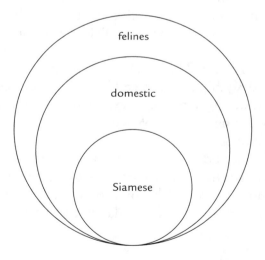

FIGURE 5.2   Circles-Within-Circles Organizer

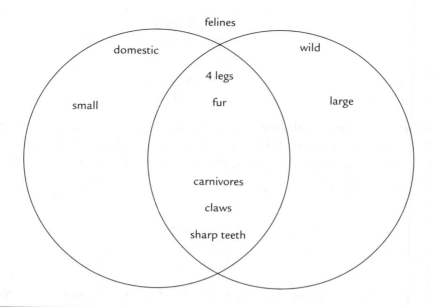

FIGURE 5.3 Venn Diagram

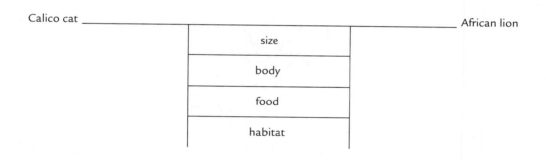

FIGURE 5.4

Poetry

Read poetry to your students, and have them read aloud as well. Play recordings of writers reading and talking about their work. Invite a local poet to your classroom to read and talk about his or her work. Everything in poetry starts from listening to it and enjoying the experience. An understanding of a variety of formats or patterns is also helpful in initiating poetry writing with students:

- *Acrostic poem:* The first letter in each line can be read vertically to form a word. Students might use their own names or the names of historical or literary characters as a starting point for their own poems. Example:

Something
Mandatory
In
Laughing
Effectively

- *ABC poem:* A poem with one word per line. The writer begins with any letter of the alphabet for the first word; the next line begins with the next letter of the alphabet. The poem may be as long or as short as desired, and the alphabet may be used backwards. Example:

  All
  Butterflies
  Can
  Dance

- *Concrete or picture poem:* An idea is expressed in both verbal and pictorial form:

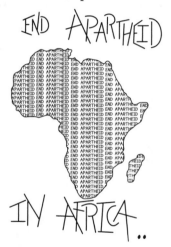

Cinquain: The five lines follow a distinct pattern. Example:

line 1: a one-word title	Buffalo
line 2: two words describe the title line	Noble, mammoth,
3: three words express action line	Stampeding, charging, dying
4: four words express a feeling line	Sadness, anger, hunger, loss,
5: another word for the title	Dishonored

Diamante: The seven-line poem has a specific format. Example:

line 1: one word title	Bicycle
line 2: two words describing the title	Sleek, swift,
line 3: three *-ing* words telling about the title	Pedaling, flying, soaring
line 4: four nouns relating to the title	Wheels, pedal, chain, seat,

line 5: three *-ing* words describing line 4	Rolling, clanking, bending
line 6: two words describing line 4	Shattered, scattered,
line 7: one word that is nearly the opposite of the title	Stranded

Wingspark: The five lines follow a specific pattern. Example:

line 1: I dreamed	I dreamed
line 2: answers the question "Who?"	Kirby Pucket
line 3: answers the question "Where?"	In the Metrodome
line 4: shows action	Hit a grand slam
line 5: describes how the action was done	Perfectly!

- *List poem:* Any number of lines in the poem list ideas, usually without transitional phrases. List poems may be based on any possible concept (beauty, ugliness, sadness, things I like, things I don't like, untrue statements about stones or pudding). Numerous variations are possible: "I wanted ... I got ..." or "I used to be ... now I am ..." List poems may also repeat a word or phrase such as "every day," "don't," or "I remember." Example:

My Junk Drawer

As I struggle to open the drawer, I find:
4 novels (unread),
20 batteries (dead),
100 feet of wire,
20 pieces of an electric train set,
1 polyester shirt I got last Christmas,
3 workbooks from fifth grade,
and the reason I can hardly open it: clay.

- *Found poem:* Lines are taken from a nonliterary source or sources such as newspapers, magazines, advertisements, labels, crossword puzzle clues, or junk mail and reshaped as a poem. Example:

Original Source

Clover Ice Cream is dedicated to perfection. We select only the highest quality, all-natural ingredients. Clover Ice Cream contains no preservatives, artificial flavors, stabilizers, additives, or colorings. This commitment to quality is why Clover Ice Cream is the finest in the world.

Found Poem

Dedicated
  to perfection
Highest quality artificial
  flavors, stabilizers,
additives ...
    finest in the
world.

- *Clerihew:* Humorous four-line rhymed verse, usually about a famous person, whose name is the first line. (Students might be asked to write a clerihew about themselves, using their own names.) Example:

Willard Scott

Is not
As fat
As all that.

- *Haiku:* A three-line unrhymed poem with seventeen syllables (5, 7, 5), usually using present-tense verbs. Example:

Goldfish in a bowl
Darting, circling, hurrying
Without arriving.

- *Haiku variations:*

  tanka: five-lines with syllables arranged in a 5–7–5–7–7 pattern
  lanterne: five lines with syllables arranged 1–2–3–4–1
  septolet: seven lines with a syllable pattern of 1–2–3–4–3–2–1

- *Free verse:* This unrhymed poetry may have any number of lines. It has no definite rhythm but is shaped on the page in a manner that gives the reader clues to its meaning. Line breaks are of particular importance. Lines can end at the end of a sentence, at the end of a phrase, or in the middle of a sentence or phrase. Words placed at the end of the line have the greatest impact. Shorter lines and white space are used to slow a poem and longer lines speed it up.

Sample Prompts for Poetry

There are many possibilities for prompts that are helpful as prewriting exercises for poetry—for example:

1. Make a long list of words naming emotions (or any other concept—a driving test, for example). Choose one of the words from the list, and make as long a list as possible of words, phrases, ideas, specific details, or incidents associated with this focus word. Include all or some of this material in a free verse poem about the topic.

2. Answer questions leading to a poem:

Line 1: What is your favorite kind of tree?
Line 2: What does this tree look like (color, shape, height)?
Line 3: What does this tree do when there's a heavy wind?
Line 4: What does this tree look like on a very dark night?
Line 5: What is the object in line 4 doing?

Birch tree,
Slender and white.
Waving to the sky,
A shivering ghost,
dancing in the darkness.

It is possible for a teacher to create a set of questions for a variety of topics—for example:

Line 1: What is your favorite season of the year?
Line 2: What objects do you think of when you think of this season?
Line 3: What colors come to mind?
Line 4: What smells or sounds do you associate with this season?
Line 5: What activities are children involved in during this time of year?
Line 6: What activities are adults involved in during this time of year?
Line 7: How does the weather change at the end of this season?
Line 8: How do you feel at the end of this season?

3. Directions for a variety of topics are useful prompts. For example, directions leading to a free verse poem based on a journey might resemble the following:

a. List as many possible journeys as you can think of—journeys that might take you only a few minutes to complete (to the teacher's desk, from the car to the house, from the hall to the principal's office, for example).
b. Underline one idea that seems to hold the best possibilities for writing.
c. Brainstorm a list of people who might be making this journey.
d. From this list, pick one person, and give him or her a name.
e. List as many reasons for the journey as possible.
f. Choose one.
g. List, using precise detail, all the sights, sounds, and smells your character might encounter on his or her journey.
h. Using as much of this brainstormed material as you wish, shape your ideas into a free verse poem—for example:

Tommy T's First Triple

Tommy T had hit his first triple,
A pitch down the center of the plate.
He swung his Easton, snapped his wrist
and smacked the ball into right center.
Tommy T had hit his first triple.
He raced to first, and the coach waved him on,
"Go to second, Tommy, go to second!"
Faster and faster raced Tommy
around second and straight for third.

The centerfielder hurled a long throw to short.
"Here," called the third baseman,
but Tommy T knew he had hit his first triple.
His cleats churned the sand.
He slid
as the shortstop's relay
hissed behind
The tag.
"Safe!"
Tommy T dusted
his uniform.
He had hit his first triple.

Form 5.11 offers helpful directions as students write found poetry.

Directions for a Found Poem

Name _____ Date _____

A found poem is a poem you create by:

· Finding words or phrases in another piece of writing; and
· Arranging them in such a way that they become a poem.

Found poetry helps you discover the possibilities of ordinary language.

1. Begin with interesting prose. For example:

   · textbooks
   · notices on bulletin boards
   · classified ads
   · obituaries
   · menus
   · magazines
   · letters
   · highway maps
   · junk mail

   Don't use other poetry or song lyrics or anything that has already been arranged on a page such as commercial advertising.

2. Select a section of the prose—the part that seems to offer the most possibilities. Lightly underline interesting words or phrases in the original source.

3. Write the underlined words or phrases in the same order on a piece of scratch paper. Leave plenty of space between words and lines as you write so you can easily rearrange them or make adjustments and changes.

4. Study the words or phrases you have written on your scratch paper. Cut out anything that's dull or unnecessary. (The words from the original should be reduced by at least half.) Change the punctuation if you need to, but try not to add any words of your own.

5. Arrange and space the words, phrases, and lines on the page. Take the whole page into consideration as you shape your poem.

   a. Play with line breaks.

      Lines may end at the end of a sentence.

They may end at the end
of a phrase
or with a key
word.

b. Arrange the words and sentences so they create a rhythm you like when you read the poem out loud.

c. Experiment with the white space.

You   can   space   words   apart   or   you   canrunthemtogether.
You can put key words

on

lines

alone

d. Poems may have any shape you want.

e. Words can be printed Large or small in color or in different **type** *faces*.

6. When the words, phrases, and lines are arranged just the way you want them, find a title, and add it to your poem.

7. At the bottom of the poem, tell where the words came from. Include the original author's name if possible. For example:

From "Blue Winds Dancing,"
By Thomas Whitecloud

Stories

We are told that students should be encouraged to write from personal experience. Trust your students to do this through fiction as well. They will write about the issues that are important to them. The following prompts are useful for stories:

1. These prompts may be used for individual students or as group prompts (in groups students pass their papers to the next student after completing each item):

    a. Write your name at the top of the page.
    b. Write a brief description of a setting for a story.
    c. Add and describe one character.
    d. Add and describe a second character.
    e. Describe a conflict between the two characters.
    f. Have one character make a statement in direct dialogue to develop the conflict.
    g. Let the second character respond.
    h. Describe the two characters engaged in some action.
    i. Write a brief dialogue between the characters.
    j. Bring the situation to a climax.
    k. Resolve the conflict. (For groups, return the sheet to the person whose name appears at the top of the page.)

2. Directions for brainstorming (may also be used as a group activity):

    a. Write down three categories of people who might be in a group—for example: construction workers, kids on a sports team, or old people in a nursing home.
    b. Circle the group that most appeals to you.
    c. Create three characters in the circled group. Name and describe them.
    d. Choose one of the characters, and write a brief description of something that happened to him or her in the past.
    e. Write a scene in which two of the three characters are talking about the third and something that happened recently to the third person. This dialogue should reveal what the two think about the third person and give clues to the personality and lives of the two speakers.
    f. Write a story based on the brainstormed material.

3. Questions for creating a character:

    a. What is his or her name? Age? Height? Weight?
    b. What unusual characteristic does he or she have?

   c. What place does she or he have in the family? (Oldest, middle, or youngest child; parent?)
   d. Who is his or her best friend?
   e. Who is a rival or enemy?
   f. What is this person's favorite food?
   g. What is this person's most hated food?
   h. What is this person's favorite activity?
   i. Is he or she neat or untidy?
   j. Does this person have a secret fear? If so, what is it?
   k. Who are this person's heroes?
   l. What is a major problem this character is facing?
   m. What are some physical habits he or she has?
   n. What is the most important thing that happened to this character in the past few months?
   o. What would someone meeting this character for the first time notice first?
   p. What is this character's biggest secret?
   q. Write a story or character sketch based on this material.

The possibilities for student writing are limitless. As you plan, be sure your students write in a variety of formats for many audiences. You'll want them to write in quantity, but you need not grade and correct everything they do. Help your students see their progress as writers and, most important, encourage them to evaluate their own writing to become independent and self-sufficient.

chapter 6

TEACHING READING *and* LITERATURE

- Approaches to the teaching of literature
- Selecting texts for student readers
- Planning for readers' responses
- Evaluating, testing, grading
- During and After Reading: Reader's Theater

Mrs. B, I just saw the old movie of Lord of the Flies. *It was in black and white but the book is so much better. It's in color.*

Many of us are teachers of English because of our love of literature. We may not remember becoming readers ourselves or recall a time when we didn't read for pleasure. We were the students who carried novels in our schoolbags to read at any opportunity. We read on the school bus, in the back of the classroom, on the porch in the summer, under the covers at night with a flashlight. We grew up loving to read.

As teachers of literature, we share what we love best with our students, and we want them to respond as enthusiastically as we do. Frequently, however, our own students have told us they don't like to read, or they "sort of" like to read, or they used to read as children but stopped when they got to high school. In frustration, we have tended to blame contemporary society, the changing family structure, or the influence and intrusion of the media for our students' attitudes. We have searched for ways to make our own teaching of reading and literature more effective. We not only want those students in our classrooms who enjoy reading to continue to be enthusiastic, but we also seek to make reading more enjoyable for those who read only dutifully, ploddingly, or not at all. In this chapter, we'll explore successful approaches to the teaching of literature, approaches that will help your students become active, enthusiastic readers.

APPROACHES TO THE TEACHING OF LITERATURE

Over the years, literature has been taught in a variety of ways, and we teachers have frequently emphasized one element in literature at the expense of others. For example, the historical approach emphasizes context, and the biographical approach highlights the author and literary form. More recently we have focused on the "new criticism," which views the text as central to the process of literary analysis. Beginning in the late 1950s and continuing through the 1960s, this analytical approach was probably the most widely used, and many college English courses concentrated on such elements as literary structure, imagery, or symbolism and regarded each work as an entity isolated from history or society. Many of us took such courses as undergraduates and graduates, and when we became teachers, we tended to teach in the same way. Our high school classrooms became smaller versions of college classrooms as we lectured and our students took notes. If our students didn't respond to our requests for meaning, we often felt obliged to fill in the silences, and we gave students our answers.

Recent research in reading has begun to exert enormous influence in the way reading and literature are currently being taught at all academic levels and, in particular, in elementary and secondary classrooms. The response-centered approach emphasizes the reader as a key element in the creation of a literary work and suggests that we have placed too much stress on getting meaning from the literature alone and too little on seeing what skills our students bring to their reading. Louise Rosenblatt's (1995) transactional view of literature has been particularly influential in this regard. She views reading not as a passive activity in which the reader receives the meaning from the text but as an active, dynamic process by which the reader and the text interact to create the literary work. From this perspective, how a reader reacts to or engages with a text is as important as what the artist "intended" (or what we teachers believe is intended). Rosenblatt also differentiates between efferent reading and aesthetic reading. Efferent reading relates to information to be acquired and is the kind of reading a student would do while reading a social studies text, for example. Aesthetic reading (reading literature) is different, and the focus, we are told, should be on what happens during the actual reading.

Does this mean that we should throw out the historical approach, the biographical approach, or a focus on the text, for example? Of course not. Each is useful and appropriate at various times. However, as our concept of the reader has changed, we've learned to place a greater value on our students' responses to literature, and we allow literary evaluation to grow naturally from these responses. We also seek to move our students beyond naive personal responses to responses that examine a text. We ask them to write and talk openly about their thoughts and feelings, to note and record important textual cues, and to make connections between literature and life. We promote analytical thinking and critical judgment without denying the pleasure of a personal response. The changes we are making in our own teaching—the enormous variety of responses we are designing for students—and our students' renewed enthusiasm for reading and literature reflect the impact of this influential research.

The Student's Role

We teach adolescents, young people emerging from the relatively untroubled world of childhood into adulthood. They arrive in our classrooms with enormous energy and endless contradictions. They know a little. They know a lot. They're innocent. They're sophisticated. They're happy. They're sad. They're filled with conflict. They're bored. They're exuberant. They're withdrawn. They challenge the authority they earlier accepted. They seek praise, yet they are highly critical of themselves and others. They want to be independent, yet they need to identify with a group. Their lives revolve around friendships and social relationships. In her highly influential book, *In the Middle* (1998), Nancie Atwell points out that this "confusion, bravado, restlessness, preoccupation with peers, and the questioning of authority are not manifestations of poor attitude: they are hallmarks of this particular time of life" (p. 25). This enormous energy of adolescence is exactly what we teachers must use in order to actively involve our students in their own learning.

The Teacher's Role

Because the best teaching of literature happens when teachers and students are involved in genuine dialogue and collaboration, your role as the teacher in the response-centered literature classroom is far different from the traditional role of lecturer at the front of the room. No longer will you do most of the talking and reading, and you will not be the final authority for every interpretation. Instead you will serve as a guide and resource who plans for and creates a learning environment that makes risk taking possible and fosters a wide variety of student responses. Here are ways that you can accomplish this goal.

Provide a Literature-Rich Classroom and Encourage Students to Read

A classroom that encourages students to become literate is filled with books (fiction and nonfiction), graphic novels, short stories, biographies, autobiographies, poetry, magazines, newspapers, writings by students and teachers—all the materials devoted readers turn to. This is also a classroom that gives students choices concerning what it is they read, time for reading, and options for a variety of responses. Atwell (1998) has pointed out that what occurs in the everyday world is what should be happening in our classrooms. She suggests that those of us who grew up loving to read and teach literature match the way we learned to read, the way we used our own reading process, against the way we teach it in our classrooms. For example, as readers we usually decided what we wanted to read. We read for pleasure and meaning, and we talked with others about what we read. We argued, exchanged bits of information, described what we liked or hated, and recommended books to others. We were captivated, and we found books we loved (Atwell, 1998). We can make this happen for our students as well.

Fill bulletin boards with reviews written by students and clipped from newspapers and magazines. Set aside a blackboard space or a large piece of paper as a graffiti board, and encourage students to comment on their reading without giving away the plot (cryptic comments help motivate more reluctant readers). Students interview teachers, community members, and other students for producing a recommended reading list or a summer reading list.

- *Should students really choose everything they read?* Some teachers allow students to choose every text they read. This requires extensive resources and real administrative artistry on the part of the teacher. The best approach is to strike a balance between whole class reading and individualized reading. You should make the selections for whole class reading, choosing the best literature your students are capable of understanding reasonably well. The choice of a common text depends, of course, on what is available to you in the book room or in a class anthology, what has preceded its study, and the needs, interests, and abilities of the students.

  Allow your students to pick their own texts for independent reading projects. Books for independent reading may be chosen from those on the shelves in your classroom or the school library. Often students bring books from home, and you can encourage them to trade with one another. Add a few books to your classroom collection each year (garage sales and library sales are good places to find inexpensive copies). Larger booksellers offer educator discounts, and with a tax-exempt letter from your school, buying new books becomes more affordable. Over time you will also want to acquire smaller sets (five or six copies) of a variety of titles for students to read in smaller groups. By offering many choices, you will be able to respond to students from the broadest possible range of ability levels and backgrounds.

- *How can I justify giving secondary students reading time in class? I've got to cover a lot of material.* If we expect our students to become readers, we have to ensure that reading happens. This involves blocks of time, and it may be our greatest gift to our students. The best approach is to build in and adjust time in connection with specific units. Some teachers work with individual students while the remainder of the class reads. Others feel reading time is so sacred that they allow no other activity to occur in its time slot, and they model reading along with their students. Reading with your students will give you time to familiarize yourself with adolescent titles, including the ones students recommend to you. However you structure in-class reading time, it's important to remember that students need time—time to read and time to get hooked on reading.

- *I always have my students write about their reading. What's wrong with asking students to write a literary analysis after they've read?* There's nothing wrong with this kind of response, but it shouldn't be the only response from students. In the past, we usually assigned writing at the end of a discussion or unit, and our purpose was to evaluate a student's understanding. Writing prior to reading or during reading can become a means of achieving understanding, a way to initiate inquiry or open a discussion. (Later in this chapter, we look at a wide variety of writing activities for students throughout the reading process.)

Allow Students to Stop Reading Something They Are Not Enjoying

As readers, we sometimes begin a book, discover it isn't for us, and set it aside. Students should understand they also have this option in their independent reading.

Emphasize Reading and Literature as Communication Rather than as a Series of Subskills

Offer complete pieces of literature to your students. Encourage them to experience the entire work, its themes, and significant issues. Excerpts from chapters, fragments, and isolated words, phrases, or exercise paragraphs are useful in some contexts for mini-lessons. They should, however, never be used as a substitute for the literature itself.

Evaluate and Monitor the Pattern of Classroom Discussions and Questions

We need to analyze carefully the way classroom discussions evolve. For example, do we encourage students to state and defend their opinions, or do we have a single interpretation in mind and lead the discussion in that direction? Fostering a sense of exploration and discovery will work toward helping students go beyond obvious answers or superficial responses and to articulate, expand, and defend their own reactions.

Questions have long been the staple of teachers' techniques for promoting comprehension. What's new is that we're learning to ask students to generate their own questions. The simplest approach at the beginning of a class period is to ask each student to write on a slip of paper a question or issue about his or her reading each considers important. You may ask students to read these aloud or collect the slips and choose one or several to share with the class. The questions become the basis for a class discussion and can take most of one class period. When you introduce this technique early in the year, students' questions at first may resemble the discussion topics in a textbook, but over time, they will learn to depend on their own resources, and their questions will become more insightful and sophisticated. Encouraging students to ask their own questions is one of the most powerful things that you can do as a teacher.

Discussion based on student-generated questions is an ideal small group exercise. Each member of the group writes a list of questions about the text. The group sorts the questions and decides whether members will consider every question, only one question, or several. Following the group discussion, one member summarizes for the whole class while you or a designated student lists the major ideas on the blackboard.

In a response-centered classroom, teachers and students really listen to each other, and authority is shared. Discussion revolves around students' feelings, questions, and responses and may result in a shared interpretation or several interpretations. There is as much student talk as teacher talk, and students are allowed to disagree with each other and with the teacher (Judy & Judy, 1983). Keep the following suggestions in mind for effective discussions:

- Allow time to elapse before responding to a student's comments. Encourage others to respond first, and don't rush to fill up the silences.
- Keep your responses neutral such as, "Could you explain in more detail?" Students are used to trying to guess what we want to hear, and comments such as, "Good point," or "I agree with you," perpetuate this kind of thinking.
- Encourage each speaker to say more, elaborate, clarify, or explain. "Why?" "What do you mean?" "Tell us more," and "I don't understand" are the kinds of replies that foster discussion.

Provide Students with a Variety of Ways to Analyze and Respond to a Text

No single approach or lesson plan is appropriate for every piece of literature. A teacher must tailor assignments and activities to each text. Nevertheless, in doing so, we seek to provide a range of response types that allow students to back up their judgments: emotional, descriptive, autobiographical, interpretive, evaluative. We also encourage students to respond in a variety of formats: essays, journals, discussion, creative writing, oral interpretation, and visual responses. (Suggestions for these options are discussed later in this chapter.)

- *Does this mean my students should never read what scholars or critics have to say?* Focusing on students' responses does not deny the importance of scholars and critics. Our students should test their responses against those of others. One approach is to distribute sample critiques after students have completed their own work and ask them to compare their responses to what critics have said about a text.

Plan for Collaborative Responses Throughout the Reading Process

Ideally you will plan for a variety of responses from your students, both individually and in small and large groups. While solo exploration is a significant part of becoming a reader, small group discussion is ideal for adolescents. Work in small groups ensures more student involvement. It also encourages students to communicate with one another in the kind of exploratory talk that allows them to take greater risks. The interaction that occurs in small groups helps students understand why they respond as they do, encourages them to develop responses independent of you, and motivates them to explore areas of agreement and disagreement with one another. Group work can occur at any time in the reading process: as a prereading activity, an activity that occurs during reading to extend the understanding of the text, or a culminating activity. (Suggestions for group activities are discussed in detail later in this chapter.)

Become Involved in the Student's Entire Reading Process

Rather than simply testing comprehension after the reading is completed, become involved in your students' entire reading process. Plan for student responses before, during, and after reading a text. Table 6.1 lists sample activities.

TABLE 6.1   Sample Activities for Students Before, During, and After Reading a Text

Before-Reading Activities	During-Reading Activities	After-Reading Activities
Webquest: Students research topics and historical information so that they better understand the context and setting for the novel.	*Creating graphic novels:* Students create visuals and text to create segments of the text as graphic novels.	*Character biography:* Create a biography about the life of a character from the reading.
Music: Use songs that have the same themes or are based on the works that your students will read. Example: Taylor Swift's "Love Story" is a version of Shakespeare's *Romeo and Juliet.*	*Reader's theater:* Students can create dramatic oral versions for the texts that they are reading in class.	*Character portrayal:* This reading strategy helps students to analyze and reflect on what they have read. Students choose a Role, Audience, Form, and Topic, and write a response to what they have read.
Shorter works: Use short stories, poems, and articles that have the same theme as the longer work that the students will read. Example: Paul Laurence Dunbar's poem "Sympathy," which is referred to at the beginning of Maya Angelou's *I Know Why the Caged Bird Sings.*	*Character bookmarks:* Sometimes it can be challenging to keep all of the characters in a novel straight. As the students are reading their novel, they can record the characters and details about the characters on a bookmark.	*Text time line:* Create a time line of the important events in the text.

(continued)

TABLE 6.1 *(continued)*

Before-Reading Activities	During-Reading Activities	After-Reading Activities
Gallery walk: Display pictures and images of the setting and historical period of the text that the students will be reading. Have the students tour the gallery and comment on what they see.	*Question and statement bookmarks:* Similar to a character bookmark, the students can record questions, comments, personal connections, or ideas on a bookmark as they are reading a text.	*Literature letters:* The students write a letter from a character's point of view to another.
Anticipation guides: A series of statements for which the students agree or disagree. These statements can focus on the students' prior knowledge or the big ideas or essential questions in the novel. The students compare their initial responses after they have read the novel.	*Sticky notes:* Using sticky notes, the students stop as they are reading (when they need to) to record insights, personal connections, and questions. These notes become even more valuable and helpful during large and small group discussions.	*Making memories:* Create a scrapbook based on the setting, events, conflict, and characters from the text.

- *How about study guides? Won't these help students as they read?* Generally study guides aren't helpful. Most don't allow sustained, extended responses to a text, and many require only obvious answers or emphasize one specific skill. These often unrelated questions may actually fragment the reader's attention rather than help a student's understanding. Although some formats can be excellent, most do little to develop the reader's understanding or appreciation of a text.
- *When do I teach skills?* Since you are involved in the students' entire process, and diagnosis and evaluation are ongoing activities, you will include mini-lessons whenever you see the need. You'll find advice on creating and teaching mini-lessons later in this chapter, along with samples you can adapt or use as presented.

Give Students Options and Choices in Responding to Literature

Provide many options and possibilities for responses and assignments. As with any other skill, students need encouragement, practice, and experience in creating their own responses to what they have read. If you tell students early in the year, "Respond to this piece of literature," their reaction is likely to be puzzlement. However, after having plenty of experience with a variety of responses, most students will perceive a long list of options, and their chief concern will be choosing a single response from all the possibilities they envision.

Plan for Student Self-Assessment and Evaluation

Assessment happens any time in the reading process—as a prereading activity to discover what information students bring to the text, as a check for understanding during the reading process, or as a culminating activity. In addition, students learn assessment skills to evaluate their own responses and the responses of others. Your goal is to reduce the need for extensive teacher evaluation as students become involved in their own evaluation process. Ideally, you will spend more time working with students as they read and respond to their reading and less time making up tests and marking papers. (See Chapter Two for a complete discussion of testing and grading.)

Encourage Students to Share Their Responses with a Variety of Audiences

Plan for your students to respond to one another and to prepare presentations for other audiences, such as adults outside the classroom. When students learn and practice a variety of responses and successfully present them to different audiences, they are more highly motivated to respond again.

SELECTING TEXTS FOR STUDENT READERS

One of the important tasks the teacher has pertains to selecting anthologies or texts for student readers. In designing his or her curriculum there are many options.

Classroom Anthologies

Many literature anthologies contain excellent selections for young readers. The sequencing of materials can be helpful to a teacher as well. In too many cases, however, the literature found in these anthologies is excerpted from a larger text or is selected because it represents a good example of a literary device. Students may gain the false impression that many poets wrote only one poem or that a famous novel contains but one chapter.

Some anthologies tend to promote knowledge about books and authors rather than fostering critical reading or a reader's personal response. In addition, the nature of the tasks that students are asked to perform in conjunction with the reading often does not reflect effective teaching practice. For example, questions at the end of the selections tend to perpetuate the reader's role as an essentially passive one and do little to encourage aesthetic reading. Too often questions are based almost entirely on recall and comprehension and call for answers that can be located directly in the text. Such anthologies often do little to build on the student's background knowledge prior to reading a selection and offer few reading strategies for the reading process itself. Most anthologies omit activities aimed at promoting small group discussion and creative dramatics and offer few suggestions for personal and imaginative writing. Too often the questions and suggested activities that follow the texts serve as an assessment of student comprehension rather than help students extend and elaborate on new learning. Questions tend to focus on isolated pieces of information that are likely to disrupt the reader's comprehension.

Does this mean that you should abandon a classroom anthology? Not necessarily. If an anthology is all that is available to you, use it, but don't feel you must cover everything. Be selective in the assignments you make, and examine the responses these materials call for. When the book selection committee meets or new texts are ordered, consider replacing or supplementing the anthology with sets of novels, poetry, drama, and nonfiction for the whole class. If your goal is to develop the habit of personal reading in your students, you'll want to give them access to the real thing—books rather than textbooks.

Literature Texts

As we choose literature texts for students, we need to keep in mind what we want students to learn and what attitudes we want them to develop. We're convinced of the value of literature for students. We believe it can stimulate their imagination, intellect, and emotions and provide vicarious experiences with new places, different times, and a wide variety of people. It can help them grow in knowledge and understanding as they ask themselves the fundamental questions people have asked through the ages. Nevertheless, what we teach is always a concern. Do we teach adolescent literature, or do we teach the classics? Some educators feel that little of adolescent literature is as good as what has stood the test of time. They believe that if students are not exposed to the world's finest writing, many will never read it. In addition, curriculum guidelines and standardized tests often require the reading of some basic texts. But we are also told that we need to provide adolescents with literature that attracts them, satisfies their interests, and at the same time challenges them. Fortunately, the quantity and quality of literature written expressly for young adults have grown enormously in the past thirty years.

Although we want students to be exposed to the best our language and culture have to offer, most teachers arrive at a middle ground. Not every piece of adolescent literature is worthy of study. Not every classic is appropriate. Some texts are simply too difficult or too remote from students' experience and may destroy their interest in reading and the possibility that they will ever read with enthusiasm. Using students' interests as a starting point, choose both classic and adolescent literature for your classroom. Select for whole class study worthy pieces, both classic and contemporary, that clearly have something to say to today's young people; allow many options for your students' independent reading.

Helpful Sources for Selecting Texts for the Secondary Classroom

Your school librarian or media specialist is your best guide as you select material for your classroom. He or she knows and has available a wide variety of selection tools and sources for recommended titles based on theme, interest, popularity, genre, and reading level. The following resources are also helpful for both you and your students as you make your selections:

Print Sources

- *Booklist*, an American Library Association publication
- *Bulletin of the Center for Children's Books*
- *English Journal*, a National Council of Teachers of English publication for secondary school teachers
- *Journal of Reading*
- *School Library Journal*

Web Sites

- Reviews of the latest titles in young adult literature: www.alan-ya.org
- Popular paperbacks for young adults: www.ala.org/ala/yalsa/booklistsawards/popular paperback/popularpaperbacks.cfm
- Books and authors of popular literature studied in high school: www.awesome library.org/Classroom/English/Literature/Middle_High_School_Literature.html
- A guide for finding children's and young adult literature: www.millikin.edu/staley/ subject/subject_guides/childlit.asp#online
- Short list of young adult literature for reluctant male readers, sorted by theme: http://scholar.lib.vt.edu/ejournals/ALAN/winter99/gill.html
- Young adult literature book list: www.seemore.mi.org/booklists
- Learn about young adult literature from this teacher's blog: http://thereading zone.wordpress.com
- Book lists for young adults: www.waterborolibrary.org/oldsite/bklisty.htm#yaclass

Appendix D in this book contains additional suggestions.

Although choosing a class novel usually depends on what is available in the book room, you may also wish to consult the following lists as you plan for collaborative and independent reading. These lists are intended to be a helpful starting point and are by no means exhaustive.

Classics

Jane Austen, *Pride and Prejudice*
Ray Bradbury, *Fahrenheit 451*
Charlotte Brontë, *Jane Eyre* and *Wuthering Heights*
Dee Brown, *Bury My Heart at Wounded Knee*
Pearl S. Buck, *The Good Earth*
Lewis Carroll, *Alice's Adventures in Wonderland*
Willa Cather, *My Antonia*
Stephen Crane, *The Red Badge of Courage*
Charles Dickens, *David Copperfield*

Alexander Dumas Sr., *The Three Musketeers* and *The Man in the Iron Mask*
F. Scott Fitzgerald, *The Great Gatsby*
William Golding, *Lord of the Flies*
Lorraine Hansberry, *A Raisin in the Sun*
Nathaniel Hawthorne, *The House of Seven Gables* and *The Scarlet Letter*
Ernest Hemingway, *For Whom the Bell Tolls*
Ken Kesey, *One Flew over the Cuckoo's Nest*
John Knowles, *A Separate Peace*
Harper Lee, *To Kill a Mockingbird*
Carson McCullers, *The Heart Is a Lonely Hunter* and *A Member of the Wedding*
Boris Pasternak, *Doctor Zhivago*
Alan Paton, *Cry, the Beloved Country*
Erich Maria Remarque, *All Quiet on the Western Front*
J. D. Salinger, *Catcher in the Rye*
Mary Shelley, *Frankenstein*
John Steinbeck, *The Grapes of Wrath, Of Mice and Men,* and *The Pearl*
Bram Stoker, *Dracula*
Harriet Beecher Stowe, *Uncle Tom's Cabi*n
Jonathan Swift, *Gulliver's Travels*
Amy Tan, *The Joy Luck Club*
Mark Twain, *The Adventures of Huckleberry Fin*n
Kurt Vonnegut Jr., *Slaughterhouse Five*
Oscar Wilde, *The Picture of Dorian Gray*
Richard Wright, *Black Boy* and *Native Son*

Mystery and Detective

Anything by the following authors: Lilian Jackson Braun, Agatha Christie, Mary Higgins
    Clark, Anna Clarke, Sir Arthur Conan Doyle, Dashiell Hammett, Tony Hillerman,
    P. D. James, Ngaio Marsh, or Dorothy Sayers
Lois Duncan, *Down a Dark Hall, Killing Mr. Griffin, Stranger with My Face,* and *Summer
    of Fear*
Elaine L. Konisburg, *Father's Arcane Daughter*
Madeleine L'Engle, *Arms of the Starfish* and *Young Unicorns*
Cynthia Voigt, *The Callender Papers*

Fantasy and Science Fiction

Douglas Adams, *The Hitchhiker's Guide to the Galaxy; Life, the Universe and Everything;*
    and *The Restaurant at the End of the Universe*
Richard Adams, *Watership Down*
Peter Beagle, *Last Unicorn*
Ray Bradbury, *Fahrenheit 451* and *The Martian Chronicles*
Marion Zimmer Bradley, *The Mists of Avalon*
Kristin Cashore, *Graceling*

Cinda Williams Chima, the Warrior Heir series
Arthur Clarke, *2001: A Space Odyssey*
Suzanne Collins, *The Hunger Games Trilogy*
Susan Cooper, *The Dark Is Rising, Susan Cooper, Greenwitch*, and *Silver on the Tree*
Jaclyn Dolamore, *Magic Under Glass*
Cornella Caroline Funke, *Inkheart*
William Goldman, *The Princess Bride*
Michael Grant, *Gone*
Shannon Hale, *Princess Academy*
Lisa M. Klein, *Ophelia, Lady Macbeth's Daughter*
Ursula Le Guin, *Left Hand of Darkness, The Tombs of Atuann*, and *A Wizard of Earthsea*
C. S. Lewis, the Chronicles of Narnia series
Lois Lowry, *The Giver*
Yann Martel, *The Life of Pi*
Stephanie Meyer, *The Host* and the Twilight series
Robin McKinley, *Beauty, The Door in the Hedge,* and *The Outlaws of Sherwood*
Terry Pratchett, *We Free Men*
Rick Riordan, Percy Jackson series and *The Kane Chronicles*
Mary Shelley, *Frankenstein*
Bram Stoker, *Dracula*
J.R.R. Tolkien, *The Hobbit* and Lord of the Rings trilogy
Megan Whelan Turner, *The Thief*
Terence H. White, *The Once and Future King*

Biography and Autobiography

Maya Angelou, *I Know Why the Caged Bird Sings*
Melba Beals, *Warriors Don't Cry*
Claude Brown, *Manchild in the Promised Land*
Man Bullock, *Hitler: A Study in Tyranny*
Richard E. Byrd, *Alone*
Truman Capote, *In Cold Blood*
John Howard Griffin, *Black Like Me*
Alex Haley, *The Autobiography of Malcolm X*
Jeanne Wakatsuki Houston, *Farewell to Manzanar*
Helen Keller, *The Story of My Life*
Mary MacCracken, *Circle of Children* and *Lovey: A Very Special Child*
Robert Massie, *Nicholas and Alexandra*
Nancy Milford, *Zelda: A Biography*
John C. Neihardt, *Black Elk Speaks*
Roger Shattuck, *Forbidden Experiment: The Story of the Wild Boy of Aveyron*
Evans G. Valens, *The Other Side of the Mountain*
Booker T. Washington, *Up from Slavery*
Donald Woods, *Biko*

Richard Wright, *Black Boy*
Elie Wiesel, *Night*

Historical Fiction

Avi, *Crispin*
Thomas Berger, *Little Big Man*
Joan Blos, *A Gathering of Days*
Hal Borland, *When the Legends Die*
Carol Brink, *Caddie Woodlawn*
Dee Brown, *Bury My Heart at Wounded Knee*
Pearl S. Buck, *The Good Earth*
Judy Blundell, *What I Saw and How I Lied*
Walter Clark, *The Ox-Bow Incident*
Howard Fast, *April Morning*
Esther Forbes, *Johnny Tremain*
Paula Fox, *Slave Dancer*
Cornelia Funke, *The Thief Lord*
Ernest Gaines, *The Autobiography of Miss Jane Pittman*
Bette Greene, *Summer of My German Soldier*
Laurie Halse Anderson, *Fever 1793*
Irene Hunt, *Across Five Aprils* and *Up a Road Slowly*
Sue Monk Kidd, *The Secret Life of Bees*
Oliver La Farge, *Laughing Boy*
Margaret Mitchell, *Gone with the Wind*
Scott O'Dell, *Sarah Bishop* and *Sing Down the Moon*
Erich Maria Remarque, *All Quiet on the Western Front*
Mary Renault, *The Bull from the Sea* and *The King Must Die*
Conrad Richter, *A Light in the Forest*
Elizabeth George Speare, *Bronze Bow* and *The Witch of Blackbird Pond*
Mary Stewart, *The Crystal Cave*
Irving Stone, *The Agony and the Ecstasy*
Mildred Taylor, *Roll of Thunder, Hear My Cry*

Historical Fiction: Twentieth-Century Wars

John Boyne, *The Boy in the Striped Pajamas*
Joseph Bruchac, *Codetalkers*
James Clavell, *King Rat*
Joseph Heller, *Catch-22*
Ernest Hemingway, *Farewell to Arms* and *For Whom the Bell Tolls*
James Michener, *Bridges at Toko-Ri*
Erich Maria Remarque, *All Quiet on the Western Front*
Nevil Shute, *A Town Like Alice*
Dalton Trumbo, *Johnny Got His Gun*

Leon Uris, *Exodus*
Herman Wouk, *The Caine Mutiny, War and Remembrance,* and *Winds of War*
Markus Zusak, *The Book Thief*

At least part of your curriculum should be devoted to texts that students select. Some will want to read books about characters like themselves facing similar problems. Many will choose escape books for pleasure reading: romances such as Silhouette and Harlequin; suspense stories such as Tom Clancy's *The Hunt for Red October*; gothic stories by Stephen King or V. C. Andrews; and science fiction and fantasy with titles such *The Hunger Games* and *The Giver*. Personal standard of choice will be modified as readers develop and mature. Their judgment will be sharpened through class work, reading reviews, and discussions with classmates. The following is a sample list of high-interest, easy-reading books for even the most reluctant reader in your classroom:

Sherman Alexie, *The Absolutely True Diary of a Part Time Indian*
Avi, *Nothing But The Truth*
Robert Cormier, *After the First Death* and *The Chocolate War*
Sharon Draper, *Forged by Fire* (a trilogy) and *Just Another Hero*
Lois Duncan, *They Never Came Home*
Neil Gaiman, *The Graveyard Book*
S. E. Hinton, *The Outsiders*
Irene Hunt, *The Lottery Rose* and *No Promises in the Wind*
Ron Jones, *The Acorn People*
James Vance Marshall, *A River Ran Out of Eden* and *Walkabout*
Harry Maser, *Snowbound*
Walter Dean Meyers, *Monster* and *Scorpions*
Naomi Shihab Nye, *Habibi*
Scott O'Dell, *Island of the Blue Dolphins*
Gary Paulsen, *Hatchet*
Katherine Peterson, *Jacob Have I Loved*
Rick Riordan, the 39 Clues series
J. K. Rowling, the Harry Potter series
Jack Schafer, *Shane*
Suzanne Fisher Staples, *Shabanu: Daughter of the Wind* and *Haveli*
Rebecca Stead, *When You Reach Me*
Janet Tashjian, *The Gospel According to Larry*
Theodore Taylor, *The Cay*
Marcus Zusak, *I Am the Messenger*
Lawrence Yep, *Dragon Wings*

Graphic Novels

Graphic novels are more than comic books. These are narrative works displayed in sequential art or comic book format. They are especially helpful for struggling readers since the visuals support comprehension of the text. Here is a list of popular graphic novels that many middle school and high school teachers are currently using in their classrooms:

Shakespeare (most of the plays are in graphic novel form)
Many classics, such as *Pride and Prejudice*, *The Adventures of Huckleberry Finn*, and *The Scarlet Letter*
Katherine Arnoldi, *The Amazing True Story of a Teenage Single Mom*
Brian Jacques, *Redwall: The Graphic Novel*
Alan Moore and Dave Gibbons, *Watchmen*
Maryjane Satarpi, *Persepolis*
Art Speigelman, *Maus*
Shaun Tan, *The Arrival*
Mary Wolfman and Damion Scott, the Teen Titans series

Michele Gorman's *Getting Graphic! Using Graphic Novels to Promote Literacy with Preteens and Teens* (2003) is a valuable resource for finding graphic novel titles and teaching these kinds of texts in your classroom.

Censorship

Some books are perhaps not appropriate for secondary students. Whether we call it selection or censorship, it is a dilemma every concerned English teacher faces. Inevitably if you are teaching literature, some of the works you use will be objectionable to someone because of either the subject matter or the style in which they are written. Consider books carefully before adding them to your lists of recommended reading. It's important for you to be familiar with the titles on your list. It's never a good idea to use someone else's list, because what might be acceptable in one community may not be in another. The best way to become familiar with adolescent literature is to read it. After all, no list can take the place of an enthusiastic teacher recommending a title. Your most helpful source in this regard is your school librarian, who is usually an avid reader able to recommend appropriate novels for students.

In most classrooms, the practice of forcing students to read something that they or their parents find objectionable can be solved by providing students with options. Most parents who find fault with a particular selection are satisfied if they are told that students can read alternative texts. Complaints can be handled individually so that no books will be censored for the whole class. It is less important that all students read a particular book than that they read and respond to something. Before ordering classroom sets for required reading, carefully consider your rationale for doing so. In addition, your English department should encourage a carefully written rationale for each required text. The following questions provide a good model for book selection:

1. For what age group is this book appropriate?
2. To what objectives does this book lend itself?
3. In what ways will this book meet these objectives?

4. What problems of style, tone, or theme or possible grounds for censorship exist in this book?
5. How will you meet these problems?
6. Assuming that these objectives are met, how will students be different because of the reading of this book?
7. What are other appropriate books a student might read in place of this one?
8. What reputable sources have recommended this book? What have critics said of it?

In addition, be sure you know whether your department or school district has a policy for dealing with challenged resources. If community members propose to ban a book in question for an entire class or from the school library, it's important that you have a school policy for dealing with this ahead of time.

Setting Up a Sequence for Teaching

You have from thirty-two to thirty-six or more weeks divided into semesters, trimesters, or quarters and from four to eight marking periods in the school year. What will be your plan? Although it is tempting to just follow an anthology from cover to cover, resist this approach.

Begin by addressing some basic concerns: What are your goals? What texts are available to you? What are your students' interests and abilities? What response activities will you include?

Planning is essential, but don't make your design so rigid that there is little room for student input or fascinating detours. Begin by deciding on some kind of organizational framework for each unit. The following sections explore typical frameworks.

Literary Types

A unit may be based on a particular literary classification:

- Nonfiction: essays, biography, autobiography
- Fiction: novels, novellas, short stories, poetry, drama

Fiction units may also be designed according to specific categories within the genre: mystery stories, science fiction, detective stories, multicultural literature, westerns, comedy, or tragedy, for example. In structuring a unit in this way, it is important that the focus be on the literature and not exclusively on the characteristics of the genre. A teacher planning a unit that involves reading several novels might use the earlier lists as a starting point—for example:

1. The whole class reads and responds to a novel from the classics list.
2. Groups of students then choose a title from the biography and autobiography list or the historical novel list.
3. Finally, students choose independent reading titles from the mystery and detective list or the fantasy and science fiction list.

Historical Survey

American and British literature has often been taught as survey courses in which texts are approached chronologically. This ordering is becoming less and less common in secondary schools because it tends to emphasize knowledge about books and authors without helping students develop an appreciation of the literature itself.

Individual Author

Units structured around a number of works by the same author can help better able students gain insight into an author. This is not as satisfactory an approach for less able students.

Thematic Units

Grouping literature by subject or theme is one of the most common and popular organizational frameworks designed by English teachers. Some popular themes are growing up, heroes and heroines, survival, death and dying, family relationships, love, alienation, justice, and war. (The selection tools mentioned earlier in this chapter offer additional themes.) A thematic structure is especially effective since you can appeal to your students' interests and at the same time involve them in a wide variety of texts and genres. However, one danger in creating thematic units is that students may encounter the same themes over and over. You'll want to consult with your colleagues at each grade level to avoid this possibility.

Suppose you or you and the class have chosen the theme of growing up. You might begin by picking a single novel for the entire class. In this case it could be Charles Dickens's *Great Expectations* or Harper Lee's *To Kill a Mockingbird.* By having chosen a theme, you have also limited the scope of student responses. In other words, you won't try to include everything there is to be said about this novel. In *To Kill a Mockingbird,* your focus will be on Scout's growing up and what she learns and comes to know as she matures. Other insights will emerge as the class responds to the text—and you will welcome them—but these will not be paramount. Next, you or you and your students will select five or six related texts—for example:

- Short stories: John Updike, "A & P," and James Joyce, "Araby"
- Poetry: Janice Ian, "At Seventeen," and William Stafford, "Fifteen"
- Drama: William Shakespeare, *Romeo and Juliet,* and Carson McCullers, *The Member of the Wedding*
- Film: *The Chocolate War* (based on Robert Cormier's novel)

You might expect every student to read one of each of these options, or you might assign students to small groups on the basis of the one text they want to read. We call these literature circles. Finally there should be a plan for students to independently read self-selected texts with a similar theme.

Many variations of literature-based curriculum are possible, and you'll want to experiment with several. Small group activities can be used as a starting point from which to individualize whole class activities—for example:

1. Each group picks an author. The members of a group read the same book by this author and collaborate in a group response.
2. Next, individuals choose an additional text by the same author for independent study.
3. Finally, the whole class collaborates in producing a group response: an annotated reading list for students in another classroom or a display piece, for example.

A good organizational framework and sequence will allow you to keep the entire class together part of the time. It will also provide opportunities for students to work together in smaller groups, and it will include student-selected independent reading options. In this classroom, you will serve as a guide and resource person. You'll determine when students read, write, speak, and listen. You'll organize the class into groups for reading or discussion or response projects, and you'll bring them back together for whole class projects. You'll provide additional material in mini-lessons when it is significant. You'll call attention to certain parts of a work and provide background information that can help the text come alive. You'll guide some of the talk and provide a wide variety of options for student response. This kind of teaching is exhilarating. When we discard the certainty of lectures, we won't necessarily control all the outcomes. We will, however, create a classroom in which we and our students learn from one another.

Literature Circles

Literature circles are a version of an adult book group that offers genuine and authentic reading experiences. Also known as book clubs and reading clubs, literature circles give students the opportunity to experience a wide variety of texts. They have these consistent elements:

- Different groups choose and read different books.
- Members write notes that help guide their reading and discussion.
- Teacher-led mini-lessons are scheduled before and after student literature circle meetings.
- The teacher does not lead a discussion of any one book. Instead, the teacher is a facilitator, fellow reader, and observer.
- Personal responses, connections, and questions are the starting point of discussions.
- The classroom has a spirit of collaboration and joy.
- When books are completed, the students present final projects that celebrate what they have read and discovered.
- Assessment is through teacher observation and student self-evaluation and is both formative and summative (usually the final project) activities and assessments.
- Literature circle groups extend for two to three weeks at most.
- The teacher-led mini-lessons cover a wide range of topics that include literary analysis, reading strategies, and social strategies that support student group work. These mini-lessons support the students' skill development for reading and analyzing texts.

The following project ideas are opportunities for students to demonstrate what they know and understand about a text. We often forget, as teachers of adolescents, that students can demonstrate what they know and understand about a text in a format other than a three-part essay:

- Create a model of a scene or important location from the text. Some examples include Boo Radley's house from *To Kill a Mockingbird* or the castle from *Macbeth.*
- Write a postcard to a friend, a family member, the author, or a character. Create artwork for one side of the postcard, and write to your audience on the other side. Perhaps Dill is at his home for the winter. What might he write to Scout while he is away?
- Create a billboard or ad for the text.
- Write a song or create an instrumental piece that represents the theme of the text.
- Create a book cover. Include a description of the book that would interest potential readers.
- Write a review and post it for other possible readers on an online bookseller Web site.
- Select a key quotation from the text, and paint or draw a picture that illustrates its meaning.
- Produce a file or video that reveals students' comprehension of the text.

Literature circles are an increasingly popular teaching strategy since it is easy to accommodate a wide variety of learners and their abilities. Harvey Daniels and Nancy Steineke's *Mini Lessons for Literature Circles* (2003) is a valuable resource for getting started with literature circles.

PLANNING FOR READERS' RESPONSES

Responses occur at any time in the reading process: before reading (to build on prior knowledge), during reading (to develop a reader's expertise), and following reading (to share some understanding of a text). You will want your students to respond in a variety of ways. Our goal as teachers has always been to integrate the language arts—reading, writing, speaking, and listening. When you plan for many response options, a true integration of these elements in your classroom is possible. Following are some responses you can adapt for students in your classroom.

Responses Before Reading

Take time at the beginning of a class period to talk informally about anything you are reading, and encourage your students to do the same. (You might have students do this in small groups as well.) At some point, have each student talk about one text he or she would enthusiastically recommend to other class members. Also consider using Steven Gilbar's *The Open Door: When Writers First Learned to Read* (1989), a treasury of recollections about reading experiences of famous authors.

Provide appropriate texts for students whose reading skills are limited. Consult your school's reading specialist and librarian for help in obtaining such texts, and invite them into your classroom to talk with students about their recommendations. Here is a list of Web sites for finding texts for your classroom:

- A short list of young adult literature for reluctant male readers, sorted by theme: http://scholar.lib.vt.edu/ejournals/ALAN/winter99/gill.html
- Reviews of the latest titles in young adult literature: www.alan-ya.org/2008/07/alans-books-july-2008/#more-150
- A list of popular paperbacks for young adults: www.ala.org/ala/yalsa/booklistsawards/popularpaperback/popularpaperbacks.cfm
- Good for searching for language arts literature: www.cde.ca.gov/ci/rl/ll/ap/litsearch.asp
- A list of books suggested by teacher editors for students at the chosen grade level: www.teachersfirst.com/read-sel.cfm
- Young adult booklists with annotations and teaching guides for selected titles: www.awesomelibrary.org/Classroom/English/Literature/Middle_High_School_Literature.html

Here are some other suggestions:

- Invite other teachers and community members into your classroom to speak about the importance of reading in their lives. Videotape these speakers for future classes.
- Read a few lines or a few paragraphs from some popular selections to draw students in. For example, the first line, "They murdered him," from Robert Cormier's *The Chocolate War* is sure to hook many readers.
- Read several paragraphs or pages of a selected text to students before they begin reading it themselves. Ask them to speculate about what will happen next or what kind of a person a character will be.
- Don't stop reading aloud to students when they reach high school. The following short stories are highly recommended by classroom teachers:

> Robert Block, "The Hell-Bound Train"
> Kate Chopin, "The Story of an Hour"
> Mona Gardner, "The Dinner Party"
> Charlotte Perkins Gilman, "The Yellow Wallpaper"
> Zenna Henderson, "The Believing Child"
> Langston Hughes, "Thank You, Ma'am"
> Richard Matheson, "Born of Man and Woman"
> Guy de Maupassant, "Old Mother Savage"
> Octavio Paz, "The Blue Bouquet"
> Quentin Reynold, "A Secret for Two"
> J. D. Salinger, "The Laughing Man"
> John Updike, "A & P"
> Donald Vining, "The Old Dog"
> Kurt Vonnegut, "EPICAC"
> Alice Walker, "Everyday Use"

- Pose a whole class or small group discussion question related to a story before the class has read it: "What would you do if someone had borrowed some expensive piece of jewelry to wear to a party and lost it?" (Guy de Maupassant's "The Necklace"); "Suppose a battered fence separates your house from your neighbor's. Should your father pay a hundred dollars to have it repaired or should he tear it down to give the neighborhood children room to play?" (Robert Frost's "Mending Wall"); "Can there be heroes in an impersonal, technological society?" (Arthur Miller's *Death of a Salesman* or Robert Cormier's *I Am the Cheese*).
- Read a story or several poems to students prior to their reading similar material. Show what good oral reading is and how it re-creates a storyteller's voice. Call on parents, talented students, members of local amateur or professional drama groups, storytellers, or community writers reading from their own work to demonstrate oral reading. Play recordings of authors and professional readers. Ask students in your classroom to prepare their own selections for oral reading as a beginning or a culminating activity.
- Use a film or recorded literature to begin a unit.
- Ask students to role-play a situation similar to one they will encounter in a text. For example, before reading Anne Frank's *The Diary of a Young Girl*, organize small groups and instruct each that they must sit together but make no noise for a designated period of time. They are not to speak aloud or do anything that will make even the slightest noise. Warn them that any noise might mean discovery and death. Finally, have students write about their feelings and describe the effect of the silence on other members of their group. Meet in small or large groups to discuss and share observations before beginning to read.
- Display picture books and art books reflecting ideas or a setting related to the literature to be read.

In preparation for reading, the following activities are useful for students:

- Write about the unit theme or topic at the beginning of a unit. Students might be asked to write about the Holocaust before reading Elie Wiesel's *Night*, for example. This will help you determine what students already know, think, or feel about a topic.
- Write in the same genre as the one to be read. For example, students write poetry before reading it, write dialogue before reading drama, or write a description of a special place before reading Maya Angelou's description of Stamps, Arkansas, in *I Know Why the Caged Bird Sings*. Writing in this manner helps students develop a strong sense of a genre's features as well as its possible variations. The comparisons are not meant to suggest that the author's version is better than the student's, but they help students appreciate the talent and craft of a successful writer.
- Research information either individually or in teams prior to reading a historical novel or older work. Students might research the Roaring Twenties before reading F. Scott Fitzgerald's *The Great Gatsby*, for example.

- Write about the same problem as that posed in a piece of literature:

   "You have just been marooned on a desert island that has vegetable and animal life and fresh water. Discuss what you must do to ensure your survival." (William Golding, *Lord of the Flies*)

   "List the names of some people and circumstances that irritate you. Then write a description of these irritating people or circumstances." (Edgar Allan Poe, "The Tell-Tale Heart")

   "Write about an event or experience in your life that has caused you to grow up a bit. Explain its impact on you. How did it affect your thinking?" (Harper Lee, *To Kill a Mockingbird*)

- Design a rating scale or a chart: "Make a list of the characteristics of an effective leader. Rank them." (William Golding, *Lord of the Flies*)

Responses During Reading

Plan discussions based on a wide variety of open-ended questions—questions generated by the students themselves about meaning, intent, and ideas. A related response is to review an important passage in a text and then pose a specific question. Students write their answers before an oral discussion so that each can formulate an opinion.

To serve as a model, read to students, but stop several times for written responses:

- How does this passage make you feel?
- What details stand out? Why?
- Does this passage remind you of an experience you have had? What might happen next? How might the story end?
- What questions do you have about the characters? the action? the setting?

There are a number of other ways for students to respond as well:

- Suggest that students draw a map to accompany a text. For example, have students consult the text to draw a map of the neighborhood in *To Kill a Mockingbird* or sketch the layout of the living quarters in *Diary of a Young Girl*. Still another option is to have students draw a map tracing the route characters follow in any story that involves a journey (*Huckleberry Finn*, for example). The National Council of Teachers of English catalogue lists a variety of historical literary maps that are useful as models.
- Either individually or collaboratively, rewrite parts of a novel as a play or radio or television script. Videotape the scene for a class presentation, or deliver it live before the class.
- Rewrite a portion of the text from a new point of view. Students might, for example, assume the role of Lady Macbeth's doctor and write the doctor's version of her

sleepwalking scene. The following is a sample assignment for *To Kill a Mockingbird* that helps readers, independently or in groups, sort and organize information in preparation for experimenting with point of view:

The Rest of the Story: Sample Assignment

A. Scout is the narrator of this story. On Halloween night, she and Jem walk from the schoolhouse to their home, "their longest journey together." Because Scout is unable to remove her ham costume, Jem leads her. She can only tell us what she hears, smells, and feels. Examine the text carefully, and make a list of everything that happens from the time Scout leaves the schoolhouse until she finally removes her costume and sees someone carry Jem into the house.

B. Boo Radley is also on the path that night. "Get into his skin," and write several paragraphs from his point of view telling us what he knows about what happened on the path that night.

Another approach is to assign students to groups, and have each respond to a single event from a different character's point of view. For example, Atticus, Sheriff Tate, Mr. Cunningham, Dill, Tom, or Mr. Underhill might each recall the mob scene in front of the jail.

- Ask students to respond to a text by adopting a newspaper format and recasting information as a news story based on the following questions:
  - Who was involved?
  - What happened?
  - When did it happen?
  - Where did it happen?
  - Why did it happen?

"Interview" the characters involved and quote them in the article. A news report could be written for a battle in Stephen Crane's *The Red Badge of Courage* or the trial in *To Kill a Mockingbird*. Students might create an underground flier designed to stir up a revolution against Macbeth. "Dear Abby" letters and responses are also useful formats. Aunt Alexandria might seek advice on how to handle Scout, or Scout might ask for help in getting along with the teenaged Jem. Since Mr. Webb (Thornton Wilder, *Our Town*) is the editor of the newspaper, he will write his daughter's obituary. Students might write it for him. A description of George and Emily's wedding for the society page or a feature article on George's high school career in baseball for the sports page are equally good responses.

- In dealing with a text that uses flashback, have students rearrange the events and list them in strict chronological order. Finally, discuss what was probably the author's reason for altering the sequence and what the story lost or gained as a result (Gunderlach, 1993).
- In dealing with a longer text, such as a novel, set target dates for reading. Plan an activity for an agreed-on set of pages, but caution those who have read ahead not to spoil the pleasure of others by discussing beyond that point. A jigsaw is a useful group activity for students working with longer texts. All students read the assigned material but each group is responsible for discussing a portion of the material. Final reports complete the jigsaw and cover all the material. To create a group jigsaw for several chapters of a novel, assign a specific number of pages to each group. Ask each to discuss its material by pointing out significant events or passages and relating these to ideas and themes generated by earlier class assignments. Finally, call on each group to summarize its discussion for the entire class.

Jigsaws can be used in a variety of ways. In discussing characterization, for example, assign a different major character to each group. Ask each to decide on three adjectives that best describe the character and explain the reasons for selecting them. Each group finds one or several passages in the text that best reveal the character's personality. Groups report to the class as a whole. Conclude with a whole class discussion of the author's handling of characterization.

Individual Responses During Reading

Too often we have had students write about literature only after they have finished reading. An alternative that allows students to respond to the text as they read is a reading journal or log. This approach is especially desirable because writing during reading encourages students to consider the kinds of questions that take readers further in understanding than they might go on their own. It helps them gather information, reflect on it, and make connections between what they are learning and their own lives. They:

- Make note of interesting points or passages or anything they want to remember to talk about later
- Jot down questions as they read
- Predict what will happen next
- Elaborate on a text by pretending
- Summarize ideas
- Evaluate any classroom activities
- Respond to prompts supplied by the teacher

A notebook for the reading journal serves to keep the entries together and organized. (Invite students to design covers for the journal that reflect themselves or the class.) The teacher reads the entries quickly and responds to provocative ideas and observations. Correctness and editing problems are not noted because the journal is intended to be a risk-free setting for experimenting with and exploring language and ideas.

Journals are also an effective evaluative tool. They will help you know your students better: why they choose particular books, why they favor some authors, and who or what influences them in selecting texts. They will also help you check on student progress and the effectiveness of classroom activities, resources, readings, and discussions. They can help you know when to present information, when to present it differently, or when to reteach a particular concept.

Asking students to read excerpts from their journals is an excellent way to initiate a discussion. Ideas and observations generated in the journal may also serve as preliminary work for a more formal response following the reading. Finally, journals encourage students to think and write about literature without the constraints of the book report form, which seldom allows students to write about their own feelings and often serves as a test of reading without fostering a love for it. The following questions may be suggested to students who are writing in journals. They can also be used as prompts for whole class or small group discussions if you do not plan to have students write in a journal:

1. What kind of a person is _____? What is your evidence?
2. If _____ were living today, what kind of clothes would he or she wear?
3. Are _____'s actions surprising to you? Can they be accounted for in the story?
4. Suppose _____ were in a [hypothetical situation]. What would he or she do? How does this differ from what you would do?
5. What do other characters say about _____ ? Why do they feel this way?
6. How does _____ treat other characters in the story? What evidence do you have?
7. How and why does _____ change in the course of the story?
8. Why do _____ and _____ relate to one another the way they do?
9. How do the other characters respond to _____ in the story? Why is this so?
10. Who are the "good" people in this text? What makes them "good"? (Who are the "bad" . . . ?)
11. What is one problem in the story? Which character has this problem, and how is he or she trying to solve it? Would you approach the problem the same way?
12. Who is the narrator of the story you are reading? Why do you think the author chose this narrator?
13. Finish this sentence: "I love the way the author . . ."
14. Have you read any other books by the author of the book you're reading now? If so, how does this one compare to the previous one you read? If you haven't read any previous ones by this author, would you like to?

15. Write a brief interview with the main character of your book.
16. Write a letter to me about the kind of story you like best. Why do you like this?
17. How did the author of your book get you interested in the story?
18. Write me a letter about the setting of the story you are reading. Why do you think the author chose this time and place?
19. What do you think will happen next? What evidence did you use from what you've already read to help you make your prediction?

As valuable as journals are, managing them can become a real concern. You'll want to avoid lugging around boxes or spending hours and hours reading them. One solution is to limit journal writing to your students' independent reading projects. As students use class time to read, pick up several journals each day, read them, write comments, and hand them back. This running commentary might constitute the entire study of an independent reading project. Form 6.1, which gives directions for keeping a reading journal, can be distributed to students when you make the assignment. Reading journals are most effective at the secondary level if the assignment is fairly structured. This is especially true for students who are keeping a journal for the first time if you want them to record their reactions on more than a superficial level. A grade may be awarded according to how many of the suggested entries a student attempts (14–17 = A, 11–13 = B, 5–10 = C, for example). Form 6.2 encourages students to become a part of the evaluation process.

Directions for a Keeping a Reading Journal

Name _____ Date _____

A reading journal is not the same as a writing journal. Your entries are to be responses to the literature you are reading. Write often, using the following suggestions as a guide. Use as many of these suggestions as possible. Think independently, and write imaginatively. Your ideas, opinions, and thoughts about your reading are important. Your journal grade will be based on the quality of your entries, as well as the variety and number of responses you write.

1. Explain how you chose your book.
2. Write about a memory or experience of your own that is similar to something you've read in your book.
3. Make a list of possible questions that arise as you read.
4. Write a reaction to something you have read.
5. Write a brief summary of several pages or a chapter. Do not, however, write a summary each time you write.
6. Become one of the characters in your book, and write a letter or poem from that character's point of view.
7. Write an interview between you and the main character of your book.
8. Illustrate a scene or draw a map or symbol that reflects your book.
9. Comment on the author's technique, choice of words, or the way he or she tells a story. Do you admire the way the author writes? Why or why not?
10. Before you have finished your book, make a prediction about how you think it will end. What makes you think it will end this way?
11. Do you think the title of this book is a good one? Why or why not? What are some other possible titles?
12. Imagine you are one of the characters in the story. Write a diary entry that reflects your thoughts and feelings about an event in your life.
13. Discuss a memorable scene from your book.
14. Write a letter to the author beginning, "I have just finished reading your novel, and I'd like you to know that ..."
15. Find and read a review of the book you are reading, and discuss your reaction to it.
16. Who else should read this book? Why? Who shouldn't read it? Why?
17. What book do you plan to read next? Explain.

Reading Journal Self-Evaluation

Name _____ Date _____

1. How many entries have you made in your reading journal since you began?
_____

2. Do you write a response nearly every time you read? _____ Explain.
_____

3. On an attached sheet, copy an entry that is fairly typical of the type of entries you write.

4. On an attached sheet, copy an entry you consider to be one of your best. Explain why you chose it. _____
_____
_____
_____

5. Write a short analysis of your reading journal. Will you make any changes in your next entries, for example, or are you satisfied with your approach to journal writing? _____
_____
_____
_____
_____

6. How do you feel about keeping a reading journal? Is this assignment helpful to you as you read and respond to literature? Please explain. _____
_____
_____
_____
_____
_____
_____

Individual or Group Responses After Reading

Traditionally many of us have asked students to write a critical analysis following their reading of a piece of literature. This is perfectly acceptable. There are, however, many other options to consider as culminating activities. These options appeal to students with a variety of learning styles. They will use their higher-order thinking skills as they recast their responses in new and delightful ways:

1. Assemble a collection of quotable quotes from the text. Groups could bind these in a booklet for a class display.
2. Illustrate a series of memorable scenes to display on a bulletin board, present to the class on an overhead projector, or bind in a booklet.
3. Create a calendar to supplement a literary work. The top third will include an appropriate illustration with a written explanation. Below, indicate the month and days and note important dates based on the text.
4. Design a time line to fit the story. Include all the math events.
5. Create a diorama or shadow box—a three-dimensional representation of a significant scene or scenes presented in a confined space such as a shoe box.
6. Act as a literary critic or review board, and prepare a review of the book to share with the class.
7. Become one of the characters in the text, and write and deliver a monologue for that character, using props and costumes. Groups should include several characters and perhaps add the author and a critic.
8. Write and deliver an interview of several characters in a story. Videotape or tape-record the interview to present to the class, or deliver it live.
9. Write a poem about each character in the book. Collect all of the poems in a class booklet. The poems might have an additional unifying format such as structure—an acrostic, for example. Another option for creating a poem is to ask each student to write a paragraph about a character and convert it to free verse with an emphasis on economy, white space, and line breaks. Students might also create found poems about a literary character based on significant lines and passages in the text itself.
10. Write a poem based on the mood, images, or feelings aroused by a story.
11. Stage an author's day. Each student shares his or her own writing orally or in some published form.
12. Write an exchange of letters between characters or authors from the same text or separate texts.
13. Compare a book's, film's, and television program's handling of the same story. How does the story change with each medium and why?
14. Suppose the author of the book you've read is a friend of yours. Write an imaginary telephone conversation between the two of you in which you discuss the book you've read.
15. Create puppets (using paper bags or socks, for example), and dramatize a scene from a piece of literature.

16. Write a TV or radio script for one of the stories you have read. Students either turn their script in to the teacher or assemble a cast and videotape it or perform it for an audience.

17. Construct objects that reflect items in the literature: shields, flags, or reproductions, for example. This might involve research as well as keeping a journal or log to document the formulation of ideas, the acquisition of materials, and a description of the object and its connection to the piece of literature. Students use speaking skills as they present and explain their objects to the class.

18. Write a short book review, and deliver it in the school's morning announcements.

19. Interview classmates and teachers. Annotate and post a recommended reading list for next year's students.

20. Write telephone-answering-machine messages or bumper stickers for several characters in a selection (Israel, 1993).

21. After reading a required text, write a letter to the district's director of curriculum recommending for or against the novel's selection.

22. Make a list of all an author had to know in order to write a particular story.

23. After reading a book about war, interview people of various ages who have served in the military during wartime. Report these findings in writing or in a panel discussion.

24. Research the life of the author; then write a script for an interview.

25. Write an autobiography for one of the characters in the text. The autobiography could span the years from childhood to the time the reader first meets the character in the text. Students brainstorm a list of make-believe interview questions and use the invented answers as the basis for the autobiography—for example:

    - In what kind of family did you grow up? How did you and your parents get along?
    - What responsibilities did you have growing up?
    - What is your most vivid childhood memory?
    - What were the fads when you were a teenager? What concerned you most when you were a teenager?

26. Create a crossword puzzle using information from the text.

27. Write a song with music and lyrics that reflect the text, and perform it for the class.

28. Choose one character in the text. Bring an object from home (don't purchase anything new) that you might give this character as a gift. Explain to the class why the gift would be appropriate.

29. Write a letter of recommendation for a job for a character in a literary work.

30. Decide what is the best book you've ever read. Write a letter to someone who doesn't like to read, convincing him or her to read it.

31. Hold a reading fair. Include displays of posters, original student writing, art reproductions, illustrations, collages, mobiles, book covers, and models. Include taped music and perform scenes from literature, invite parents and friends, or take the entire production to a class of younger students.

The sample assignments in Forms 6.3 to 6.6 are excellent options to consider as you plan response projects for your classroom.

A Booksellers' Day

Name _____ Date _____

Your assignment has been to read a book independently. You were asked to select your own book, choosing one that is worthwhile and truly enjoyable. After you have completed your independent reading, we will hold a classroom booksellers' day on _____. Each of you will try to "sell" your book in a book talk. Plan to use visual aids to accompany your "pitch," as well as props, costumes, and/or music. Visual aids might include:

· Advertising posters
· A book jacket of your own design
· Advertising fliers to distribute to the class (I'll help you make copies.)
· Bumper stickers
· Lapel buttons
· Bookmarks
· Business cards
· A magazine spread
· Transparencies for the overhead projector (I'll show you how to make these.)
· Your own videotaped advertisement
· An ordinary object that represents the book in some way

　The following is the suggested format for your talk:

1. Set up your props and materials.
2. Introduce the book. Show it to your audience. Be sure to give the title and author. Write the title and the author on the board, or refer to it in one of your visual aids.
3. You may want to provide some background about the author. This should be only a brief portion of your presentation. Be sure to tell your audience what source you have used for this information.
4. Briefly summarize the book. Spend no more than a minute or two on this portion of your talk. (Decide whether you should reveal the ending.)

5. Read a brief excerpt from the book. The passage you select should be a significant passage that describes a main character in some way, represents an important point in the plot, or reflects the author's style.

6. Review the book. This is the important part of your talk. You might comment on the book's theme, problem, conflict, character development, or believability. Your opinion counts. What did you like? What might other readers like? Relate your talk to the visual material included in your presentation. Make a recommendation to other students. "Sell" this book to those you believe would enjoy it.

7. If the book has been made into a movie and you have seen it, you might also want to compare and contrast the book and the film. If you wish, you can bring in the video and show a short clip (no more than two minutes). This could count as a visual aid. If you plan to do this, make arrangements with me ahead of time to have a video player and monitor in the room.

The following scoring sheet will be used in evaluating your presentation:

1.	Visual aids	10 points
2.	Props or costume or music	10 points
3.	Introduction and conclusion	5 points
4.	Information about the author	5 points
5.	Brief plot summary	5 points
6.	Excerpt from the book	5 points
7.	Review and "selling" of book	10 points
	Total	50 points

Independent or Group Response Projects for a Novel

Name _____ Date _____

We have come to understand that there are many ways we can respond to literature. After you have finished your novel, choose one of the suggested projects. You may complete this assignment independently, or you may organize a group and work cooperatively.

   Presentations are scheduled for _____. Choose one of the following options:

1. Design a time line to fit the story. Use illustrations, and include all the main events.

2. Draw several cartoon strips showing the main parts of the story. What happened in the beginning, the middle, the end?

3. Plan a filmstrip with 15 to 25 frames to retell the story with pictures and text. The frames should recount the story in sequence. The first frames will be the title and credits. The last frame will be "The End."

4. Create and produce an alphabet book. Show knowledge of characters and events through the letters of the alphabet.

5. Write a poem about each major character in the book. Collect all poems in a bound book. Include illustrations.

6. Make a "wanted" poster for a character in the book. Include a drawing, a physical description, a list of the character's misdeeds, the reward being offered, and any other important information.

7. Write and deliver a monologue for one or more characters. Use props and costumes for the presentation.

8. Prepare a newspaper account of a major event in the book. If a group works on this project, produce a complete issue.

9. Prepare a short presentation to introduce this book to next semester's class.

10. Assume the role of a prosecuting attorney, and put one of the characters from the book on trial for a crime. Prepare your case on paper, give all your arguments, and support them with facts from the book. Students working in groups may present the trial before the class, taking the roles of the accused, the judge, the defense attorney, the prosecuting attorney, and witnesses.

11. Create a game similar to Trivial Pursuit or Pictionary that reflects the details of your novel.

12. Create a high school yearbook with the main characters from the novel as graduating seniors. Clip out pictures from magazines or draw your own. Write a brief profile for each "senior," including the highlights of his or her school activities. Bind these pages as a book.

13. Design and create a pop-up book based on the text.

14. Write a telephone answering machine message for each major character in your book.

15. Write letters of recommendation for the major characters in your book.

16. Design your own response project. Plan it and have it approved by the teacher.

A Novel Response

Name _____ Date _____

Title of novel: _____ Author: _____

Number of pages: _____ My rating: 1   2   3   4   5   6   7   8   9   10
(1 is low and 10 is high)

Characterization

1. Who is the main character? _____

2. What kind of person is the main character? Copy several sentences to support your statement.

_____

_____

_____

_____

_____

3. List the things you liked best and those you liked least about the main character:

   Best:

   Least:

4. Compare yourself to one of the characters in the book. How are you alike or different?

5. Which character in the book changed the most? In what ways did he or she change?

6. Pretend you are the main character in the story. Write a brief description of another character from the main character's point of view.

Plot

7. In no more than fifty words, summarize the plot.

8. What is one problem in the story?

   Which character has this problem?

   What does he or she do to solve it?

9. Could the story have ended differently? Explain.

Setting

10. List as many words and phrases as you can find that tell where the story takes place.

11. Pretend you are one of the characters in the story. Complete this chart listing the sights, sounds, smells, tastes, and textures you experienced in the story.

Sights	Sounds	Smells	Tastes	Textures

Responding to a Book

Name _____ Date _____

1. Why did you choose this book to read?

2. How did the author capture your interest as you began the book?

3. What did the author do to keep your interest as you read further?

4. Are there any similarities between this book and your own life? Explain.

5. What character would you like to be in this book? Explain.

6. What would you and your favorite character talk about in your first conversation?
   Begin the conversation:

7. Do you think the title fits the book? Why or why not?

8. What questions would you like answered after reading this book?

9. What seems to be the major point the author wants you to remember?

10. Who else should read this book? Why? Who shouldn't read this book? Why?

Responses to Poetry

As you invite students to read and respond to poetry, it's especially important that you avoid questions like, "What is this poet trying to say?" or "What is the hidden meaning in this poem?" Encourage students to be open to alternatives, and remind them to consider an entire poem, not just a line or phrase. Students should understand that a poem does not have to have a message. It may simply be someone's sharing of a view or a moment.

Questions for a Poem

1. How did this poem make you feel?

2. What idea is the author concerned about?

3. Does the poem make you aware of something you did not know before?

4. Are there any surprises in this poem?

5. What is the most important word in the poem?

6. What colors do you associate with the poem?

7. What sound do you associate with the poem?

8. What are some things that are puzzling to you about this poem? Did you solve any of the puzzles? Which ones and how?

9. What questions would you like to ask the poet? Have each class member write one question he or she has about the poem and base an entire class discussion on students' questions.

Responses After Reading a Poem

1. Read a poem; then limit students' responses entirely to questions.

2. Rewrite some element of a poem in another format and compare the two. For example, after reading "Out, Out" by Robert Frost, students might write an obituary entry for the young boy in the poem and compare the two texts.

3. Draw an illustration for a poster and include the poem as a part of the presentation. Explain the relationship between the two.

4. Make a poem visual and help clarify its meaning by creating a mobile, which should balance when hung in the classroom.

5. Make a collection of favorite poems and bind these in a book to present to the school library. Include illustrations. Books might also be based on themes such as nature, heroes and heroines, or growing up.

6. Keep a poetry journal. Include personal reactions and anything the poetry brings to mind.

7. Bring a picture to class that captures your response to a particular poem. As a whole class assignment, request a picture from each student. Class discussion is based on the

question of which picture the author might select for an illustration. If students work in groups, a reporter presents the group's choice to the class and explains and justifies this decision to the class.

8. Each day one student presents a written response to a poem. The subsequent class discussion involves a reaction to both the student's response and the poem. Following each discussion, writers revise their papers if necessary. Publish a class booklet of the revised writings.

9. Choose a poem and design a multimedia presentation about it to present to the class. The presentations should include costumes, props, or any additional material that will make the presentation effective (sound and lighting, for example).

10. Create a collage representing the dominant impression of a piece.

11. Write a poem in the same style but on another subject.

12. Write a poem expressing the same point of view but in another style.

13. Write a letter to the poet sympathizing with the poet or arguing with the poet's point of view.

14. Choose a phrase or line in the poem, and use it as a starting point for a personal writing.

15. Design, create, and model a poetry T-shirt. Using fabric paints, decorate a shirt with favorite published and personal poetry. Hold a "fashion show" and award prizes (Paprocki, 1993).

The assignment in Form 6.7 is an effective way to encourage students to interact with one another as they read and respond to poetry. The teacher's role is that of observer. Do not question, make comments, or become a part of a discussion. Sit back and allow students to function independently. They can handle this assignment successfully.

Responding to Poetry

Name _____ Date _____

In this poetry unit, you will be given a collection of poems. Read the poems, and choose one that appeals to you. Register your choice with me. (If you have another poem in mind, be sure you have it approved by me.) On scheduled days, you will present your response to the poem you have chosen to the class as a whole. Plan for your response to take from 3 to 5 minutes. Responses should follow this format (but not necessarily in this order):

1. Indicate the title of your poem and its page number in the collection. (If you have obtained permission to use another poem, distribute copies to each class member.)

2. Read the poem to the class.

3. Call on someone to read the poem a second time. Plan ahead and be sure the person who does this is a willing, confident reader.

4. Present your response to the poem to the class.

5. Ask for comments, questions, and suggestions. Encourage students who have other observations about the poem to make their additions. Aim for a brief discussion period.

   Types of responses to consider:

A. Create a list of at least fifteen thoughts that arise from the poem. Each sentence should begin with the phrase, "I wonder ..."

B. Write a several-paragraph response to the poem. Carefully edit it, and give a copy to each class member.

C. Write your own poem in response.

D. Write a monologue. Become a character from either inside or outside the poem. For example, if the poem is about a teenager, you might become that teenager, or you could invent and become the teenager's parent, or principal, or teacher, for example. Distribute copies of the monologue to each person in the class.

E. Write a letter to someone about the poem and distribute copies to everyone.

F. Write a dialogue in response to the poem. Be sure each classmate has a copy.

G. Write a list of at least fifteen statements pointing out what you like about the poem. Each sentence will begin "I like ... " Distribute copies.

H. Create and display a poster featuring both the poem and an illustration. Explain the relationship.

I. Make your poem into a mobile that balances when hung. Explain your reasoning and the process you followed in creating your response.

J. Create your own response.

The due date for your poetry response is _____, and it will be evaluated in the following manner:

First reading of poem (3 points)   _____

Second reading of poem (2 points)   _____

Presentation of your response to the class (10 points)   _____

Questions and comments elicited from the class (5 points)   _____

Total (20 points)   _____

Some More Thoughts About After-Reading Activities

After-reading activities assist students in extending meaning. These activities provide the opportunity for students to:

- Ask questions about what they don't understand in the text.
- Connect the text to personal experience.
- Provide opportunities to visualize the text.
- Explore and summarize the text.
- Identify key characters, main plot events, and other details like symbols.
- Develop inferences about the text.
- Develop final conclusions about the text after careful reflection of what they have read.
- Participate in larger discussions about the text and express their opinions about the text in a larger audience.
- Identify the author's point of view and opinions.

EVALUATION, TESTING, AND GRADING

Unfortunately, grades and tests often have the effect of undermining much of what we want to encourage and nurture in our classrooms—risk taking, exploration, and discovery. They often do little to help students learn something more about a subject, and they tend to label students rather than help them work from their strengths. Consider some of the following alternatives:

1. The students make out a set of examination questions based on their reading, and the teacher chooses questions from those submitted for the class test.
2. Let testing take a game format such as Stump the Experts or Jeopardy. Students working in groups write questions about a shared literary work and present their questions to other groups. In the Jeopardy format, contestants are given the answer, and their response must be the correct question. In response to the study of a Shakespeare play, student questions might resemble the following:

Answer	Question
a. Boy actors	a. Who played women's parts in Shakespeare's plays?
b. Stratford-upon-Avon	b. What is Shakespeare's birthplace?

3. Ask students to write an exam including a short-answer section and an essay question for a text they have read. The students then take the exam themselves as they prepare an answer key.
4. Ask students to respond to a new text by using a familiar response. The multimedia presentation suggested earlier as a response to a poem is a good activity for the end of a unit or grading period.

5. Require students to collect samples of their work over a period of time for a portfolio. The portfolio is a good alternative to traditional testing because it records a student's growth over time. (See Chapter Two for a discussion of student portfolios.)

Forms 6.8 (on page 205) and 6.9 (on page 207) provide additional resources and handouts for teaching literature in your classroom.

DURING AND AFTER READING: READER'S THEATER

Readers' theater is a powerful tool for readers, especially for struggling readers. Students are assigned characters' roles and are encouraged to develop the characters through voice and movement. The students do not just read the scripts—like actors, they are expected to portray characters. People have an innate interest in stories. Telling and listening to stories is what makes us human beings. The origins are traced all the way back to the paintings found on the caves of our prehistoric ancestors. Reader's theater is minimal theater that builds on this foundation for storytelling and puts literature into a simple dramatic form that engages an audience. It supports students' developing reading skills by

- Creating pictures or images as the text is being read
- Encouraging reading fluency through multiple readings
- Creating interest and skill in reading
- Encouraging reading for meaning and inferences

The fact that "reader" is in the title for reader's theater reveals that the reader is the main focus of this strategy. There are no props, costumes, or strategies. Reader's theater is presentational, not representational, and the images from the text are created not on the stage but in the minds of the readers.

It is also a helpful tool for struggling readers and students with special needs in that it is another way in which to examine and experience text. Given the linguistic complexity of many of the classic literary texts that are a mainstay in our literature curricula, it is an effective strategy for supporting students as they attempt to decode and interpret text.

This example of reader's theater is from *King Arthur and the Knights of the Round Table: The Tale of Sir Gawain and the Green Knight* translated by Sir Thomas Mallory.

Arthur: Though shalt promise me by the faith of thy body, when thou hast jousted with the knight at the fountain, whether it fall ye be on foot or on horseback, that right so ye shall come again unto me without making any more debate.

Griflet: I will promise you as you desire.

Narrator: Griflet took his horse in great haste, and dressed his shield and took a spear in his hand. He rode a great wallop till he came to the fountain and thereby he saw a rich pavilion and thereby under a cloth stood a fair horse well saddled and bridled, and on a tree a shield of divers colors and a great spear.

Griflet smote on the shield with the butt of his spear, that the shield fell down to the ground.

With that, the fair knight came out of the pavilion.

Griflet:	For I will joust with you.
Knight:	It is better ye do not, for ye are but young and late made knight and your might is nothing to mine.
Griflet:	As for that, I will joust with you.
Knight:	That is me loath but sith I must needs, I will dress me thereto.
	Of whence be ye?
Griflet:	Sir, I am of Arthur's court.

Tips for Creating Reader's Theater Script

1. Sources for reader's theater include novels, poems, short stories, and essays. You may also pull scripts from Web sites such as Screenplays for You (http://sfy.ru).

2. Select a text for the reader's theater script. Choose a text that supports many different voices. Assign readers for the different parts and begin to edit.

3. Suggestions for editing the script for performance:

   a. Omit superfluous characters.

   b. Decide who will be the narrator.

   c. Decide whether a reader can portray multiple roles.

   d. Create a focus for the script.

   e. Edit the text so that only the essential information that develops the story is included.

4. Practice and rehearsal

   a. All parts should be clearly marked.

   b. Assign numbers for readers.

   c. Does the script flow?

   d. Is there a balance of voices between the readers?

5. With the edits, does the script logically flow?

6. Script format

   a. There is a title page with text title and author.

   b. Characters are clearly designated in the script.

   c. Performance directions are clearly marked.

Reader's Theater Evaluation

Text Selected and Author _____

Readers: _____

Introduction to the Reader's Theater Selection

Tone (5 points)

- The actors created the proper tone for the reader's theater selection.
- The audience became interested in the selected piece.

Development and use of script (5 points)

- The script is edited and developed so that the audience understands the plot and characters of the selected text.

Performance (5 points)

- The author's performances effectively employ voice and gestures to develop the different characters and plots of the reader's theater script.
- Pauses and utterances are appropriately placed.
- Readers clearly rehearsed and developed their performances.

There is no single way to ensure student interest and involvement in literature. Don't hesitate, however, to try an occasional unorthodox technique that could help students approach literature creatively. Spend time talking with parents and administrators about what you and your students are doing in your classroom. Invite guests into the classroom for oral and dramatic activities or culminating projects. Think of yourself as an explorer, and pay close attention to the students around you. Keep a journal or a record of what's occurring in your classroom. Don't ask too many questions to which you already know the answer, and involve students in lesson planning and problem solving. When something doesn't work, don't be afraid to ask, "What would make this better?" Then listen to your students' answers.

Prereading Anticipation Guide for *Romeo and Juliet,* Act I, Scene I

Before you read, predict which of the statements about scene 1 is accurate. Write *Yes* in the Before column if you predict the statement to be accurate. As you read scene I, write *Yes* in the After column if the play proves the statement and *No* if the play disproves the statement. In the line number column, write the number of the line(s) on which you found the answer.

Synopsis: *Romeo and Juliet* occurs over a five-day period. It is Sunday morning in the public street in Verona, Italy

Before (Yes or No?)		After (Yes or No?)	Line Number
	Sampson and Gregory are Capulet's servants.		
	Sampson says he refuses to excuse insults.		
	Sampson expects insults from the Montague servants.		
	Abraham and Balthasar are Montague's servants.		
	Sampson bites his thumb at Abraham and Balthasar. This is an insulting gesture.		
	The servants fight with insults, not swords.		
	Benvolio is Capulet's nephew and Juliet's cousin.		
	Benvolio enthusiastically joins the sword fight.		

(continued)

(Continued)

Before (Yes or No?)		After (Yes or No?)	Line Number
	Tybalt is Montague's nephew and Romeo's cousin.		
	Tybalt loves peace, hell, Montagues, and Benvolio.		
	Another sword fight begins. Members of the Capulet and Montague families join the fight.		
	Lady Capulet tells her husband that he is too old to fight.		
	Lady Montague encourages her husband to fight.		
	In lines 56–78, Prince Escalus criticizes both houses for having three street fights and sentences anyone who engages in more street fights to death.		
	Everyone leaves the street except Lord and Lady Montague and Benvolio.		
	In lines 81–90, Benvolio tells his aunt and uncle a lie about the street fight.		
	In lines 94–105, Benvolio says that Romeo was out walking an hour before dawn.		
	Lord Montague wonders why his son shuts out the daylight and prefers to be outside at night.		

During- or After-Reading Activity: Story Boards

Directions: Choose eight of the scenes from your novel that you think are most important to retelling the story. Draw these scenes to summarize what happens underneath the illustration.

Caption _____ Scene One	Caption _____ Scene Two
Caption _____ Scene Three	Caption _____ Scene Four
Caption _____ Scene Five	Caption _____ Scene Six
Caption _____ Scene Seven	Caption _____ Scene Eight
Summary:	

chapter 7

TEACHING LISTENING
and SPEAKING

- Teaching listening
- Conversing with one person
- Conversing in small groups
- Conversing in large groups
- Presenting individual speeches

Yes, Kevin, you're allowed to talk. It's a speech class.

The traditional approach to teaching the language arts has been to treat listening, speaking, reading, and writing as separate strands. Today, however, researchers and teachers point out that these are inextricably interrelated processes that are best taught integratively rather than separately (Beers, Probst, & Rief, 2007). This emphasis on the integration of speaking, listening, reading, and writing in the English classroom is a concern for many teachers who feel they lack the background and experience to teach listening and speaking skills in their classes. The good news is that if your students read and write together in response groups, they are already using all the language arts. They write a piece to bring before the group, read that piece, and listen to peer responses. Simultaneously their peers listen, write responses, and react orally. If you also encourage your students to respond to literature in a variety of ways both written and oral—independently, in small group discussions, and in oral presentations to the class—they are also practicing listening and speaking skills (Beers, 2007).

Despite the fact that you are providing plenty of opportunities for speaking and listening in your classroom, you also want your students to become more skillful speakers and listeners. This chapter discusses a variety of activities that will help you teach these skills as your students read and write together.

TEACHING LISTENING

Although students may spend the greatest portion of their class time listening, many have become efficient at not listening at all. For many, listening means being quiet and paying passive attention to the teacher. As teachers, we realize how much individual success in society depends on the ability to listen and speak well. We want our students to become active, involved listeners who will become articulate members of society. Consider using one or more of the following activities as you introduce a brief listening unit early in the year. Each lesson will take approximately one class period.

Lesson One

1. Introduce the familiar game telephone. One person (a student or the teacher) begins by turning to the next student and quietly relaying a short, spoken phrase or set of directions. This is passed along to each member of the class. The last student to receive the information repeats the message he or she has heard to the entire class, and this is compared with the original. Naturally the messages undergo interesting evolutions as they are passed along. Students have fun, and the exercise makes a strong argument for the necessity of paying attention.
2. Direct everyone to sit quietly for two or three minutes and mentally make a list of all the sounds they hear: "Close your eyes, and focus your attention on what you hear. Keep listening for everything: sounds in the distance and sounds up close—even your own breathing." After the time has elapsed, ask students to contribute to a list of words naming the sounds they have heard. Define onomatopoeia (words that imitate the sounds they name), and point out examples of these words as you record them on the blackboard.
3. Pair students. Direct each to carry on a quiet conversation with a partner with their eyes closed. Suggest that they pay close attention to each word of the partner. Notice the tone, volume, and pace of the partner's voice. Check to see if the words are in complete sentences or short fragments. At the end of the conversations, ask the pairs to respond to this experience either as freewriting or orally. Many are likely to say they felt closer to the partner as they really listened to the other person, undistracted by other sounds and their own thoughts. Point out that the best listeners pay close attention to and show respect for the speaker's words (Hayes-Jacobs, 2006).

4. Locate a recording of a song to which the students would not know the words. It is best if you can provide the actual written lyrics. Play the song once without interruption while the students write down as many of the lyrics as possible. Then play the piece again, pausing after lines to allow students time to write. Finally, hand out the actual lyrics so that students can see if they listened correctly, and play the song again. Discuss the need for concentration and purpose when listening (Mills, 2009).

Lesson Two

1. Pair students.
2. One member of each pair moves his or her desk to face the blackboard. The second student moves his or her desk to face away from the board. The student facing the board is the "speaker," and the student facing away is the "listener."
3. Tape to the board a sketch similar to one of the following:

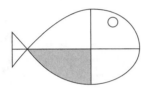 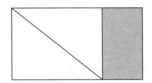 

4. The speaker describes the sketch to the listener who (without looking at the board) reproduces it on a piece of notebook paper. The listener cannot talk or ask questions, but concentrates on listening as carefully as possible to the speaker's instructions. The speaker should not look at the listener's sketch.
5. When each sketch is completed, ask the students to compare theirs to the original.
6. Have the partners exchange roles, and try the exercise again with another figure (Kozacik, 1989).
7. Ask each pair to evaluate their efforts as speakers and listeners.

Lesson Three

1. Explain that the day's activities are concerned with listening and the characteristics of good listeners.
2. Ask students to find a partner they do not know well. (If there is an uneven number of students, you should become someone's partner.)
3. Write a series of topics for discussion on the blackboard—for example:
   • What is it like to grow up in a small town, a large city, a closely knit neighborhood? (Choose one for this lesson.)
   • The proudest moment of my life and why.
   • What I'd like to accomplish in my life and why.

- My greatest fear and why.
- Pick a topic of your own.

4. Direct one student in each pair to speak with his or her partner on a chosen topic for three to five minutes. The second student is to listen and encourage the speaker.

5. After the time has elapsed, students exchange roles for another three to five minutes.

6. For a brief time (forty-five seconds to one minute), students again exchange roles as they continue with the original topic or discuss a new one. This time, tell the students acting as listeners to give negative feedback.

7. Repeat.

8. In a round-the-room session, ask the following questions:

   a. What did your partner do to encourage you as a speaker?
   b. What did your partner do to discourage you as a speaker?
   c. Tell us one new bit of information you learned about your partner.

9. Ask everyone to contribute to a definition of good and bad listeners. Record the suggestions on the blackboard. These may resemble the following:

   a. Good listeners

      - Are supportive and kind
      - Let the speaker know they hear what is being said
      - Ask useful, interesting questions
      - Show they are interested
      - Look at the speaker

   b. Poor listeners

      - Interrupt
      - Criticize or argue
      - Concentrate on another activity
      - Speak to someone else

Lesson Four*

Gibberish is a foundational improvisation game that teachers listening skills. Students use a made-up language in a variety of games and scenes. There are many kinds of gibberish exercises, and the concept is very adaptable.

The basic version of the game follows:

1. Divide students into pairs.
2. Instruct the students to give commands to their partners in made-up sounds. No language can be used. Only vocal sounds that don't resemble a recognized language like English, Spanish, or Chinese may be used.

---

* Adapted from McKnight, K. S., & Scruggs, M. (2008). *The Second City guide to improv in the classroom: Using improvisation to teach skills and boost learning.* San Francisco: Jossey-Bass.

3. Instruct students to take turns issuing commands to their partners. Once the partner understands the command, she can execute it. Examples are "Wave to the teacher," "Have a seat," or "Pass the butter."

The point of the exercise is for the partners to use and listen for intonation and hidden meaning in the made-up language.

Lesson Five[†]

Bippity, Bippity, Bop is a fast-paced game played in a circle. It requires players to listen and work together to avoid ending up in the center of the circle. Students develop skills such as listening, following directions, and working as a team or group.

Instructions for the Basic Game
1. Up to fifteen players form a circle.
2. One student goes to the center.
3. The center player approaches any player in the circle, makes eye contact, and says, "Bippity, bippity, bop."
4. This chosen player must say "Bop" before the center player says it.
5. To trip up the circle players further, the center player can skip "Bippity, bippity" and just say "Bop." If the center player beats the circle player and says "Bop" first, they trade places.

Throughout the year, continue to emphasize active listening skills. Make a practice of giving oral instructions carefully and clearly—but give them only once. Answer any questions about the meaning of the instructions, but don't repeat the instructions. At first students may grumble about this policy, but they will quickly become more attentive listeners.

Encourage students who are not part of an oral presentation to practice good listening skills. Following an oral presentation, have each write a brief summary or a list of main ideas. This assignment need not become an extra correcting burden. Simply give every student a few points for having done the summary, or call on a few students to read their summaries aloud while you comment on them orally. For more formal speaking activities, expect all students to respond on an evaluation form.

CONVERSING WITH ONE PERSON

The most common person-to-person communication in many language arts classrooms takes place between you and a student in a writing conference. It also happens easily between two students who are deliberately paired off to interview one other, act as peer editors for one another's writing, or brainstorm together.

[†] Adapted from McKnight, K. S., & Scruggs, M. (2008). *The Second City guide to improv in the classroom: Using improvisation to teach skills and boost learning*. San Francisco: Jossey-Bass.

Rehearsals

As a prewriting activity, encourage your students to explain their writing plans to their partners. This is sometimes called "rehearsing" a writing. As the author explains what he or she intends to say, the topic becomes more focused. The partner's questions also help the writer clarify his or her goals. Talking about writing is also a good speaking and listening activity because students don't know it's an exercise, and their conversation is relaxed and spontaneous.

Focused Discussions

At the beginning of a class, pose two or three open-ended questions pertaining to the day's reading assignment. Display the questions on an overhead transparency, interactive white board, or LCD projector, or write them on the blackboard. Ask students to work independently to answer each question. Next, have students work in pairs to share and compare answers with their partners. Remind everyone to listen carefully to the partners' answers and explanations. Finally, ask each pair to create a new answer that is superior to their initial individual answers. Collect only the pairs' final effort. These may be graded or used as a springboard for further class discussion (Johnson, Johnson, & Holubec, 1991).

Interviews

Because we live in an information age, the ability to acquire information is one of the most important skills we can teach students. In addition to knowing how to do library research, students should understand that information can also be acquired from expert testimony. Interviewing skills, which can be practiced and learned, are invaluable for every student.

Preparation for an interview is important. A student who will conduct an interview should:

- Research the subject to be able to ask good questions
- Choose an opening question and organize follow-up questions
- Avoid questions that can be answered yes or no
- Ask follow-up questions for clarification
- Restate answers to ensure an understanding of what has been said
- Persist politely to get needed information
- Take good notes

As a part of a year-long course design, structure a series of practice interviewing exercises such as the following.

Activity One

As an opening class activity, pair students and ask each to consider a single question—for example:

- What television commercial do you like best (or least)? Why?
- If you could meet any person living today, who would you meet and why?

- What is the title of a novel you could recommend to other students in this class? Why?
- What is the most dangerous thing you have ever done?

Students interview one another and report what they have learned to the class as a whole.

Activity Two

Use improvisational role-playing activities to develop interviewing skills. For example, place slips of paper in a container naming types of people such as doctor, dentist, author, someone from history, or a character in a well-known story. One student in a pair draws out a slip. After time for brainstorming, the second student interviews the partner as if the partner were the character named on the slip.

Activity Three

Structure activities so that the students must acquire information through interviews to share with the class. For example, before a research project, give specific students or students working in groups the responsibility of finding out how to use particular resources in the library. Students interview the librarian and report orally to the class. (This could also result in a written set of directions for using the source.)

Activity Four

As part of a unit, invite a community expert into your classroom. Instead of having the expert deliver a lecture or give a talk, structure the visit so that students must obtain information by interviewing the guest. A variation of this activity is to ask several guests to visit the classroom at the same time. Students are appointed to small groups, and the guests take turns being interviewed by each of the small groups in a round robin.

Activity Five

Research projects may be based on interviews. For example, students interview a family member or interesting person in the community and write a personality profile. Collect the profiles in a polished class publication. Projects such as this also involve letter writing (a request for an interview, a confirmation letter, and a thank-you letter) in addition to plenty of cooperative planning for editing and publishing the booklet. (The I-search paper discussed in Chapter Five also relies heavily on interviews.) Form 7.1 is helpful for students as they prepare for such an interview.

CONVERSING IN SMALL GROUPS

Working and conversing in small groups is an essential skill students can learn through careful guidance and repeated practice.

Guide for an Interview

Name _____ Date _____

1. The name of the person I plan to interview is:
   _____

2. The topic of my interview is:
   _____

3. Read up on this topic. List as much as you know about this subject:
   _____
   _____
   _____

4. Think about the preceding list. Now begin a new list. What do you want to find out?
   _____
   _____
   _____

5. Decide on an opening question. Write it here.
   _____

6. Make a list of questions for your interview on the back of this sheet. Remember:

   a. Questions should be open-ended, not the kind that can be answered by a yes or no. For example, instead of asking, "Did you decide to become a lawyer for the money?" a better question is, "Why did you decide to become a lawyer?"

   b. Questions should be specific, not general. For example, instead of asking, "What is your opinion on the law and teenagers?" a better question is, "Does the law treat teenagers differently than adults?"

   c. Ask for the facts. For example, instead of saying, "Tell me about capital punishment," a better choice is, "Under what circumstances might a teenage criminal be treated as an adult?"

During the interview, listen carefully and always ask for more detail. Jot down the answers as quickly as you can, without worrying about spelling or punctuation. Give the person you are interviewing plenty of time to talk. Don't interrupt or tell your own stories or stick so close to your list of questions that you miss what the person is saying. If something interesting comes up, follow that line of thought, but keep in mind the purpose of your interview. People are interesting. They will give you good information and tell you wonderful stories if you give them the chance.

Cooperative Skills

Many experts suggest that small group work is one of the most important processes to happen in classrooms. They point out that students are challenged to define, clarify, qualify, elaborate, analyze, and develop the thinking and verbalizing skills needed for reading and writing (Hayes-Jacobs, 2006). (See Chapter Four for a complete discussion of cooperative learning activities.) It's important, however, to remember that students seldom have the social skills needed to converse effectively in groups. They must learn to:

- Value the contributions of all group members
- Take turns speaking
- Listen to other speakers
- Disagree with another student's words without criticizing the speaker
- Respond to the previous speaker
- Organize a group to meet a goal
- Encourage others to join in

Whenever students work in groups, observe and monitor them. Reserve time at the end of each group activity to discuss your observations, emphasizing what each group has done well. Ask students to evaluate their own performances. With our busy schedules, it's tempting to skip this part of the lesson, but it's something you must not do. Your students can and will learn to function well in groups if you give them the opportunity to regularly assess their performance.

Gender Differences

As we plan for listening and speaking activities in our classrooms, we intend to make the kinds of classroom decisions that are best for all our students. One concern we may have is equal treatment of boys and girls. For example, researchers point out that when boys and men talk with one another in all-male groups, they often compete for dominance and assert their status by the length of time they keep the floor, and interruptions or hostile comments are frequently seen as normal interaction. Males tend to ignore the comments of previous speakers and usually make strongly assertive statements. They also tend to play devil's advocate and seldom reveal personal thoughts or feelings. Men tend to speak at the lower end of their speaking range, and in this culture, the lower range is the one that carries authority (Gurian, 2002).

Girls and women are more likely to support a speaker by providing reinforcements such as positive comments or nonverbal cues such as head nods. If a woman interrupts a speaker, this is not seen as an attempt to gain the floor but is more likely to be a request for elaboration. Women are more likely to make an effort to get everyone in the group to participate. In speaking, women tend to make false starts, use a questioning intonation when making a statement, have hesitant pacing, and use an excessive number of qualifiers. Women tend to speak at the higher end of their speaking range.

There are implications in all this for our classroom. We are told teachers tend to value class contributions delivered in the assertive "male style" regardless of content and to penalize lack of participation in discussion. We need to be aware of this. We also need to be alert to classroom dynamics. If, for example, certain boys consistently dominate class discussions, we can insist that all students spend two or three minutes thinking over the question or topic before a discussion is initiated (Gurian, 2008). We can ensure that both sexes get practice asking both supportive and challenging questions. We can encourage slower, louder, and lower speaking in those who tend to be uncertain and high-pitched. We can stress the value of listening and design activities that call for both cooperative and competitive activities.

Cooperative Activities

In addition to the cooperative activities discussed in Chapter Four, consider using small group discussions in the following ways.

Embedded Discussions

Embedded discussions are those that can be used within another activity. For example, an entire class may study a novel. In place of a large group discussion, appoint students to small groups, and give each group its own open-ended question. The small group appoints one member a recorder and another the reporter, and they discuss their question for a specified time. Finally, the reporter for each group reports to the class as a whole. For example, if a class were discussing Harper Lee's *To Kill a Mockingbird*, you might devise group questions such as the following:

- Explain what a mockingbird is, and explain which characters might be thought of as mockingbirds.
- One of the themes in this novel is getting into someone's skin to understand him or her. Which characters in this novel do this or should do this? Explain your answer.
- The author places limitations on the narrator's ability to tell the story. What are they? What is their purpose?
- Scout grows up in this novel. How does she change, and what does she learn?

Panel Discussions

Small group discussions are excellent preparation for more formal panel discussions later in the year. Panel discussions involve students in library research, cooperative work, and oral presentations without the grading burden of the traditional research paper.

Students are assigned to groups of four or five, and each group brainstorms a list of topics the members are interested in researching (the early history of their community, for example). Once the group has agreed on a topic and received your approval of it, members begin their research, breaking the general topic into subtopics for which individual students are responsible. Whenever necessary, you will teach mini-lessons pertaining to research tools, summary writing, note taking, and interviewing. Finally, after the library research has been completed and school and community experts have been interviewed, each student prepares his or her information for the group's oral presentation to the class.

Students should understand that they may consult notes as they speak, but they should not read from a script. Group members help one another as they practice and rehearse their oral presentations. Finally, each group makes its presentation to the entire class. Although there are many variations, this is the usual format for a panel discussion:

1. Opening remarks by the group's moderator, including an explanation of the topic and the reasons for the group's choice of the topic, for example
2. Introduction of speakers by the moderator, along with an explanation of the subtopics
3. Presentations by panel members
4. Audience participation, usually in the form of questions to panel members
5. Conclusion or summary by the moderator

In addition, you may also ask each group to submit a bibliography. Although it involves more reading and grading on your part, you may also ask students to submit individual summaries of their research. Ideally you will award both individual and group grades.

Cooperative Controversies

As teachers, we are reminded we need to provide a framework in which students can think and work and listen and speak, and then we must back away, encourage their opinions, and avoid playing the expert. This activity, known as a cooperative controversy, encourages this to happen. It is an ideal activity to couple with a unit concerning library research or interviewing. In addition, it does not create an unmanageable paper load.

Here is how it works:

1. Arrange students in groups of four.
2. Direct groups to brainstorm for a topic based on controversies they see in their school or community. A sample list might resemble the following:

   • Progress being made in recycling in our community is too slow.
   • Our school should adopt a pass-fail grading system.
   • Our school should have an open campus.
   • Adopted children should be encouraged to find their birth parents.

3. After each group has decided on a topic, assign half of the students in each group to the pro side and half to the con side of the question.
4. Students conduct library and Internet research and interview experts. All members of the group collaborate by sharing information about the issue in one or several strategy sessions.
5. On a specified date, the small groups convene to present the information each has gathered to others in their small group. When the pro side presents its arguments, the con side records them. When the con side presents its arguments, the pro side makes a record of these arguments.
6. The sides are switched, and the groups meet again in strategy and research sessions.
7. The new pro side presents its arguments, and the new con side records them. The new con side presents its arguments, and the new pro side records these.

8. Finally, each group works together to consider and discuss what has been learned and to write, individually or as a group, a report that includes a balanced discussion of both sides of the controversy and all supporting evidence (Johnson, Johnson, & Holubec, 1991).

Asking students to look at issues from more than one point of view helps them move away from rigid, preconceived positions. The small group format encourages students to actively think, learn, speak, and listen to produce well-reasoned and well-documented writing.

Group Improvisations

Stories are everywhere, and students can and should be encouraged to create, expand, and improvise stories in a variety of ways:

1. The entire class may be involved in a group story. One student is asked to begin the story. In a round-robin, every other class member contributes one sentence to the story, which ends when the last student contributes. Stories can be fun and silly, but with practice, students get better and better at this, and a cohesive plot and story structure emerge.
2. Pair students. The first student begins telling a story; when the teacher says, "Stop," the second student continues the story. The two continue to take turns telling the story as directed by the teacher. This can also be used as a writing exercise and works especially well with computers. Pairs who first write their stories should also be asked to read them aloud.
3. Read an unfamiliar story to the class, but stop before the ending. Groups collaborate in brainstorming, writing, and acting out an ending. After the last version is presented, conduct a whole class discussion about the different versions.
4. Suggest story endings such as, "Finally, he knocked on the door," or "She picked up the phone," or "She said, 'I stole the jackknife.'" Groups brainstorm, create, and enact a complete story.
5. Read a summary account of a scene to each group or invite a group to invent its own. Summary accounts involve the three W's: Who is in the scene? Where is the scene? What is the relationship? ("An old man who has just lost five dollars meets a ten-year-old boy in the park," or "A thirteen-year-old girl oversleeps, but her mother still insists she go to school," are summary accounts.) Groups brainstorm possibilities for each scene, expand on the story, and enact it for the class.
6. Assign each group a specific setting—taxicab, elevator, emergency room, theater lobby, or supermarket checkout line, for example. Group members decide what type of person each will represent (driver, executive, doctor, traveler from abroad, farmer, child, parent) and improvise a scene.
7. Place single words printed on separate cards in a container. Individuals or groups draw a card and tell a story suggested by the word on the card. A variation of this exercise is to fill a bag with a collection of found objects. Each student or group draws one object and tells a story based on that object.

8. A group selects a character it has studied in a piece of literature during the year. It then writes and performs a skit that places this character in a contemporary setting and reflects the theme or idea in the original work. (One of the boys in William Golding's *Lord of the Flies* may work at an American fast food restaurant, for example.)

CONVERSING IN LARGE GROUPS

A good class discussion is actually a conversation with much interaction taking place among students as they share different points of view. The immediacy of responding to and questioning each other is not possible in writing, so class discussion can make the literature your students read and study especially meaningful. The following suggestions will help you foster successful large group discussion:

1. Seat students in a large circle so that every student can see every other person in the room.
2. From time to time, choose student leaders. Discussions are often more honest when students lead them.
3. Ask students to generate a list of questions pertaining to the topic before the discussion begins. Choose the questions that offer the most possibilities. Base the subsequent discussion on these student-generated questions.
4. Have students freewrite about a question before discussing it. This gives all students equal time to think about a topic, and discussions are often better because students have thought the question through. If you do not plan to have students write before a discussion, allow plenty of wait time following a question to give an opportunity for reflection.
5. Discourage interruptions, wild hand-waving, and distractions when someone is speaking. Students should volunteer by raising their hands, but also call on those who don't. Occasionally give participation points based solely on the number of times a student responds, but point out that the best discussions include contributions from everyone.
6. Keep a record of who has spoken. This can be as simple as a check next to a student's name on a seating chart. A student can serve as a monitor as well. We need to do this because we tend to think we have called on many more students than we actually have. If a student tends to monopolize every class discussion, let him or her act as a monitor occasionally. Another option is to begin the discussion period by giving each student two or three "speaker's tickets." Explain that once students have spent their tickets, they cannot speak again until all others have spent theirs.
7. Don't let the "I don't know" student off the hook. Rephrase the question, ask for a personal response, or come back to the student later in the discussion. Gentle persistence with a reluctant student will pay off over time.
8. Acknowledge a speaker in some way. Although you should avoid making comments that evaluate students' responses, you need to let them know you have heard. "What do you mean by . . . ?" or "Can you give me some examples?" are helpful types of responses.

9. Plan for closure at the end of a class discussion. For example, ask students to turn to a partner and do one of the following:

- Identify two important points raised in the discussion.
- Comment on an idea in the discussion that was interesting or thought provoking.
- Suggest one question that still has not been answered.

The partner discussion further ensures that every class member is involved. One member of each pair may report to the class as a whole.

PRESENTING INDIVIDUAL SPEECHES

Formal speeches by individual students to the entire class can be enormously time-consuming. Although it is possible to divide your classes into smaller groups so that several speeches can be given at one time, this means finding three or four rooms if they are available and videotaping the speeches so you can evaluate them. If you teach in a school where you cannot leave students unsupervised, recruiting parent volunteers is a possibility. The logistics of all of this is discouraging, however. On the other hand, we're usually not happy with the one-speech-per-semester approach, and we fear that such a requirement tends to reinforce students' apprehension about public speaking.

The following short, less threatening activities will encourage individuals to speak frequently without creating an overwhelming logistical or grading burden for you.

Announcements

Announcements usually include information about who, what, where, when, and sometimes why and how. If students have this information, they can be and should be responsible for making all classroom announcements. For practice, they can have fun inventing announcements too. Invented announcements are particularly good for involving shy or reluctant students.

Simile

Brief speeches based on comparisons encourage students to reveal something personal as they learn about this literary device:

1. Begin with a class discussion of what a simile is: a comparison between two unlike things using *like* or *as*. In this instance, students would compare themselves to any real or fictional thing except another person, for example, "My life is like a winding journey," or "She spreads sunshine like a sunflower."
2. The introduction includes the speaker's name and the object of comparison. ("My name is Jane, and I'm like a house cat.")
3. The simile is supported by two main points that explain the comparison: "I am independent and like to sleep a lot. I am affectionate and loving to my family when I am around them."
4. The concluding sentence restates the first.

Introductions

Point out the rules of formal introductions, and provide opportunities for your students to practice these in your classroom. Traditional introduction guidelines are as follows:

1. Determine whose status is lesser or greater by age (older people have more status) and position, rank, or job (presidents, principals, generals, and so forth).
2. Introduce a person of lesser status to a person of greater status.
3. State the name of the higher-ranking person first.
4. The person making the introduction should provide a conversation opener such as an item of mutual interest the two individuals share.
5. The person of greater status extends his or her hand first if there is a handshake. The person of lesser status does not extend a hand if the higher-ranking person does not.
6. One should establish eye contact with the person to whom one is being introduced.
7. A person of lesser status always rises, if seated, and the person of greater status should also rise as a mark of friendship.
8. The two build on the conversation starter to continue the conversation.

Activities for Introductions

1. Direct students to write on a slip of paper the name of a person living or dead, real or fictional, famous or ordinary. The information should also include the person's age, job, or rank. Collect the slips in a container, and have each students draw one and introduce the person named on the slip to the class.
2. Turn interviews with student partners into introductions to the class. If the class is large or the students seem especially insecure about speaking in front of the whole class, form groups of six or eight for practice before beginning the whole class activity.
3. Select characters from a piece of familiar literature, and call on students to introduce each to the whole class. This is an excellent activity prior to writing more formal character descriptions based on literature.
4. Expect your students to introduce classroom guests to the class. This will involve some interviewing skills as well.

Directions

Exercises and practice in giving both written and oral directions help students to understand and use precise language. Simple class activities can lead to more formal demonstration speeches.

Begin by providing information about the nature of directions:

- Directions are usually given in chronological order.
- If they are lengthy, directions may be organized in segments or steps.
- If manipulatives are involved, practice is important.
- The speaker states the benefit of being able to follow the directions.

- The conclusion is usually a summary and a reminder of the usefulness of the information.

Here are some activities for practicing directions:

Activity One: Drawing
1. Students are paired.
2. One student draws a simple design and gives the partner oral or written directions for drawing the same design.
3. The second student follows the directions to produce a similar design.
4. The students compare the two designs.

Activity Two: Movement
1. Pair students. One student is blindfolded.
2. The second student accompanies the blindfolded student and gives him or her oral directions for getting from the classroom to another location in the building.
3. The students exchange roles.
4. The partners discuss and define the characteristics of effective directions.

Activity Three: A How-To
1. A student talks a partner through an unfamiliar procedure, such as how to do origami, knit, make an art project, play a game, compute square roots, or build a model out of plastic interlocking blocks.
2. An interesting variation is to place a barrier between the two students so they can hear each other but cannot see each other.

Demonstrations

Using how-to books checked out of the library or based on skills they already know, students demonstrate a skill to the class. Demonstrations, with oral explanations, might include setting up a tent, decorating a cake, crocheting, riding a horse, using the proper techniques for operating shop tools, or applying CPR, for example. Teaching a skill or concept (such as finger plays or songs) to younger students is another good approach.

Alternatives to Book Reports

As a response to a reading and literature unit based on biographies, students become the subjects of their biographies. Wearing self-designed costumes and using simple props, each presents an oral narrative based on his or her reading. The following is a helpful format for this project:

- Family background
- Formal and informal education
- Contributions to humanity
- Impact on society (Urban, 1989)

The same approach may also be used with fiction by asking students to talk about their book from the point of view of one of its main characters. Form 7.2 is an evaluation form for such an activity. Encourage the listeners in the class to complete an evaluation form as well.

Reading and Storytelling

Impromptu reading in the classroom may happen occasionally, but taking turns around the room can be deadly. Instead, as part of your lesson design, have students select excerpts from a piece of literature and study and rehearse the selection to read to the class. Such a project works well with a poetry unit, for example.

Invite a storyteller from the community into the classroom to model formal storytelling. Students should understand an effective storyteller is concerned with the rate, volume, and pitch of the voice, as well as the physical aspects of facial expression, gesture, and eye contact. A good storyteller creates distinct voices for each character. After observing an expert storyteller, students can be expected to create and practice their own stories and deliver them to an audience in a variety of ways: cassette tape, puppet theater, videotape, or live. Reader's theater is an excellent extension of this. Student-written plays, stories, and poems can be prepared and delivered to audiences outside the classroom—to other classrooms, parent-teacher association meetings, or student assemblies, for example. Students should practice their stories in small groups prior to a whole-class activity. Use Form 7.3 for storytelling evaluation.

Speeches to Inform or Persuade

Assignments that require students to inform or persuade can consume a great deal of class time if they are made as separate assignments. However, in an integrated classroom in which literature, writing, speaking, and listening are all being taught, it is possible to ask students to prepare speeches in conjunction with other assignments. For example, if students have completed an I-search or research paper or a cooperative controversy, they are well prepared on a subject. It's logical to consider assigning an informative or persuasive speech as a follow-up assignment. Use Form 7.4 for evaluating these speeches.

Additional Suggestions

Students need to have many successful oral experiences early in a course to build confidence for more challenging speaking assignments. Discussions with partners, conversations in small groups, impromptu group exercises, and whole group round-robin exercises give students experience and confidence for more formal speaking activities. Assignments that encourage students to incorporate costumes or props such as maps, charts, or pictures are especially successful for shy students who are reluctant to speak before a group.

Early on, deemphasize the importance of grades. If grades must be given for a formal activity, devise a checklist or grading grid for each assignment. Encourage your students to rehearse in small groups before speaking to the entire class, and involve every class member in the subsequent evaluation.

Oral Report on a Book

Name _____ Date _____

Scale: 1 = weak,   2 = fair,   3 = average,   4 = good,   5 = excellent

1. Content	1	2	3	4	5
2. Volume	1	2	3	4	5
3. Rate	1	2	3	4	5
4. Enunciation	1	2	3	4	5
5. Costume	1	2	3	4	5
6. Props	1	2	3	4	5

Comments:

_____

_____

_____

Total possible: 30 points

Your score: _____

Evaluator: _____

Storytelling Evaluation

Name _____   Date _____

Scale: 1 = weak,   2 = fair,   3 = average,   4 = good,   5 = excellent

Vocal

Rate	1	2	3	4	5
Volume	1	2	3	4	5
Pitch	1	2	3	4	5

Physical

Facial expression	1	2	3	4	5
Gestures	1	2	3	4	5
Eye contact	1	2	3	4	5
Characterizations	1	2	3	4	5
General impression	1	2	3	4	5

Comments:

_____

_____

_____

Total possible: 40 points

Your score: _____

Evaluator: _____

Evaluation Form for an Informative or Persuasive Speech

Name _____ Date _____

Scale: 1 = weak,   2 = fair,   3 = average,   4 = good,   5 = excellent

Introduction					
Captures the audience's attention	1	2	3	4	5
Provides background information	1	2	3	4	5
Body					
Presents information clearly	1	2	3	4	5
Makes information interesting	1	2	3	4	5
Uses supporting evidence	1	2	3	4	5
	(for a total of 45 points)				
Conclusion					
Summarizes main points	1	2	3	4	5
Delivery					
Uses effective vocal delivery (volume, rate, quality)	1	2	3	4	5
Uses effective physical delivery (eye contact, facial expression, gestures)	1	2	3	4	5
Responses to questions					
Clarity of answers	1	2	3	4	5

Comments:

_____

_____

_____

Total possible: 45 points

Your score: _____

Evaluator: _____

chapter 8

USING TECHNOLOGY *and* MEDIA *in the* CLASSROOM

- What is media literacy?
- Twenty-first-century literacies
- Encouraging responsible use of computers and the Internet
- Types of media
- Re-creating media literacy

Ms. R—I really like the tech stuff n class. This is really how I use writing in my life. It makes me smarter, don't u think?:)—Email message from seventh-grade student to his teacher in "text" dialect

Our students today are technology rich. They have immediate access to resources through computers and handheld devices. The Internet has revolutionized accessibility to information. Gone are the days when we searched for hours for sources to complete research papers. Instead of teaching students how to get their hands on resources, we need to teach them how to synthesize and use all that they have available to them.

This chapter defines a term that all English teachers need to be familiar with: *media literacy.* It provides an overview of the media that you might use in your classroom and includes suggestions for resources that support the integration of media and technology in the classroom.

WHAT IS MEDIA LITERACY?

As students are exposed to hundreds of images and depend on technology in their everyday life, they must also develop skills to sift through this information in a brief amount of time. Their ability to use this information in ways that allow them to express themselves and how they understand their world is important. We call this ability *media literacy*. Media literacy is a set of skills that students can use for accessing, evaluating, and producing various media forms. Students who have developed skills in media literacy understand the production, commercial nature, and ability of media to influence an audience or viewer. Our twenty-first-century students should have opportunities to develop technology-driven literacy skills in the same ways that they use the other language arts: reading, writing, speaking, and listening.

TWENTY-FIRST-CENTURY LITERACIES

The importance of media literacy in the English classroom has also been recognized by the National Council of Teachers of English (NCTE). In 2008, its executive committee adopted the following abilities that students need to have today:

- Develop proficiency with the tools of technology
- Build relationships with others to pose and solve problems collaboratively and cross-culturally
- Design and share information for global communities to meet a variety of purposes
- Manage, analyze, and synthesize multiple streams of simultaneous information
- Create, critique, analyze, and evaluate multimedia texts
- Attend to the ethical responsibilities required by these complex environments

ENCOURAGING RESPONSIBLE USE OF COMPUTERS AND THE INTERNET

Before you get started in using online resources in your classroom, it is a good idea to give the students a handout and pledge about the responsible use of technology and the Internet (see Form 8.1). Use this as a basis for discussion concerning the ethical use of online resources. At the end of the discussion, collect the signed copies of the contract and keep them for your records.

Internet and Computer Responsible Use Agreement

Please read the following, and if you agree to meet these expectations for responsible use of school computers and the Internet, sign and date in the space provided.

Posting

· Before I post anything on the Internet, I agree not to display information or images that could be embarrassing or damaging to me or anyone else.

· I will not post any personal information like cell phone numbers, home phone numbers, home addresses, or inappropriate pictures or videos.

· I will respect other people who are online.

· I promise not to post anything offensive or threatening.

· I will not post images that could embarrass or hurt another person.

· I promise not to post anyone's personal information and use it in a malicious way.

· I will think before I print. I will print only final drafts and information that I absolutely need.

Student's name and signature _____

Date _____

TYPES OF MEDIA

When we invite our students to think about media, we are exposing them to a wide variety of texts and images. Television, magazines, Web sites, social media, video games, and advertising are a few examples. Today, more than ever, our students need to learn how to read, interpret, and comment about the texts that they experience daily. Technology-based media is an integral part of our teenage students' lives and we need to make this connection in the classroom.

Print Media: Magazines and Books

Just as we want to expose our students to a wide variety of texts in the classroom, we also need to support students to develop their ability to discern the point of view and hidden meanings in other print sources. As they read magazines that target their demographic, they need to be able to analyze the messages and images. Magazines send powerful messages to teenagers about societal expectations for appearance, roles, and behaviors. You might want to consider creating lessons using magazines to sharpen students' analysis skills of texts. Here are some ideas:

- Bring to class a variety of magazines marketed to the teenage audience. Have the students analyze the covers, and identify what they see. Next, have the students analyze the images for hidden messages. Also have them look at the headlines and comment on the topics and features of the magazines. What does this information reveal about the magazine's expectations and assumptions about teenagers?
- Have the students examine three different news magazines from the same time period. The students can identify one news story and compare and contrast how the story is reported in each of the magazines. This exercise teaches about point of view and the differences of interpretation or bias depending on the source that reports the story.
- Select fashion magazines that cater to women and fashion magazines that cater to men. Have the students analyze the images and advertising. What do the images imply that society expects from men and women? How are men and women portrayed in these magazines?

Movies

Young adults love to go the movies, and if we exclude this medium from classroom teaching, we are missing out on an important opportunity for students to develop their literacy skill sets. We want students to understand how easily they may be influenced by the print media and that film may create the same kind of impact. Students need to develop the skills to discern these influences. Provide them with opportunities to analyze and critique film and develop awareness of what they choose to see and why.

The movie viewing guide in Form 8.2 can help support your students' critical movie viewing.

Movie Viewing Guide

Movie Terms

Flashback: the plot moves back in time to show events that happened earlier than those that were already shown in the movie.

Point of view shot: a movie shot or angle from the view of a character's eyes.

Wide angle: using a wide-angle lens to capture a wide range of elements.

Identify the following people who created this movie:

Screenplay author

Director

Actors who portray the main characters

Actors who portray key minor characters

The Movies

What is the overall mood of the movie? How does the director create the mood?

What kinds of film techniques are used in the movie? How do these techniques affect your viewing of the movie?

How does the director establish the setting of the movie?

Who tells the story in the movie?

After you finish viewing the movie, choose a scene from the movie and carefully observe the characters. How do the characters make their characters believable?

Television

Television, a major influence in our lives, reflects society and the people in it, yet we rarely discuss it in our English classrooms. A report on teenagers and television in 2005 indicated that American teenagers are exposed to media content for about eight and a half hours a day, three of them spent watching television (Navarro, 2005). Because students are so engaged in media and television viewing, it makes sense to teach them media literacy. In doing so, we can move them away from passive viewing into critical analysis.

Just as students keep a log of their independent reading, they can do the same for television. Taking notes while viewing television is challenging, but they should be encouraged to jot down notes during commercials. When students become more critical in their television viewing, they become more objective and knowledgeable about the influence television has in shaping our opinions and ideas, and this can lead to profitable class discussions. Sometimes this awareness of how people and events are portrayed in television carries over to discussions about literacy elements as well. Yet even if it doesn't, students gain tremendous knowledge about media and how they influence our thinking (Considine, 2002).

The television viewing log in Form 8.3 can get students started in their critical television viewing. Form 8.4, a character analysis graphic organizer for a television program, is useful in offering students an opportunity to bridge television characters with text-based characters found in literature. Form 8.5 is a graphic organizer for students to create their own media literacy, in this case, a television show. This is intended as a prewriting writing activity. The next step would be for the students to draft a screenplay for a pilot episode and eventually produce a videotape if the teacher chooses to expand the assignment.

Television Viewing Log

Title of program	Date	Time show started/time show ended	Major conflicts faced in the show: Comment on whether you think it is an accurate or realistic portrayal	Identify and describe the main character	What is the setting for the program? Is the setting an accurate and realistic portrayal?	Which audience do you think this program is attempting to reach?	Do you have any additional opinions about the program that you viewed?

Television Character Analysis Graphic Organizer

Directions: Note the requested information to help you analyze the character from your selected television program.

Name: _____

Date: _____

Title: _____

Author: _____

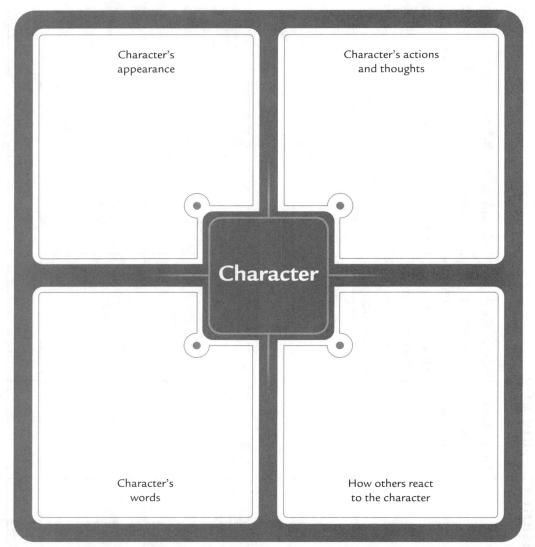

Character's appearance

Character's actions and thoughts

Character

Character's words

How others react to the character

Adapted from *The Teacher's Big Book of Graphic Organizers*, Katherine McKnight, © 2010 by John Wiley & Sons, Inc. Reprinted with permission of John Wiley & Sons, Inc.

Creating a Television Show

Directions: Use this graphic organizer to preplan your television program.
Draw a picture of the setting of your story.

Name: _____

Date: _____

DIRECTIONS: Write down and illustrate the key events in chronological order.

1	2	3
4	5	6

Adapted from *The Teacher's Big Book of Graphic Organizers*, Katherine McKnight, © 2010 by John Wiley & Sons, Inc. Reprinted with permission of John Wiley & Sons, Inc.

Music

With the invention of portable musical playing devices, carrying an entire music library is easy. Our playlists reveal much about our own identities. In the English classroom, music is a powerful tool for teaching literature. Not only is there a synergy between music and poetry, many themes in prose literary works have inspired contemporary songs. Some suggested strategies for using music in the English classroom include these:

- Students select a song and complete an analysis of the song that uses literary terms such as plot, conflict, theme, and mood (see Form 8.6).
- Use songs as a prereading activity. There are strong connections between many literary works and songs (see Table 8.1). When students explore the themes and stories that composers present in the music, you will also meet the needs of auditory learners and those with musical and rhythmic intelligences. Students will be able to learn about the text prior to reading it. This schematic scaffolding will support the student's comprehension of the text. Select popular songs that depict the same themes in the assigned literature. Have the students listen to the songs and read the lyrics. The students are likely able to identify the similar themes and conflicts that are depicted in the literature they are about to read.

Video Games

Yes, video games do have a place in our English classrooms. Like other forms of media, there are connections between video games and twenty-first-century literacy. In our technology-driven world, written text is one example of communication. Our ability to read images, that is, our visual literacy, has become increasingly important (Gee, 2003). For example, images are taking up more and more space in textbooks, and students need to be able to understand their meanings. Video games require us to quickly assess, reassess, and discern meaning of visual images. We can use video games to teach students literacy, as suggested in the following activities:

1. Encourage students to create advertisements for video games. Develop a vocabulary graphic organizer of the terms and jargon of video games. Who are the advertisers targeting when they use certain words from video game dialect? Some examples of video game jargon include:

   Newb: Newbie, someone who is new to the game. In the online gaming world, this is a derogatory word and used as an insult if a player is not performing well.
   Mobs: Computer-controlled enemies.
   Frag: Short for *fragmentation*; used when an enemy is completely destroyed and obliterated.
   Slam: Completely beat the computer-controlled game.
   Off the hook: Usually refers to a new game that is extremely popular and in demand.

2. Video games are often criticized for violence. Conduct research that examines this concern, and write a persuasive paper on this issue.

3. Have the students create a video game (on paper) based on a work of literature. Students can research the video game industry and discuss its societal impact.

RE-CREATING MEDIA LITERACY

Developing students' skills in media literacy goes beyond critiquing. Online media forms such as wikis, nings, and blogs give students the opportunity to create their own media literacy. Table 8.2 (on page 243) explains how to use these in the classroom.

ADVICE FOR GETTING STARTED

Be an explorer and consistently ask, 'Can I use this in my classroom?'' As teachers, we support and guide our students to understand the messages and information that are transmitted at a rapid rate. Your lessons will fill with technology as you make this your focus.

Here are some ideas for classroom projects for integrating media and technology:

- Have students look at major news Web sites and determine the reliability and point of view of the reporting.
- Choose a major event like Hurricane Katrina and research how it was reported in the media.
- Examine several political cartoons and how the content could influence society.
- Gather print advertisements from many different magazines and discuss how gender is portrayed in the visual images.
- Explore how editing, point of view, camera angles, framing, pace, visual rhythm, repetition, contrast, music, and even opening credits contribute information to the viewer.
- Have students view several versions of the same story or play (for example, *Hamlet*) and discuss the filmmaker's adaptation.
- Have students conduct a media audit by examining different visual media and discussing how different ethnic groups are portrayed. Are these representations accurate or stereotyped?
- Students may research how social networking sites affect communication.
- Use social networking Web sites as a means to analyze a character. For example, if Beowulf had a social networking site, what would he post on his site? What might a status posting look like, who would his friends be, and what might be in his information posting?
- Students create a movie based on a global issue such as global warming, health issues, or education and literacy.
- Have the students conduct a scavenger hunt and gather information and images of teens in media and advertising. How do advertisers market to teens? What assumptions do they make about teens? Are these accurate or stereotyped?

Song Analysis Graphic Organizer

Directions: Use the following graphic organizer to document your analysis of the song that you selected

Name: _____

Date: _____

	Name 1	Name 2
Attribute 1		
Attribute 2		
Attribute 3		

Adapted from *The Teacher's Big Book of Graphic Organizers*, Katherine McKnight, © 2010 by John Wiley & Sons, Inc. Reprinted with permission of John Wiley & Sons, Inc.

TABLE 8.1 Classic Songs

Author	Text	Song Title and Artist
Edwin Arlington Robinson	"Richard Cory"	"Richard Cory" by Wings
Maya Angelou	*I Know Why the Caged Bird Sings*	"Caged Bird" by Alicia Keys
Emily Brontë	*Wuthering Heights*	"Wuthering Heights" by Kate Bush
Samuel Taylor Coleridge	"Kubla Khan"	"Xanadu" by Rush
	"The Rime of the Ancient Mariner"	"The Rime of the Ancient Mariner" by Iron Maiden
Dante	"The Inferno"	"Dante's Prayer" by Loreena McKennitt
John Donne	Poems by John Donne	"Rave on John Donne" by Van Morrison
Nathaniel Hawthorne	"Young Goodman Brown"	"Shohhoth's Old Peculiar" by The Kindly Ones
Homer	*The Odyssey*	"Tales of Brave Ulysses" by Cream
		"Home at Last" by Steely Dan
		"Lotus Eaters" by Moloko
Aldous Huxley	*Brave New World*	"Brave New World" by Iron Maiden
John Milton	"Paradise Lost"	"Song of Joy" by Nick Caves
George Orwell	*1984*	"1984" by David Bowie
Edgar Allan Poe	"The Cask of Amontillado"	"The Cask of Amontillado" by Alan Parsons Project

(continued)

TABLE 8.1 *(Continued)*

Author	Text	Song Title and Artist
	"Lady Legeia"	"Vanishing Act" by Lou Reed
	"Murders in the Rue Morgue"	"Murders in the Rue Morgue" by Iron Maiden
William Shakespeare	*Romeo and Juliet*	"Romeo and Juliet" by Dire Straits
		"Romeo and Juliet" by Indigo Girls
		"Kissing You" by Des'ree
	The Tempest	"Prospero's Speech" by Loreena McKennitt
	Sonnet 142	"The Miseducation of Lauryn Hill" by Lauryn Hill
Sophocles	"Oedipus Rex"	"Oedipus Rex" by Tom Lehrer
Alfred Lord Tennyson	"The Lady of Shallot"	"Left Me a Fool" by Indigo Girls
J.R.R. Tolkien	*The Lord of the Rings*	"Ramble On" by Led Zeppelin
Mark Twain	*The Adventures of Huckleberry Finn*	"Barefoot Children in the Rain" by Jimmy Buffett
Mark Twain	*The Adventures of Tom Sawyer*	"Tom Sawyer" by Rush
William Wordsworth	The Lucy poems	"Lucy" by The Divine Comedy
W. B. Yeats	"Before the World Was Made"	"Mofo" by U2

Source: McKnight, Katherine, and Berlage, Bradley. (2008). *Teaching the classics in the inclusive classroom* (pp. 34–35). San Francisco: Jossey-Bass.

TABLE 8.2   Media Forms and Classroom Applications

Form	What Is It?	How Can I Use It in My Classroom?
Wiki	Collaborative Web sites where users can discuss a specific topic or network as a group. A well-known example is Wikipedia.	Can provide students the opportunity to discuss any topic. Use it for an online literature circle group or to work on collaborative projects.
Ning	Online social networking sites like Facebook and Twitter.	Can be used to promote a school event, or students could use this platform for a creative project. For example, students could create a ning for a literary character.
Blog	A contraction of the term *web log*. These are different from wikis and nings in that blogs are created by an individual. Although others can respond to the blog, the focus is on the author/creator.	Could be used as an online journal, learning log, discussion area, or literature diary.
E-mail	Electronic mail	An effective way for teachers to communicate with students and parents.

- The hero (Beowulf and Odysseus, for example) is a character common in literary works, and movies are no different (Iron Man, Shrek). Students can compare and contrast how heroes are portrayed in movies.
- Since technology has given us tremendous access to so much information and to each other, issues of privacy have become a hot topic. How do we protect our identity and privacy in this technological age? Have students explore this question and examine the security of personal information and identity.
- The music industry invests tremendous resources in promoting images of artists. Explore the connections between music and image.
- Political elections today are deeply influenced by technology. Specifically explore how the 2008 presidential campaign used social media networks and e-mail. What impact does technology have in the election process?

There are many sources for integrating media literacy into your English Language Arts classroom. Here are some Web sites that can help you to discover materials for classroom use.

- Media Awareness Network, which provides support and resources for developing greater awareness of media and how it affects society: www.media-awareness.ca/english
- Copyright-Free Photo Archives—27,000 images from NASA, NOAA, and FWS: http://gimp-savvy.com/PHOTO-ARCHIVE
- DHD Multimedia Gallery—selection of images and sounds: http://gallery.hd.org/index.jsp
- Images of space from NASA: http://grin.hq.nasa.gov
- Images of American political history: http://bill.ballpaul.net/iaph/main.php
- American Memory from the Library of Congress: http://rs6.loc.gov/amhome.html

chapter 9

WORKING *with* OTHERS

- Working with parents
- Working with teachers and administrators
- Working with community resources

The students were working in small groups when Principal Henry came to the door. "I'm here to observe you," he said, "but I'll come back when you are teaching."

We work in a setting filled with active, energetic adolescents. We're surrounded by fellow teachers, administrators, and support staff. There are only rare moments during the day that we can truly call our own. And yet one of the most common complaints from teachers is a sense of loneliness and isolation, a sense of "going it alone." We spend seven to eight hours each day in the small area known as our classroom and seldom see the teachers at the other end of the building. We wonder about the experiences our students have in other classes across the curriculum, and we know we are in touch with too few parents. We hope for a sense of community, a feeling of working as a team, because we want the best for our students and ourselves. We work to become better teachers and seek validation that we're teaching well. We believe many good things are happening in education across the nation, and we want to make the same happen in our schools. Fortunately, there is much we can do to work toward these goals.

WORKING WITH PARENTS

Every study that has ever been done concerning parental involvement shows that students do better in school when their parents are involved in their education (Grant & Ray, 2009). Some parents gladly give you the support you need, some want to help but don't know how, some are angry at schools in general, and some just don't seem to care. Although parents and their situations may differ, you can work to make each parent a positive factor in contributing to a student's success in your classroom. Consider using some of the following strategies as you work to increase parental involvement.

Beginning of the Year

Don't wait until a problem occurs to contact parents. Begin working even before the school year gets under way to gain their support. Mail a postcard greeting to all parents and incoming students before the first day of school. Keep the message simple and upbeat. Introduce yourself, and let your students and their parents know you are looking forward to the year and working together. The message can be as simple as the following:

To the family of: _____

    I was pleased to learn _____ will be a student in my English classroom this fall. I am looking forward to a wonderful year, and I hope you are too.

                            Sincerely,

                          _____

    On one of the first days of school, have each student address an envelope. Then mail or e-mail each parent a letter introducing yourself and your class. The sample letter to parents in Form 9.1 is useful in this regard. Note the information at the bottom of this sample letter: parents are to sign the letter and have their child return it to school.

Sample Letter to Parents

To the parents of _____

    My name is _____, and I will be your child's English
teacher this year. I am looking forward to the coming school year and am pleased
_____ will be in my classroom. I believe that it is important for
parents and teachers to work together to ensure the best education possible for each
student. I encourage you to visit our classroom and to contact me whenever
you have a comment, question, or suggestion. Please phone the school office at
_____, and I will respond as quickly as possible.
    I look forward to a happy and successful year as we work together.

                            Sincerely,

                            _____

I have read the above letter. I can be reached at _____

The best time to phone is _____

Parent/guardian's name (please print) _____

Parent/guardian's signature _____

Student's name (please print) _____

Date _____

Comments:

_____

_____

_____

_____

_____

You can also include additional information in your introductory letter—for example:

- Educational philosophy
- Class requirements
- Grading system
- Homework policy
- List of materials the student will be reading
- Major projects and deadlines
- Students' responsibilities
- Your contact information (work phone number and e-mail address)

If the cost of mailing these letters is prohibitive, ask the students to deliver them to their parents, and include a student bonus point coupon or a tear-off sheet that parents sign and return. E-mail is free, and often parents respond more through electronic communication. Provide a space for comments and any additional information that will be helpful to you.

Back-to-School Night and Parents' Workshops

A back-to-school night can be one of the most important events of the school year because it is your single best opportunity to meet parents, explain your policies and program in detail, answer questions about your class, and emphasize the importance of parental involvement in students' learning. Unfortunately, parents of older students aren't as likely to attend as those of younger students. There are, however, some ways to increase attendance. Involve your students in decorating the classroom, posting welcome signs, and designing and delivering invitations. Generate enthusiasm they can pass along to their parents. The sample invitation in Form 9.2 has a simple format that students can decorate and personalize. An RSVP tear-off sheet will help commit parents to attendance.

You might feature a raffle drawing or offer bonus points for students whose parents do attend. E-mailing the back-to-school-night information helps keep track of the messages and responses. You might also want to use a social networking site like Evite so that you can maintain a record of which parents are attending this important event (see www.evite.com).

Sample Invitation to Back-to-School Night

An Invitation to: _____

    You're invited to a Back-to-School Night.

Place: _____

Date: _____

Time: _____

    Please join us for Back-to-School Night to meet the teachers, visit classrooms, and learn what you can do to help your child have a successful school year. I'm looking forward to meeting you and explaining our class plans and goals for the coming year. Do plan to attend.

_____ I will be attending.

_____ I won't be attending.

Name _____

Parent of _____

It's important that you carefully plan your back-to-school-night presentation to parents. This is not a time to talk about individual students but rather to explain your educational philosophy and discuss general information that will be helpful to every parent. The following format will help you organize an effective presentation:

1. Introduce yourself.
2. Welcome everyone, and stress the significant role parents play in their son's or daughter's academic success.
3. Explain your academic program for the semester (or year). Mention major assignments and important deadlines.
4. Stress the importance of good attendance.
5. Briefly describe your discipline plan.
6. Describe your homework policy.
7. Explain your grading policy.
8. Explain how parents can help their students at home and request their support.
9. Ask for questions and suggestions.
10. End on a positive note by emphasizing the importance of parents and teachers working together for the success of each student.

You may find that the people you want most to attend are the ones who don't. Consider sending a follow-up note to these parents, summarizing your information and again encouraging them to contact you with any questions, concerns, or suggestions. Electronic communication also helps to keep parents informed about their son or daughter.

In addition to a back-to-school night, encourage your colleagues to host a departmental workshop for parents. Involve the entire English department. Send invitations and invite parents to learn more about the department and the language arts curriculum. Introduce staff members and offer teaching demonstrations. Involve teachers, parents, and students in writing and sharing together.

Phone Calls and E-Mail

Contact parents by phone or e-mail when a student is doing something well. Don't let the large number of students you teach prevent you from making this effort. Simply keep the phone call or e-mail brief, and be precise and positive about a student's achievement, a good grade, an act of kindness, or some special quality. Once you've established positive communication, it's much easier to contact parents later if necessary. Unfortunately, most parents report they hear from a teacher or the school only when there is a problem.

Notes, Cards, Letters, Presentations, and Newsletters

Keep the lines of communication open. If you cannot reach a parent by phone, send a note or card or an e-mail. Letters and e-mail are helpful in keeping parents up-to-date about long-term assignments or student achievement. Design several assignments with parents in mind. (A writing assignment that involves interviewing a family member works well.)

With the student's permission, mail or e-mail a copy of a final draft along with a cover letter explaining the assignment to his or her parent.

Invite parents and community members to class on days when students are sharing their work or presenting culminating response projects. Inform the local newspaper as well, and suggest it run a feature highlighting a particular classroom activity. Celebrate students' successes and include parents in these celebrations.

Duplicate and mail or e-mail a monthly or quarterly classroom newsletter to parents. Include samples of students' work and explanations of assignments and class activities. Involve students in its production. Submit students' work to the district newsletter as well.

Problem Solving

It's difficult for parents to hear their child isn't doing well in school. No one likes to hear bad news, and parents frequently feel they have little power to make a situation better. When a student begins having academic or behavioral problems, document what is happening. Keep a record of your observations in precise detail and include notes on your responses. Don't wait too long to contact parents. A parent who finds out about a student-teacher disagreement from the student without any information from the teacher is likely to become angry and may be slow to forget.

Before making a phone call, outline exactly what it is you have observed and the steps you have taken to solve the problem. Be tactful and professional, offer solutions, and ask for parental input. It's important that parents recognize you have the desire and the ability to work with them to help their son or daughter. Be sure to follow up your initial call with at least one additional progress report.

Reporting Student Progress

Rather than mailing deficiency notices to the parents of students who are failing, send a computerized periodic progress report with a brief personal note to every parent. If you do not have access to a computer grading program, develop a simple personal form similar to that in Form 9.3.

Student Progress Report

Name _____ Date _____

Course _____ Teacher _____

Number of absences _____

	Excellent	Average	Poor
1. Attitude			
2. Initiative			
3. Ability to get along with others			
4. Dependability			
5. Quality of work			

Grade _____

Comments/suggestions:

_____

_____

_____

_____

_____

_____

_____

_____

If you take the time to confer with students about their grades before mailing forms such as this, you can avoid misunderstandings. If you and the student disagree about a grade, check your calculations and either change the grade or explain why the grade is what it is. Then ask the students to tell their parents what their grade is going to be and why.

Parent-Teacher Conferences

A regularly scheduled parent-teacher conference isn't a good time to surprise parents with negative information about their child's performance. You'll want to deal with problems as soon as they occur or alert a parent before the scheduled conference date. Although scheduled conferences days limit the time you can spend with any one parent, they can be productive if they are well planned. Because you are likely to involve your students in self-evaluation throughout the year, it's especially important that you do this before a formal conference. The student self-evaluation in Form 2.5 is especially useful. (Many teachers encourage students to attend the conferences as well.) Your goal is for parents to leave these conferences with a clear picture of how well their son or daughter is doing. Keep the conference informal and positive. The following format is helpful in conducting a successful conference:

Guidelines for a Parent-Teacher Conference
1. Open with a positive comment concerning the student and his or her contribution to the class.
2. Show samples of the student's class work as well as his or her self-evaluation. A student-assembled portfolio is ideal for this.
3. Point out the student's academic strengths.
4. Discuss the student's academic weaknesses.
5. Ask about the parents' expectations for the student.
6. Set goals for the next grading period.
7. Suggest help that can be given at home to overcome weaknesses.
8. Ask for additional parental questions and input.
9. End the meeting on a positive, upbeat note.

All of us want a good education for our students. Show parents they are important in achieving this goal, and encourage and enable them to participate. Most will respond positively in any way they can.

WORKING WITH TEACHERS AND ADMINISTRATORS

Cooperation is a key part of every profession. Businesspeople virtually never work alone; health care teams in hospitals practice in consultation with one another. Likewise, the ideal school district consists of many people working as a team. English teachers have an especially strong motive for cooperating with their fellow teachers. Because English overlaps all other fields, working with other teachers is vital. Naturally we hope that every instructor in the school will reinforce the attitude that English class is important.

Teachers

An English department is a group of people who are united in common concerns—their teaching area and the education of their students. A well-organized, smoothly functioning department accomplishes a great deal and improves the professional life of all its teachers. As an individual teacher, you can help your department function effectively. Attend department meetings, stay involved, and share responsibility. An ideal department has good organization, strong leadership, well-thought-out philosophy and goals, and time for its members to plan and evaluate curricula and share and exchange successful teaching strategies. Unfortunately, in far too many schools, the ideal department does not exist. Many departments meet so infrequently and are so powerless that they are simply a collection of people who teach in the same discipline and jealously guard their ideas and teaching materials for fear that someone else will use them.

There are some things, however, every teacher can do to work cooperatively with others:

- Seek out colleagues with similar philosophies and goals, and help and encourage one another. Plan together, and set some ground rules for the use of shared ideas. Make it a policy to return borrowed materials promptly and in good condition.
- Along with teachers in the same or compatible disciplines, write proposals for special projects or pilot programs. (See Chapter Ten for a discussion of grant writing.)
- Keep administrators and counselors informed about what is happening with these projects and in your classrooms.
- Ask for advice from teachers you admire and respect and in turn support others in positive ways.
- Make an effort to balance negative discussions with humor and a positive outlook.
- If you are a more experienced teacher, encourage and help new teachers.
- If you are a new teacher, find other beginning teachers. Share experiences and encourage one another.
- Become a part of the school's formal mentor program if one exists.

School relationships can be fragile. If we've worked together for a time, we've gotten to know one another's personal lives. Some of us repeat the same stories over and over. We each have our ups and downs: sickness, emotional crises, and other difficulties. We occasionally get on one another's nerves. Despite this, we need friends and a support system for commiseration as well as celebration. We need to nurture these friendships, especially when we consider the many hours and days we spend together. Who else really understands what it's like to interact with 150 teenagers day after day?

Substitute Teachers

For those times when it is possible to predict in advance when a substitute teacher will be needed, provide directions and materials tailored to your teaching unit and objectives. Ideally, you will also confer with the substitute teacher in advance. Substitutes generally like to talk to the teacher prior to working in the classroom. The following checklist is helpful as you write lesson plans for a substitute teacher:

❏ Seating chart or some other means of identifying each student.
❏ Directions and materials for taking attendance.
❏ A statement of goals and objectives for the day's lesson.
❏ All necessary teaching materials and handouts and an explanation of where they are located.
❏ A step-by-step set of directions for presenting the lesson. (Don't anticipate or expect that most substitute teachers will have the same knowledge of your English class or your school's policies as you do. The more you write, the better. Plans that say, "Do independent study" or "Study for the test" are too vague to be helpful.)
❏ A clear statement of what students are expected to do or produce.
❏ An explanation of how the substitute teacher might help and work with individual students.
❏ An explanation of what students are to do with their completed work. (For example, is the work to be exchanged with other students and corrected and collected, kept in the student's folder until a following day, handed in and graded by the substitute, or handed in for the classroom teacher to evaluate and grade? Be sure an answer key is provided if the substitute teacher is to do the grading.)
❏ An explanation of what students are to do if they complete their work before the end of the class period.
❏ An assignment for the following day.
❏ Information about students with special needs, students who have the potential to cause problems, or students who otherwise require special handling.
❏ The name and location of a nearby teacher to turn to or talk to if problems arise.
❏ An explanation of extra duties if these are a part of your own assignment on a particular day (hall duty or detention, for example).
❏ A notation of any school activity (such as an assembly) that might disrupt the normal schedule.

It's not always possible, of course, to predict when you will need a substitute teacher. For the times when it is necessary for a substitute teacher to be called on short notice, keep a clearly marked resource file for substitute teachers in a conspicuous location. Also include in it one or two sets of manageable classroom activities or lesson plans for emergencies. (Many of the suggested activities discussed in the first chapters of this book can be adapted as a substitute teacher's emergency lesson plan.) An additional source you might also add to this resource file is *More Lesson Plans for Substitute Teachers: Classroom-Tested Activities from the National Council of Teachers of English* (National Council of Teachers of English, 2002). This is an excellent collection of single-class-period activities designed for the nonspecialist English substitute.

Substitute teachers are one of the most powerful public relations tools a teacher has. Although confidentiality is expected, it is only natural that substitutes will make judgments about the school system and your effectiveness as a teacher based on their experiences in your classroom. A substitute teacher who finds a poor lesson plan or none at all, cannot find the necessary materials, or is not given enough information about classroom routines cannot help but feel negative about your classroom or the entire school. By creating the best environment possible for substitute teachers, you will not only enhance your image as a teacher, but you will also ensure that educationally sound and manageable activities continue to happen in your classroom when you are away.

Administrators

Observe any faculty lounge, and most of the criticism you'll hear there is directed at the administration. "They just don't understand us," we complain. Aren't all those assemblies, announcements on the intercom, and classroom interruptions an administrator's plot to destroy our effectiveness? Administrators are a perfect target for our frustration or anger. We hate it if they appear to "hide" in their offices and never really know what's going on in the school. We hate it if they appear indifferent to our problems and lack immediate solutions. We hate it if an administrator observes and evaluates our teaching and classrooms but knows little about our subject area. We hate it if administrators don't write well, if messages from the office are filled with sentence fragments, run-on sentences, or jargon. Most of us have spent a great deal of time complaining about inefficiency and bureaucracy. Some of us thrive on it.

The criticisms leveled against principals are endless. These are not true of every administrator, of course, and to be really fair, we should look at the school day from their point of view. Most are intelligent, fair, and professional. Their first interest may be improving instruction, but the nature of their work is to spend long hours handling paperwork, taking care of attendance and discipline problems, and talking with irate parents. They're caught between the district office and the teachers. Many don't have a strong support system of their own or the immediate positive feedback that most classroom teachers can expect.

There are a number of ways to make working with principals and other administrators more productive:

- Be the best teacher you can be. That's the first priority. Good administrators will recognize and have confidence in your expertise, and they will support you.
- Be reliable and professional. Show up for assemblies. Arrive at and leave school on time. Volunteer for your share of committees. Carry your weight.
- Avoid constant complaining. Know what changes are realistic, and then work toward a positive solution. When you have a legitimate problem, one that an administrator can solve, seek him or her out—when you are calm, reasonable, positive, and optimistic.
- Differentiate between a passing problem and a long-term problem. Don't overuse a principal. Work to solve classroom problems yourself before asking for assistance with one that won't go away. You might, for example, discuss a discipline problem with a colleague or counselor before involving a principal. Keep your priorities in mind, and don't use up your goodwill on things that aren't essential.
- Express your satisfaction and thanks for something done well.

Administrative Observation

In many schools, a formal plan for an administrator's observation of a teacher's performance is designed cooperatively by the school district's teachers and administrators and is agreed on contractually. If this is the case in your school, be sure you understand the procedure for such an observation. But if administrative observation and evaluation of your work in the classroom consists primarily of a principal dropping in from time to time, there are some ways you can make an observation more productive and helpful. You can, for example, ask that an administrator evaluate your work in a more formal way. Request a formal observation and set a date. Design a lesson plan that will be helpful to anyone observing your work, and submit the plan to the observer before the date of the observation. Ideally, a lesson plan for a formal observation will include the following information:

- An explanation of your objectives: What will the students know or be able to do following this lesson?
- An explanation of where you are in the course or unit: Is this an introductory, middle, or culminating activity?
- A description of the teaching methods you will use: Will you demonstrate, lecture, ask the students to work cooperatively in groups, or provide a practice exercise?
- An explanation of the learning activities in which the students will be involved: Will students work independently, with partners, or in groups? What will they do?
- An explanation of your evaluation process: How will you assess your students? How will you know they have learned?
- A description of any special circumstances of which the observer should be aware: unusual behaviors or students leaving class during the period, for example.

A detailed lesson plan helps an observer respond fairly and helpfully, particularly if English is not his or her discipline. Following such an observation, ask to meet formally with the observer, and invite comments and suggestions and set personal goals.

Support Personnel

Some of the most important people in any school are those who perhaps receive the least recognition: secretaries, cooks, janitors, bus drivers, teacher's aides, and technicians. They contribute significantly to the effectiveness of a well-run school. Treat these people with courtesy and respect. Don't expect or demand unnecessary favors. Do learn and follow the prescribed procedures when requesting services. Be pleasant and grateful for the support and help when it is given.

WORKING WITH COMMUNITY RESOURCES

Many school districts have a formal community resource volunteer program. These are excellent programs that offer community members' knowledge, expertise, and talents to students in the classroom and enable a teacher to draw on the wealth of resources within the community. Most formal programs offer a catalogue that lists widely varied topics and saves a teacher time in searching for volunteers. Most also have a formal request form for the teacher to fill out and send it to the community resource office. The office makes the original contact with the volunteer, arranges the time and date, and confirms this information with the teacher. These programs also ask the teacher to complete a formal evaluation of a presentation to help plan better programs as well as give volunteers assistance in improving their presentations.

If your district has no formal resource program, begin making your own list or a departmental list of community resource people. As your students explore a specific theme in literature, for example, invite community people with expertise in this area to speak about their own experiences or knowledge of the topic. Invite local poets and writers, college and university staff members, and business leaders into your classroom. Contact human resource departments of large companies, or go directly to the owners of small businesses. You might, for example, create an entire unit in which you ask several volunteers to speak about the importance of writing in their lives. Include cross-discipline resources as well. Invite artists, art historians, musicians, actors, and performing groups into your classroom.

If you are making arrangements on your own, you'll need to be sure the guest has the following information:

- Financial remuneration, if any. This must be cleared with the administration in advance. (See Chapter Ten for a discussion of grant applications.)
- Topic and suggested format. Are you requesting a lecture, a discussion, or a performance?
- The age and grade level of the students.
- A brief description of your curriculum and its relation to the topic.
- A schedule. Are you expecting the guest to meet with one class, several, or the entire student body? Will the presentation be given once or several times? Indicate the exact times and length of each presentation.
- A map of the school indicating where parking is available and clearly showing the site of the presentations. Provide a guest parking permit if one is required.
- Details of lodging, meals, and transportation if applicable.

Resource people offer endless possibilities for curriculum enrichment. It is well worth your time to add this dimension to your curriculum.

chapter 10

AVOIDING BURNOUT *and* BECOMING *a* MORE EFFECTIVE TEACHER

- Staying healthy and fit
- Becoming a more effective teacher

Message from principal (former deputy sheriff): Cap infractions will no longer be tolerated.

Stress is a part of all our lives. Some is positive and necessary. We may be excited and tense watching a baseball game or acting in a community theater production, for example. Good stress peps us up and produces healthy relaxation. In contrast, stress involving persistent anger, frustration, or worry can threaten our health and lead to professional burnout. Individuals in the helping professions are especially prone to this condition since we give of ourselves and tend to receive too little positive response in return. Ironically the teachers who are most frequently affected by varying degrees of burnout are often the most productive, dedicated, and committed professionals.

STAYING HEALTHY AND FIT

Low-level burnout causes us to feel less enthusiastic, less energetic, less fulfilled. After a short time, these feelings usually go away. Unchecked, however, they can intensify. We may experience shortness of temper, impatience, lapsed concentration, and sleepless nights. In time we may lose our ability to cope with minor daily problems, suffer chronic fatigue, and become more and more detached and cynical. Sadly, some of the best teachers leave the profession because of unchecked, destructive burnout.

As teachers, our professional lives are intense and hectic. To be effective, each of us must develop a personal system for resisting, deflecting, or reducing the effects of stress and burnout in a demanding profession. Every one of us, new teachers as well as more experienced teachers, must consciously guard against burnout. The following suggestions will help you stay healthy and productive.

Vary Your Routine

We often work in isolated settings, and our lives seem to be ruled by bells or buzzers signaling each class period. There may be little you can do about the school's rigid six-or seven-period day, and worrying about things you can't control wastes your energy. However, you do control what happens in your classroom each period. You set the tone and design the schedule. Personalize your environment. Don't be afraid to have fun. Vary your routine, be yourself, keep a sense of humor, and trust your instincts. Occasionally set aside a lesson you have planned, and do something unexpected: games, puzzles, discussion, or a film, for example. Rearrange the furniture and desks from time to time.

Experiment Once in a While

Try a new approach or technique or new materials. Don't be afraid to fail. A lesson doesn't have to be perfect the first time you do it. Avoid using the same lesson plans, the same unit plans, the same semester- and year-long schedule over and over. Few are so perfect that they deserve being set in stone.

Vary Your Lunchtime Routine

Instead of eating with the same people day after day, seek out other colleagues and locations. Talk with people who stimulate you intellectually. Occasionally lock your classroom door and eat alone, read, or listen to the radio. On another day, go for a walk. Although thirty minutes is obviously not long enough for a civilized meal, eat at a nearby fast food restaurant once in a while or plan ahead with colleagues and have food delivered to the teachers' lounge.

Interact with Colleagues and Students Between Classes

If you've lapsed into a pattern of complaining, make an effort to talk to people in a more positive way. Remember to give genuine praise when you see the successes and accomplishments of others. Support your colleagues' projects and special interests, and they will support yours.

Set Priorities and Manage Your Classroom Efficiently

Most of us feel overwhelmed by all that we believe must be accomplished in limited time. You'll feel confident and in control if you manage your time efficiently—for example:

- Prioritize your objectives and set realistic goals.
- Simplify and focus your curriculum.
- Eliminate tasks and assignments that have become obsolete.
- Revise assignments that are time consumers rather than time savers. If the end product isn't worth the effort, eliminate the task entirely, or rework it so that it's manageable and valid.
- Set reasonable long- and short-term deadlines.
- Organize and manage your classroom so that students take responsibility for routine clerical tasks. Give students immediate feedback by letting them correct some of their own work.
- Expect your students to write frequently, but don't feel you must read and correct everything they do. If you grade individual papers, ask students to select one of several writings for evaluation, and even then, concentrate on and respond to only one or two elements in the writing. The long hours we have traditionally spent marking student papers have seldom translated into proportionate learning on the part of our students.
- Work efficiently during the school day, and make a policy of taking as little school work home as possible. When you do have papers to correct, avoid spending too much time chatting with coworkers. Work during your prep period and lunch period. Occasionally plan days for students to read or work quietly as you evaluate and grade material at your desk.
- Make daily and weekly to-do lists. Crossing items off when they're completed will help you realize what you've accomplished.

Pamper Yourself

Too often we teachers become so obsessed with our self-imposed deadlines and high expectations that we neglect ourselves. To be effective, you must have a healthy diet, plenty of sleep, and exercise. It's never easy to force yourself into physical activity after arriving home exhausted and spent. Nevertheless, teachers who exercise daily discover renewed energy. Practice relaxation exercises, walk, take part in aerobic exercise, or join a health club. Resist the temptation to devote excessive hours entirely to school work.

Keep a folder of your successes: thank-you letters from students and parents, notes from principals commending your performance, copies of student work that has special meaning. Don't lose sight of your accomplishments. Writing in your own journal will help you keep your perspective and clarify problems, which often shrink when they are expressed in writing.

Get Involved in Outside Activities

Keep a balance between your work and your life outside the job. Separate teaching from your private life as much as possible. When you're away from school, don't worry about ungraded papers and unfinished lessons or talk about your classroom endlessly. Treat yourself to the things you enjoy—a good meal, a trip, some time alone. Develop interests that are different from education, and use the summer break and weekends to change your daily routine and pursue these interests. Volunteer for projects that you can realistically handle and enjoy. Develop friendships away from school with people who are not teachers. When you are with colleagues, avoid constant shop talk.

Consider Other Options

If you feel locked into a less-than-ideal position, investigating other possibilities will both help you realize your worth and clarify other opportunities:

- Participate in a faculty exchange.
- Arrange for a change of responsibility or teaching assignment within your district.
- Consider teaching abroad. The Fulbright Exchange Program arranges overseas teaching opportunities. Contact the United States Information Agency (http://dosfan.lib .uic.edu/usia).
- Take a sabbatical for further study.
- Use a leave of absence to explore other options.
- Keep an up-to-date résumé so that you're prepared when other positions or options become available.
- Join the National Council of Teachers of English (NCTE). Attend its conferences and consider presenting about your students and classroom.

Be sure to guard your job security, however. Don't, for example, resign in frustration. You may discover you can't find anything else you like as well.

BECOMING A MORE EFFECTIVE TEACHER

As teachers, we are members of one of the great professions. Each of us has the responsibility to be as effective as we can be. Each of us needs to grow professionally.

Self-Evaluation

We spend much of our time judging and evaluating the performance of others: students, peers, parents, and administrators. Even so, it's never quite easy to look at ourselves critically. Yet we must if we want to be effective in our classrooms. The following suggestions are helpful ways for you to evaluate your own work in the classroom as you seek to improve your professional skills:

- Once a semester make an audio- or videotape of one of your classroom sessions. Review the tape. Did the planned activities actually occur? Did they have the intended outcomes? What do you do well? What might you improve? Set personal goals each semester.

- Team with a supportive colleague and observe one another's classrooms. Sit down together and honestly analyze each other's work. Note strengths as well as areas needing improvement. Talk about teaching strategies and better ways to teach.
- Establish a class suggestion box and encourage students' suggestions.
- Invite student evaluation of assignments and units rather than asking for a single evaluation at the end of the semester or year—for example:

  - What do you like about this activity?
  - What did you find most effective in the way we approached this activity?
  - What do you feel is the most important thing you learned as you completed this activity?
  - What should I change or do differently if I use this activity another year?
  - Elicit group discussion and evaluation midway in a course for example:

    - What about this class has been best at helping you learn the material?
    - What can we do to improve this class?
    - Is there anything you do not understand? What would you like to have reviewed or clarified?

- Plan for an end-of-the-year evaluation. You might, for example, ask students to write letters to next year's students describing your class, explaining what to expect in terms of assigned work and classroom environment and offering advice on how to succeed. The course evaluation in Form 10.1 provides a helpful format. In using a form such as this, however, keep your students' responses in perspective. Don't be destroyed or even dismayed if one out of a hundred students hates his or her desk, dislikes you, and can't stand change. No teacher can succeed with every student, although we all try.
- Write your own end-of-the-year evaluation.
- If you are a less experienced teacher, seek out a mentor. If you are a more experienced teacher, work with a less experienced teacher. Mentorships, formal or informal, can include any of the following elements:

  - Regularly scheduled confidential meetings.
  - Discussions concerning lesson plans, questions, problems, attendance, grade reporting, classroom management, or motivation strategies. Discussions on a variety of topics might also occur in a joint dialogue journal.
  - Observations of each other's classrooms.
  - Sharing classroom materials, professional books, and magazines.

Course Evaluation

Name of Course _____ **Date** _____

Please react to the following statements by circling the number that corresponds to how you feel about this class.

	I agree				I disagree
1. Directions are clearly given.	5	4	3	2	1
2. Grading is done fairly.	5	4	3	2	1
3. There is adequate time to complete assignments.	5	4	3	2	1
4. New ideas are accepted.	5	4	3	2	1
5. I have a chance to express my ideas.	5	4	3	2	1
6. The teacher gives extra help when needed.	5	4	3	2	1
7. The teacher knows the subject.	5	4	3	2	1
8. The subject is interesting.	5	4	3	2	1
9. The subject is not my favorite, but the teacher makes it interesting.	5	4	3	2	1
10. I have learned a lot in this class.	5	4	3	2	1

11. Please complete the following sentence: My favorite assignment was

_____

_____

_____

_____

12. Please complete the following sentence: If I taught the class, I would

_____

_____

_____

_____

_____

Staying Current

The most effective teachers never stop being curious, never stop reading, and never stop learning. Be informed about educational issues. Know what is happening at the local, state, and national levels. Understand your contract. Encourage your local teachers' organization to take progressive stands on issues.

Fortunately we have many options for professional growth. The NCTE and its state affiliates are organizations that every English teacher should join. The NCTE publishes a half-dozen magazines, including the *English Journal,* geared specifically to keep secondary teachers abreast of current trends and research. It also publishes pamphlets and books on curricular and other matters and makes available to its members large numbers of teaching aids. *Notes Plus* offers many practical, hands-on activities that a teacher can use immediately.

In addition to its publications, the NCTE holds national conventions that offer significant opportunities for continuing education in both formal sessions and in discussions with other teachers from throughout the country. These conventions allow us to hear and respond to the leaders of our profession and provide a much-needed professional stimulus to all teachers of English.

As a professional, consider acquiring an advanced degree. Enroll in college and university courses in your own or complementary disciplines.

You'll also want to begin or add to your professional library. As you do so, consider the following publications:

Periodicals

Contemporary Education: School of Education, Indiana State University, Terre Haute, IN 47809

Educational Leadership: Association for Supervision and Curriculum Development, 1250 North Pitt Street, Alexandria, VA 22314

Education Digest: Prakken Publications, Inc., 416 Longshore Drive, Ann Arbor, MI 48107

English Journal: National Council of Teachers of English, Urbana, IL 61801

Kappan: Phi Delta Kappa, Eighth and Union, P.O. Box 789, Bloomington, IN 47402

New York Times Book Review: 229 West 43rd Street, New York, NY 10036

Notes Plus: National Council of Teachers of English, Urbana, IL 61801

Speech Communication Teacher: Speech Communication Association, 5105 Backlick Road, Building E, Annandale, VA 22003

Teacher Magazine: Editorial Projects in Education, 4301 Connecticut Avenue NW, Suite 250, Washington, DC 20008

Books

Atwell, N. (1998). *In the middle: New understandings about reading, writing, and learning.* Portsmouth, NH: Boynton/Cook.

Beers, K. (2002). *When kids can't read: What teachers can do: A guide for teachers 6–12.* Portsmouth, NH: Heinemann.

Daniels, H., & Steineke, N. (2004). *Mini-lessons for literature circles*. Portsmouth, NH: Heinemann.

Gurian, M., Stevens, K., & King, K. (2008). *Strategies for teaching boys and girls: A workbook for educators*. San Francisco: Jossey-Bass.

Heacox, D. (2002). *Differentiating instruction in the regular classroom: How to reach and teach all learners, grades 3–12*. Minneapolis: Free Spirit Publishing.

Rief, L. (1992). *Seeking diversity*. Portsmouth, NH: Heinemann.

Weaver, C. (Ed.). (1998). *Lessons to share: On teaching grammar in context*. Portsmouth, NH: Boynton/Cook.

Wilhelm, J. D. (2007). *"You gotta BE the book": Teacher engaged and reflective reading with adolescents* (2nd ed.). New York: Teachers College Press.

Applying for Grants, Workshops, and Seminars

Improve your professional skills by attending local in-services and workshops. Most districts have staff development funds earmarked for individual and schoolwide or districtwide projects and encourage teachers to develop projects either cooperatively or individually. Be sure you understand how these funds are allocated in your district. Why not, for example, apply for funds to pay for a substitute for your classroom for a day while you observe teachers in your own or another school?

Apply for summer institutes and seminars. The Fulbright Seminars Abroad program is open to secondary school teachers. Application forms are available from:

Fulbright Seminars Abroad Program
Center for International Education
U.S. Department for Education
400 Maryland Avenue SW
Washington, DC 20202
(202) 245–2794
www.fulbrightteacherexchange.org

The National Endowment for the Humanities offers summer seminars and institutes for teachers. For general information, guidelines, and application forms contact:

National Endowment for the Humanities
Division of Education Programs, Room 302
1100 Pennsylvania Avenue, NW
Washington, DC 20506
www.neh.gov/projrcts/si-school.html

In addition, a wide variety of grants are available from a variety of other sources. These grants are usually appropriated to institutions or in some cases to individuals for specific purposes. In making an application, work with your district's designated grant writer. If your district has no such person, you'll need to become knowledgeable about the grant-writing process.

Identify Your Need and Goal

Student scores in your school may be low in a particular area, and a needs assessment may have indicated a specific problem. Your district or department may have determined a series of educational priorities. Any of these areas can become the focus of a grant application.

Know the Type of Grants Available

A variety of grants is available: research grants, development grants, literacy grants, demonstrations grants, and replication grants. Determine which type of grant will best address your situation. For example, a replication grant can be used to duplicate an existing successful program in another school. A research grant is intended to help you develop a program specifically designed for your individual situation.

Select the Appropriate Funding Source

Many publications offer information about available funds:

- *Education Grants Alert* is a weekly report on funding opportunities for K–12 programs. www.grantsalert.com.
- *Foundations and Corporate Grants Alert* and *Federal Grants and Contracts Weekly* detail areas of grant availability, application requirements, and dates and amounts awarded. www.grants.gov/assets/EducationGrants.
- *The Foundation Directory and Foundations Grants Index Bimonthly*, published by the Foundation Center, describes thousands of corporate, community, and independent foundations that award grants. http://www.grants.gov/applicants/email_subscription.jsp.
- *The Federal Register*, a daily government publication, provides an up-to-date report of federal grants. www.gpoaccess.gov.

With so many grants available, it's important that you determine the most appropriate funding source for your project. By carefully analyzing each grant listing, you will be able to determine which program areas this source is funding, as well as information pertaining to proposal requirements, application dates, eligibility, and dollar amounts awarded.

Submit a Clearly and Concisely Written Proposal

The format and degree of comprehensiveness required in a written proposal vary from source to source, and you will need to read the particular guidelines. Most proposals, however, usually include the following components:

- Cover letter
- Title page
- Narrative description
- Needs
- Objectives
- Activities

- Personnel
- Evaluation procedures
- Budget

Many grant writers suggest that one of the best ways to include all the components and specific information necessary for a good proposal is to focus on who, what, where, when, and how and relate each to the overall purpose and goal of the project. It's also important that you present a realistic and reasonable scenario regarding program implementation and cost. Mail your proposal by registered mail, return-receipt requested, before the deadline. Most grant proposals are submitted online or via e-mail. Be sure to follow the grant deadline and procedures accurately.

Appendix E in this book offers additional suggestions.

SAMPLE UNIT PLANS

THEMES IN AFRICAN AMERICAN LITERATURE

This unit on African American literature with a thematic focus was developed by teacher DiSheen Smith. The thematic focus is developed through the following essential question: What social issues help define a cultural/ethnic identity—specifically, an African American identity?

Description of the Unit

This unit deals with the examination of social identity in poems, speeches, and novels written by African American authors. As they read the texts both aloud and independently, students will be responsible for annotating the text and deciphering the meaning behind the texts. Students will determine how these ideas and philosophies relate to the social climate of the time period and how these issues relate to the social climate of the twenty-first century. Once the social identity has been determined, students are to connect the social identity of the texts to their own social identity. Students will read the Prologue and Chapter One of *Invisible Man* by Ralph Ellison, "We Wear the Mask" by Paul Laurence Dunbar, "I've Been to the Mountaintop" by Martin Luther King Jr., and "Man Know Thyself" by Marcus Garvey. Students will have gallery walks, view videos, do worksheets, and engage in small group discussions that will help develop their thoughts.

Objectives for Students

- Demonstrate the meaning of social identity verbally and in a written form
- Identify in the text where social identity is influenced by society
- Identify how social identity of the text connects with them as individual
- Determine why is important to know one's social identity and how it fits in a global society
- Be able to write a well-constructed essay with textual support of what the role of the black man has been in society and how that has contributed to his social identity with support from the text

College Readiness Standards (www.act.org/standard)

- Identify the basic purpose or role of a specified phrase or sentence
- Determine relevance when presented with a variety of sentence-level details
- Identify the central idea or main topic of a straightforward piece of writing
- Identify a clear main idea or purpose of any paragraph or paragraphs in uncomplicated passages
- Discern which details, though they may appear in different sections throughout a passage, support important points in more challenging passages
- Use context to understand basic figurative language
- Draw simple generalizations and conclusions about people, ideas, and so on in uncomplicated passages
- Maintain a focus on the general topic in the prompt throughout the essay
- Provide an adequate but simple organization with logical grouping of ideas in parts of the essay but with little evidence of logical progression of ideas

General In-Class Activities

- Gallery walks
- K-W-L sheets
- Popcorn reading
- Sustained silent reading (SSR)
- Group activities
- Post-reading activities

Formative Assessment Description (Checking for Understanding)

- Worksheets
- Do-nows

- Class participation during reading and Q&A
- Graphic organizers
- Reciprocal teaching
- TPS (think-pair-share)
- Exit slips

Common Assessment Description (Summative Assessment)

Students will choose from three prompts and construct a well-written five-paragraph essay answering one of the following questions:

- In a well-written five-paragraph essay, use *one* of the two quotes listed below from Marcus Garvey's "Man Know Thy Self" and connect their meaning to the story of *Invisible Man.* (Synthesis Essay)

   "For man to know himself is for him to feel that for him there is no human master. For him Nature is his servant, and whatsoever he wills in Nature, that shall be his reward. If he wills to be a pigmy, a serf or a slave, that shall he be. If he wills to be a real man in possession of the things common to man, then he shall be his own sovereign."

   OR

   "When man fails to grasp his authority he sinks to the level of the lower animals, and whatsoever the real man bids him do, even as if it were of the lower animals, that much shall he do. If he says 'go.' He goes. If he says 'come,' he comes. By this command he performs the functions of life even as by a similar command the mule, the horse, the cow performs the will of their masters."

- In a well-written five-paragraph essay, explore the three strategies that Dr. King told his followers needed to be intact in order to redefine the social identity of the black person in America. (Analytical Essay)
- Carefully explore the image at www.afscme.org/about/1029.cfm and in a well-written five-paragraph essay, describe three ways the photo captures the social identity of the garbage workers. (Visual Essay)

The students use a graphic organizer to plan their essay and DiSheen developed a rubric as an assessment tool for this assignment (see Forms A.1 and A.2).

Essay Graphic Organizer

Date _____   Period _____

Main Idea and Supporting Details Organizer

Name _____

Place Main Idea Here

Supporting Detail 1   Supporting Detail 2

Essay Rubric

Name _____ Date scored _____

	High (3 points)	Medium (2 points)	Low (1 points)	Rock Bottom (0 points)
Answering the prompt	The prompt is answered completely	The prompt is partially answered	The prompt is restated but not answered	There is no direct mention of the prompt
Clarity of the thesis statement	The thesis statement is clearly identified in the introduction	The thesis statement is identified but is not placed in the introduction	The thesis statement is unclear and lacks the author's position	There is no thesis
Making claims	At least three claims are made concerning the question	Two claims have been made concerning the question	Only one claim has been made concerning the question	There are no identifiable claims made by the author
Textual support	Textual evidence is used to support each claim	Textual evidence is used to support two of the claims	Textual evidence is used to support one claim	No textual evidence is used to support claims
Physical organization	Essay is physically organized into 5 paragraphs	NA	NA	NA
TOTALS				

Score (15) _____ /15

Calendar Unit Overview

DiSheen created a brief calendar that outlined the activities and content that she would cover each day in class:

	Day 1	Day 2	Day 3	Day 4	Day 5
Week 1	"We Wear the Mask"—Dunbar	"The Mask That I Wear" design activity and What is Social Identity?	Who is Ralph Ellison? How do I annotate?	*Invisible Man*, Prologue—Ellison	*Invisible Man*, Prologue—Ellison
Week 2	"Invisible Man" Prologue—Ellison	*Invisible Man*, Chapter One—Ellison	*Invisible Man*, Chapter One—Ellison	Civil rights gallery walk and American Federation of State, County and Municipal Employees (AFSCME) video with viewing guide	"Mountain-top"—MLK
Week 3	"Mountain-top"—MLK	"Mountain-top"—MLK	Do you know yourself? What do you know about yourself? Gallery walk	K-W-L Marcus Garvey and the 1920s	"Man Know Thyself"—Marcus Garvey
Week 4	"Ain't I a Woman"—S. Truth "Ain't I a Woman" student poem	"Nikki-Rosa" and "Ego Trippin"—Nikki Giovanni	Review and linking my identity to the poem's depiction of identity. Mini review of main idea and supporting details	Review and preparation for essay exam	Essay exam

In-Class Activities

DiSheen gives the students an outline of in-class activities so that her expectations are clear. You might want to consider doing this when you begin a major unit. On the first day of the unit, she hands the students the following "In-Class Expectations" sheet:

Welcome to Ms. Smith's African American Literature Class

Explanation of in-class activities

Do now is an opening activator to get the students thinking about the topic or issue at hand.

Group biography exercise: Each student will be given a fact about the author to research. Students will get into groups of 3 to 4 and use their facts to create a mini-biography within their groups. Facts will be diverse, and students will have to be creative to make them interesting and fun. Then as a class, students will share their group biographies and use those to compile a class biography to be displayed in the class during the unit.

VIPs: Very Important Points. Students select a minimum of three (or a specified number) points in the text that they think are very important to the main idea of the text. After everyone has selected points, we share the points out loud as a class. Students will use thumbs-up/thumbs-down voting to say if they agree or disagree that point should be considered as a main point. Students should be able to verbally explain the use of textual support to defend their claim. As a class, we compile a list on chart paper and keep it posted in the class during the remainder of the unit.

Design the Mask: Students are to design the mask based on part of their identity that they have to hide. Students are to describe what the mask represents and place the explanation on a sticky note. Mask will be displayed in the class.

Annotation: Students will use exclamation marks next to text that they feel is an interesting statement. Students will use question marks for text they do not understand or to represent questioning of the author's thoughts. Students will use check marks to represent that they already were familiar with the issue or idea or that they understand what the author is trying to say. Next to each annotation, there needs to be some type of explanation or question mark next to the symbol or text. Explanation of the text can be done three ways: students talking to the text, students talking to the author, and students talking to themselves (respectively, t/t, t/a, and t/s). Students will also highlight any text or write notes on anything the teacher or class may deem as important.

Class discussions: Used as verbal forums for students to express their opinions and gain clarity about text, issues, ideas, philosophies, and any other academic-based information. Students are expected to participate, and participation will be factored into their class participation grade.

Journal reflections: Students will be given questions and asked to reflect on them. They will need to bring journals to class to use for discussions; journals will be submitted on the final day of the unit. Students will be graded based on a rubric. Journal entries, unless specified, are reviewed for content, mechanics, and elaboration. However, if a student shows too much deficiency in grammar, that will be handled on a case-by-case basis.

Exit slips: Used as a tool to check for understanding. They will be weighted in the class assignment and class participation category.

During the second week of the unit, DiSheen showed a documentary about the AFSME strike in Memphis, Tennessee, in 1968. She created for her students the viewing guide in Form A.3.

AFSCME Viewing Guide

Name _____

Directions: As you watch the videos about the AFSCME strike, answer the following questions. Answers should appear in chronological order.

1. Why were the garbage workers striking?
2. What does the acronym AFSCME stand for?
3. Where did the strike take place?
4. What three groups forged together to fight for the garbage workers?
5. What were the "struggles" of the garbage workers?
6. Why did Rev. James Larson ask Dr. Martin Luther King to come to support the strike? (Hint identity)
7. What was the most important thing to the garbage workers?
8. What did you learn from this video, and why is it important?

During the second week of this unit, DiSheen has her students participate in a gallery walk. In this activity, the students examine pictures that are posted in the classroom. As the students consider each picture, they complete Form A.4, a graphic organizer.

Gallery Walk Questionnaire

Name _____ Date _____ Period _____

Directions: As you walk around the class, please think about the photos that you will be viewing. Answer each question for EACH photo. Your questionnaire MUST BE COMPLETE by the end of the allotted time period.

	Have you seen the photo before? If so, where (e.g., the Internet, history class)?	When you look at this photo, how do you feel (e.g., mad, sad, happy)?	Where do you think this photo was taken (e.g., Paris, Chicago, Egypt)?	What do you think is going on socially in society (e.g., woman's movement, civil rights, voting rights)?	What is happening in the picture? (e.g., a riot, a party, a speech)?
Photo 1					
Photo 2					
Photo 3					
Photo 4					
Photo 5					
Photo 6					

DISCOVERING MY IDENTITY

The following unit, developed by Lauren Stanczak, focuses on students' discovering their identity through memoirs. The thematic focus employs two essential questions: How does our past affect our identity? How is our identity shaped by our experiences?

Description of the Unit

This two-week unit focuses on finding identity through memoir and discovering who we are and where we are from. As a young adult, there's nothing more important than finding those answers. The unit comprises a series of formative assessments designed to help students complete their cumulative assessment: writing a personal memoir. Essentially the "Where I'm From" poems, photo essays, interview, submission, and Learning to Love You More (LTLYM) assignment are a form of scaffolding. However, the biggest activity in this unit is the introduction to thematic literature circles, in which the students participate in two rounds. The introduction and practice of literature circles is meant to improve reading comprehension, reinforce student-centered learning, and create a community of readers within the classroom. The process of self-exploration in this unit will help build a safe and intellectually curious classroom community in which students learn to value themselves and each other.

At the beginning of the unit, students will receive a schedule with assignment deadlines and the rubric for the cumulative assessment. The students are expected to participate in classroom activities, use time management effectively to complete the unit portfolio, and treat each other with respect.

Unit Schedule

These teaching and learning strategies are used in the following unit:

- Foldables are three-dimensional graphic organizers. For information about creating foldables for your classroom go to http://foldables.wikispaces.com.
- To create a photo essay carousel, each group of three to four students is given a sheet of poster paper with a different picture. Give the students thirty seconds to write down any ideas, comments, or reactions that they have to the picture. Each group should have a different color marker. When the time is up, the students will pass their poster paper to the next group. Repeat the opportunity for students to respond to the picture in thirty seconds. This process is repeated until all of the groups have responded to each poster paper/picture. (See http://readingquest.org/strat/carousel.html for carousel templates and resources.)

	Monday	Tuesday	Wednesday	Thursday	Friday
Week 1	Introduce memoir with Foldables	Interview techniques and questions Introduce photo essays	Photo essay carousel Close reading of *Mango Street* vignettes	Introduce literary circles with teacher modeling Choose texts	Literary circles with insert notes and role sheets Self-evaluation and debriefing
Week 2	Literary Circle book talk New literary circle groups SSR	Learning to Love You More assignment Computer lab and camera workstations	Literary circles and found poetry Debriefing	Field trip to Harold Washington Library's Teen Center Round robin	Share Learning to Love You More (LTLYM) assignments Reflection Book talk Submit portfolio

FOCUS ON POETRY AND THE PERSONAL MEMOIR

Jessa Resiner is a passionate teacher who integrates contemporary poetic words and creative writing assignments in her unit. This four-week unit addresses the following essential questions: What kind of world is this? How do we understand ourselves and our place in the world?

Description of Unit

This unit aims at exploring identity and how identity is shaped by the world around us. By defining self through memoir poems and exploring the concept of the world through poetry, students will be able to compare and contrast themselves to the world around them. They will be able to understand and analyze their existence within the context of the world. The two elements of this essential question relate to the college readiness standards of the main idea built off supporting details and comparing relationships through an examination of supporting details.

Essential Unit Questions

- *Essential questions:* What kind of world is this? How do we understand ourselves and our place in the world?

- *Essential concepts:* Curiosity versus inquiry; vulnerability versus resilience; reliability versus treachery; metacognition versus naiveté

Objectives for Students

By the end of this unit, students will be able to:

- Define figurative language including simile, metaphor, rhyme scheme, rhythm, onomatopoeia, and personification.
- Identify figurative language in poetry.
- Analyze figurative language's effect on poetry.
- Apply and use figurative language in their own poetry.
- Identify and define the main idea using supporting details in poetry.
- Compare/contrast poems and their use of figurative language.
- Compare/contrast main idea of poems.

College Readiness Standards Covered in This Unit (www.act.org/standard)

- English skills

  - Word choice in terms of style, tone, and economy
  - Sentence structure and formation
  - Organization, unity, and coherence
  - Topic development in terms of purpose and focus
  - Word choice in terms of style, tone, clarity, and economy
  - Sentence structure and formation
  - Conventions of usage
  - Conventions of punctuation

- Writing skills

  - Using language
  - Organizing ideas
  - Developing a position
  - Using language

- Reading skills

  - Meaning of words
  - Supporting detail
  - Sequential, comparative, and cause-effect relationships
  - Meaning of words
  - Generalization and conclusions

- General in-class activities/strategies per subject area

Throughout this unit, every day is designed to have elements of constructivism and teacher-centered and student-centered activities. Each day aims to include many different learning modalities—most frequently hearing, writing, discussing, and kinesthetic activities. Each day aims to have the structure of "I do, we do, you do." Throughout the unit, I will scaffold to enable students to have the majority of the class focused on their practice. Also, every day students will read poetry and write. I want students to experience poetry through their own creation, through fun, and through the canon. Two main components of every day will be:

Discussion
- Class discussion on the themes and messages of the work
- Discussions on figurative language and the effect on the work

Journals
- Student journals will be focused on writing their own poetry applying figurative language.
- Student journals will be focused on brainstorming definitions of figurative language.

Formative Assessment Descriptions (Checking for Understanding)

- *Journals:* Journals will be collected weekly.
- *Annotations:* Annotations will be collected as poems are completed to check for application of annotation routine and for depth of thought.
- *Final Paper:* "Writing Your Memoir Through Poetry." Students will need to write a final paper in poetry. They will need to define their story through poems. See Form A.5.
- *Poetry review portfolio:* Students will complete poetry portfolio in groups to demonstrate their understanding of figurative language in poetry.
- *RAFT:* To check for understanding of poetry book students are reading.
- *Discussions and class participation:* Using students' comments and active participation as a gauge for how well they understand the text and the reading skills. Also, this gives me ways to make sure that they are in fact reading.
- *Reading quizzes:* Short reading quizzes as needed.
- Reading guides to be completed as needed to check for reading.

Writing Your Memoir

The story of your life is not your life. It is your story. —John Barth

Throughout the next week, we will be working on writing our own memoir through poetry.

A memoir is a narrative composed of personal experiences. A memoir is made up of noteworthy life stories. So, your job will be to pick important events that have affected your development as a person. Think about how you got to be who you are today. Think about how where you've been will affect where you're going in the future.

In at least five poems, you must examine where you have come from, where you are now, and where you are going in the future.

These five poems must follow the plot pyramid. You will need to compose a poem that represents EXPOSITION, RISING ACTION, CLIMAX, FALLING ACTION, and RESOLUTION. Using a plot diagram can be helpful as you plan your poems.

Of these five poems, three need to be based on poems written during class (for DO NOWS or group work).

What should your poems be about? How do you go about choosing noteworthy moments?

· Think about big moments in your life.
· Think about emotional points in your life.
· Think about turning points.
· Think about important decisions.

As you write . . .

Remember that poetry doesn't need to have a regular rhythm, line length, or rhyme scheme. Poetry can rely on the natural rhythms of speech. So, use your speech, your language, while keeping every poem school appropriate!

Remember that a good poem begins on the inside, in the middle of the action. So, try to start all of your poems inside an experience, feeling, observation, or memory.

Remember that poetry can invent and follow its own form, pattern, and rules. So, be creative!

Remember that breaks in lines emphasize to the reader moments to pause. So, make sure you're giving your reader clues about what's important!

Remember to conclude strongly! The conclusion of a poem should resonate with the reader after he or she has finished. The ending of every poem should leave a reader with a feeling, idea, image, or question. So, play around with your ending to find one that works!

Remember that this is your story—these are your first-person experiences to make sure your *I* is present and is thinking, feeling, seeing, and acting.

And most important, find your voice as a poet and as a writer!

Checklist:

Make sure you have each of the items listed below before turning in your assignment

· One poem representing exposition
· One poem representing rising action
· One poem representing climax
· One poem representing falling action
· One poem representing resolution
· Three poems based on do nows or group work
· Two examples of revisions

INTRODUCING SHAKESPEARE: *ROMEO AND JULIET* GRAPHIC NOVEL

Pearl Park created this thematic unit, "Crimes of Passion," with *Romeo and Juliet* as the core work. She explains that her unit is an introduction to Shakespeare using the graphic novel *Romeo and Juliet* to introduce students to the power of images and to the tragedy of the play. Students will learn about graphic terminology and how the images are portrayed to reveal or emphasize certain aspects of a story. The students will explore crimes committed out of passion and will also consider ethical dilemmas in relation to the text and their own lives. The students will engage in meaningful debates and discussions regarding moral dilemmas. As a culminating project, the students will design their own graphic scene in cooperative groups. This will be presented and shared with the class.

This unit addresses the following essential questions:

- Can all crimes of passion result in tragedy?
- What makes an event tragic?
- How do images, such as those in a graphic novel, influence the story?

Student Objectives

Students will understand:

- How the portrayal of graphic images emphasizes certain ideas of a story
- The different ethical dilemmas in *Romeo and Juliet* and in articles
- What constitutes a tragedy
- What constitutes a crime of passion

Key Knowledge and Skills Students Will Acquire as a Result of This Unit

Students will know:

Key terms: *tragedy, ethical dilemma, crime, passion,* and graphic terminology
What components are necessary to make up a tragedy and a crime of passion

Students will be able to:

Analyze graphic images in order to understand what they represent
Express opinions in regard to controversial issues regarding moral dilemmas

TWENTY ASSESSMENT SUGGESTIONS

Traditional assessments like quizzes, tests, and some kinds of essays heavily rely on a student's ability to memorize, recall, and record information. Twenty-first-century learners need to be able to analyze and synthesize the huge quantities of information that are available at our fingertips. As a result, how we grade students can be challenging at times. Learning some tools and strategies for evaluating students and their mastery of skills and knowledge can help diminish some of our anxiety.

Education assessment is the process for documenting students' knowledge and skills. Assessment is usually separated into formative and summative. Summative assessment is generally conducted at the end of a unit of study: large unit tests, final projects, or more comprehensive writing assignments like essays or research papers, for example. Formative assessments are generally shorter and administered during the course of study. These are learning aids that help teachers determine how students are performing on a particular skill—for example, quizzes, exit slips, or beginning-of-class activities. It is important that all assessments, formative and summative, are reliable and valid. This means that the assessments consistently and accurately measure the intended learning outcomes. The following activities can be used as formative assessments for your students. They are effective alternatives to quizzes and tests.

1. *Reader's theater.* From an assigned text, have students create a script and perform it. Use a rubric to evaluate the script and performance.
2. *Story trail.* Instead of giving students a pop reading quiz to determine if they completed the reading assignment, have the students create a story board. Give the students a story board graphic organizer with four to six events. Make sure that they explain why they chose the event rather than summarize the event.

3. *Text time line.* To support students' understanding of the major events of a text, have the students create a time line for the major events in the text.
4. *Graphic organizers.* The students visually depict what they know and understand—for example, about vocabulary and texts.
5. *Exit slips.* The teacher poses a question at the end of the lesson, and the students write a response for three to five minutes on an index card. As the students leave the class, they turn in the exit slips. Some effective exit slip prompts are, "What did you learn, and why is it important?" and "What do you think will happen next in the story?"
6. *Gist.* A content literacy strategy in which the students summarize a lesson or text in exactly twenty-one words.
7. *RAFT.* A writing activity that is especially effective for students to understand and articulate a specific point of view or empathy:

   R = Role of the writer. Who are you as the writer? Are you Benjamin Franklin or Abigail Adams?
   A = Audience. Who are you writing this for? Congress? Other patriots?
   F = Form. Your writing could be an essay, letter, poem, song, or something else.
   T = Topic. What are you writing about? Maybe you are explaining the role of women in the newly created United States or about the challenges of the American Revolution.

8. *Questioning the author.* Have students imagine that they are able to ask questions of the author. The strategy is designed to move students beyond simple recall to higher levels of comprehension and understanding by making inferences, analyzing, and responding on a more personal level. The basic format uses these five questions:

   - What do you think the author wants to tell you?
   - Why is the author telling the reader this message?
   - Is the author stating the message clearly?
   - How could the author articulate the message more clearly?
   - What message would you have said?

9. *Vocabulary slides.* Have students create index cards for each vocabulary word like the sample shown in Figure B.1.
10. *Cornell notes.* Instead of a pop reading quiz, have the students create a two-column organizer with the following headings: on the left, "Questions/Key Points," and on the right, "Notes/Details." As the students read, they should record the most important information and questions in the left-hand column and the most important information and details in the right-hand column.
11. *Webquest.* Students research topics online in an Internet-based scavenger hunt.
12. *3–2–1.* Students list three things they have learned, two interesting things, and one question that they still have.
13. *Compare/contrast chart.* In a two-column organizer, students list the similarities and differences between two concepts.

Name: _____

Date: _____

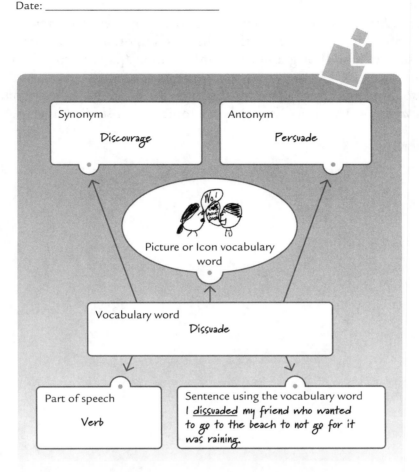

FIGURE B.1 Sample Vocabulary Slide

Source: Adapted from *The Teacher's Big Book of Graphic Organizers,* Katherine McKnight, ©
2010 by John Wiley & Sons, Inc. Reprinted with permission of John Wiley & Sons, Inc.

14. *Graphic organizers.* Organizers that require students to summarize are important tools
for learning. They prompt students to demonstrate what they know and understand
and how to synthesize and generalize this information.

15. *Question generator.* Students bring questions to class discussions. In this way, they
demonstrate what they already comprehend and extend their understanding.

16. *Reading and learning logs.* Students record and document what they are learning and what it means.
17. *Bio poem.* Students create a biographical poem for a key character.
18. *Posters.* Students create posters that illustrate important literary concepts (plot, character, theme, mood) or grammatical information (parts of speech, active and passive voice).
19. *Podcasts.* Students create a podcast that presents research that they conducted.
20. *Create a movie.* The movie is based on a topic or text studied in class.

STRATEGIES *for* DIFFERENTIATED INSTRUCTION

Differentiated instruction is rooted in the belief that one size does not fit all. Students have a wide variety of needs and abilities, and we teachers need to create environments in which all students can master and demonstrate a wide variety of skills and content. Here are strategies to do just that:

1. *Use all modalities for learning:* kinesthetic, auditory, visual, social-emotional, musical, dramatic, spatial, and others.
2. *Graphic organizers.* Use these learning tools to support students' organization of ideas and to personally connect information. Students learn better in pictures and graphic organizers are visual representations of information.
3. *Choice board.* Give students a variety of activities and assessments so they can practice new skills, develop new knowledge, and demonstrate what they have mastered and learned.
4. *Curriculum compression.* Depth is far better than breadth. Decide what the most important content is in a curriculum, and prune what remains.
5. *Flexible grouping.* Change student groups on a regular basis. Students benefit from working with a wide variety of learners.
6. *Learning centers.* Create opportunities for students to develop and practice their skills. Learning centers are important for adolescent learners because they give these young people the opportunity to physically move around the classroom, which helps maintain their focus and attention.
7. *Tiered activities.* Students can demonstrate different levels of mastery in tiered activities. These are designed to engage students at different levels of mastery, which will eventually lead to overall mastery among the students.

8. *Mastery learning.* Instead of a percentage or letter grades, create rubrics that indicate mastery of specific skills. Provide students with the opportunity to increase their mastery to acceptable and exemplary levels. Remember that assessments are learning tools, not punishments.

9. *Be a diagnostician.* The most effective teachers figure out the abilities of their students and then teach accordingly. In the first week of school, conduct a reading and writing diagnostic. Many schools already conduct diagnostic testing at the beginning of the school year. If yours does not, look up reading fluency snapshots. Reading fluency snapshots prompt students to read a passage and respond to questions that increase in difficulty. Briefly, the more questions that the student is able to answer, the higher the level of fluency. For writing, have the students write on a given topic, and create a rubric of skills that the students should have mastered at a given grade level.

10. *Highlighters and sticky notes.* Let students use highlighters on handouts and books (when possible) to identify key phrases and vocabulary. Give them sticky notes to jot down their questions, comments, and insights as they read an assigned text.

11. *Large print.* Allow struggling readers to use large print versions of the assigned textbook. Most publishing companies provide large print versions of texts.

12. *Audio.* Let struggling readers listen to the text. Listening while reading the text helps students with comprehension. Most textbooks have an audio version, and nearly every novel has an audio version.

13. *Rip up the textbook.* Often the textbook is too visually stimulating. Tear out sections of the book, and turn them into smaller chapter books. This helps struggling readers who are feeling overwhelmed by a huge textbook.

14. *Graphic novels.* If there are graphic novel versions of the texts that you plan to assign in class, use them.

15. *Readability.* Check the reading levels of the texts that you assign, and make sure that you are using different texts at different reading levels.

16. *Plastic sheets.* Let students use clear plastic sheets over the textbook so they can make markings that will help them to understand the text.

17. *Glossary.* Photocopy the glossary of the textbook and turn the pages into mini-books for an easy reference for struggling readers.

18. *Color plastic sheets.* Many students with visual processing disorders or dyslexia benefit from color overlays for reading material.

19. *Use yellow paper.* It is less visually jarring than white paper.

20. *Think-pair-share.* Students need time to think. When you pose a question, give the students the opportunity to turn to a neighbor and discuss it.

21. *Students asking the questions.* Traditionally teachers, not students, pose the questions. Model how to create effective questions, and turn the task over to the students. You will be surprised and pleased to discover that the students' questions are most frequently like yours, and they often pose questions that you may have never considered.

22. *Mini-lessons.* Use mini-lessons, each never more than ten minutes, to teach grammar, vocabulary, literary elements, and reading strategies.

23. *Interest.* Group students by interest rather than ability level. Studying and learning about what interests us is highly motivating.

24. *Posing big questions.* Have students create and develop their own big question, and then allow them to explore, research, and write about it.

25. *Community and service projects.* Get students out of the classroom and into their community. Have them develop community and service projects based on what they have learned in the classroom. For example, after studying *Romeo and Juliet*, ninth-grade students interviewed residents of a retirement home about love. The culminating activity was a jointly planned Valentine's Day party, where the students gave their new friends a book that they created from the interviews. The book was the students' written version of the love stories that the retirement home residents had shared.

26. *Reflection.* Giving students the opportunity to reflect on their learning helps them remember and retain information.

27. *Extension projects.* For major projects, give students the opportunity to do extra assignments or more challenging ones.

28. *Revise and redo.* Give students the opportunity to revise their work. They will learn from revision and will be more likely to master the skills that they are learning.

29. *Portfolios.* Demonstrating growth in developing knowledge and skills is the most valuable assessment. Portfolios that showcase students' best works is empowering for learners.

Here are some good sources on differentiated instruction:

Bender, B. (2002). *Differentiating instruction for students with learning disabilities.* Thousand Oaks, CA: Corwin Press.

D'Amico, J., and Gallaway, K. (2009). *Differentiated instruction for the middle school language arts teachers: Activities and strategies for an inclusive classroom.* San Francisco: Jossey-Bass.

Fattig, M., and Taylor, M. T. (2007). *Co-Teaching in the differentiated classroom: Successful collaboration, lesson design, and classroom management, grades 5–12.* San Francisco: Jossey-Bass.

Fisher, D., and Frey, N. (2007). *Checking for understanding.* Alexandria, VA: Association for Supervision and Curriculum Development.

Fogarty, R., & Stoehr, J. (2008). *Integrating curricula with multiple intelligences: Teams, themes, and threads.* Thousand Oaks, CA: Corwin Press.

Forsten, C., Grant, J., and Hollas, B. (2003). *Differentiating textbooks.* Peterborough, NH: Crystal Springs Books.

Gardner, H. (2006). *Multiple intelligences.* New York: Basic Books.

Gurian, M. (2002). *Boys and girls learn differently! A guide for parents and teachers.* San Francisco: Jossey-Bass.

Gurian, M., Stevens, K., and King, K. (2008). *Strategies for teaching boys and girls: A workbook for educators.* San Francisco: Jossey-Bass.

Heacox, D. (2002). *Making differentiation a habit: How to ensure success in academically diverse classrooms.* Minneapolis: Free Spirit.

Heacox, D. (2002). *Differentiating instruction in the regular classroom: How to reach and teach all learners.* Minneapolis: Free Spirit.

Hollas, B. (2007). *Differentiating instruction in a whole-group setting.* Peterborough, NH: Crystal Springs Books.

Jensen, E. (2005). *Teaching with the brain in mind* (2nd ed). Alexandria, VA: Association for Supervision and Curriculum Development.

Marzano, R. (2006). *Classroom assessment and grading that work.* Alexandria, VA: Association for Supervision and Curriculum Development.

Sousa, D. (2001). *How the brain learns.* Thousand Oaks, CA: Corwin Press.

Tomlinson, C., and McTighe, J. (2006). *Integrating differentiated instruction and understanding by design.* Alexandria, VA: Association for Supervision and Curriculum Development.

Tomlinson, D. (2003). *Differentiation in practice.* Alexandria, VA: Association for Supervision and Curriculum Development.

Tomlinson, D. (2003). *Fulfilling the promise of the differentiated classroom.* Alexandria, VA: Association for Supervision and Curriculum Development.

Tomlinson, D. (2001). *How to differentiate in mixed ability classrooms.* Alexandria, VA: Association for Supervision and Curriculum Development.

Wormelli, R. (2006). *Fair isn't always equal.* Portland, ME: Stenhouse Publishers.

YOUNG ADULT LITERATURE TITLES

The popular young adult novels listed in this appendix come from teacher suggestions.

Author	Title	Age Range	Brief Synopsis
Abouet, M.	*Aya*	14–16	The title character lives on the Ivory Coast of Africa in the late 1970s, prior to the civil war that decimated the country.
Alexie, S.	*The Absolutely True Diary of a Part-Time Indian*	14–16	Junior deals with prejudice from those in his new white high school and from those he left behind on the reservation.

(continued)

(Continued)

Author	Title	Age Range	Brief Synopsis
Beah, I.	*A Long Way Gone: Memoirs of a Boy Soldier*	16–18	When civil war comes to the author's country, Sierra Leone, he learns to survive as a twelve year old in this dangerous world. This was originally published as an adult novel and contains violence, but it is taught in high schools because the story is a powerful one about overcoming tremendous obstacles.
Beals, M.	*Warriors Don't Cry*	12–14	The story of the African American teenagers who attended Little Rock High School in 1957.
Black, H.	*Valiant: A Modern Tale of Faerie*	14–16	Valerie learns that her new friends in New York use "faerie glamour" to get what they want and are suddenly missing and turning up dead.
Blundell, J.	*What I Saw and How I Lied*	14–16	This National Book Award novel blends mystery and historical fiction to tell the story of Eve. A teenager vacationing with her parents in Palm Beach after World War II observes them making unusual business deals.
Brashares, A.	*The Sisterhood of the Traveling Pants*	14–16	The first of a four-book series that tells the story of four friends who share a pair of magical jeans over the summer.

Author	Title	Age Range	Brief Synopsis
Bryson, B.	*Shakespeare: The World as Stage*	16–18	A witty exploration of Shakespeare's work and life.
Collins, S.	The Hunger Games trilogy	14–16	In this dystopian fantasy, two teenagers representing each district must fight until only one is left standing.
Curtis, C. P.	*The Watsons Go to Birmingham*	9–12	A Flint, Michigan, family goes on a road trip to the South during the volatile summer of 1963.
D'Orso, M.	*Eagle Blue*	14–16	Told through the eyes of the high school basketball team, this true story explores the small village of Fort Yukon, Alaska, and the struggle to maintain its culture and heritage.
Follett, K.	*Pillars of the Earth*	16–18	An epic tale about power and class that takes place in twelfth-century England.
Fleischman, S.	*Escape: The Story of the Great Houdini*	9–12	The story of the great magician Harry Houdini.
Gaiman, N.	*Stardust*	16–18	A contemporary fairy tale that features two young lovers.
Green, J.	*Looking for Alaska*	14–16	This Printz Award–winning novel follows the life of Miles in his first year at an elite Alabama boarding school.

(continued)

(Continued)

Author	Title	Age Range	Brief Synopsis
Gruen, S.	*Water for Elephants*	15–18	Tells the story of the challenging circus life.
Guerrero, E., and Krugman, M.	*Cheating Death, Stealing Life: The Eddie Guerrero Story*	16–18	The life of the famed WWF wrestler Eddie Guerrero is told.
Haddon, M.	*The Curious Incident of the Dog in the Night-Time*	16–18	Christopher, who has Asperger's syndrome, sets out to solve two mysteries: who killed a dog and what happened to his mother.
Hanssen, J.	*Freedom Roads: Searching for the Underground Railroad*	12–14	Chronicles the historian's quest to document and understand the struggle for freedom through the Underground Railroad.
Hesse, K.	*A Light in the Storm: The Civil War Diary of Amelia Martin*	12–14	A fictional diary kept by a lighthouse keeper's daughter on Fenwick Island, Delaware, during the Civil War.
Hidier, T. D.	*Born Confused*	14–16	Dimple is trying to assimilate as an Indian American girl until she meets a boy who exposes her to the charms of their Indian heritage.
Hosseini, K.	*The Kite Runner*	16–18	Amir flees Afghanistan and then returns to his native land as an American citizen and attempts to atone for the betrayal of his best friend before he fled.

Author	Title	Age Range	Brief Synopsis
Kidd, S. M.	*The Secret Life of Bees*	16–18	As she searches for the truth about her mother's death, Lily finds answers, love, and acceptance from the Boatwright sisters.
Kodahata, C.	*Kira-Kira*	12–14	In this Newbery-winning book, two Japanese American sisters grow up in post–World War II America.
Lee, M.	*Necessary Roughness*	12–14	Korean-American teens move from Los Angeles to an all-white town in Minnesota. Their new life prompts them to examine their identity.
Laiz, J.	*Weeping Under This Same Moon*	14–16	Based on a true story about a teen, Hannah, who learns about the plight of the Vietnamese boat people and helps them.
Martin, S	*Born Standing Up*	16–18	Steve Martin's autobiography about his life as a comedian.
McCaffrey, A.	Dragonriders of Pern trilogy	14–16	Famous trilogy of dragon tales.
McCarthy, C.	*The Road*	16–18	A father and son embark on a dangerous journey to the sea after an apocalyptic catastrophe.
McCormick, P.	*Sold*	14–16	Lakshmi manages to escape a brothel in the Calcutta slums.

(continued)

(Continued)

Author	Title	Age Range	Brief Synopsis
Medley, L.	*Castle Waiting*	16–18	The author takes traditional fairy tales and creates new fantasy stories in a graphic novel version.
Mortenson, G., and Relin, D. O.	*Three Cups of Tea: One Man's Mission to Promote Peace One School at a Time*	16–18	Mortenson vows to build schools throughout Pakistan and Afghanistan when the people of a mountain village shelter and nurse him back to health after his failed attempt to climb K2.
Myers, W. D.	*Monster*	16–18	Written in a screenplay format, this is an award-winning story of a young African American man caught up in a robbery.
Myers, W. D.	*Sunrise over Fallujah*	16–18	Told through the eyes of Robin, a young soldier who believes in his country and volunteers to fight in the Iraq war. He soon realizes when he is in the war zone that fighting for freedom is not always clearly defined.
Na, A.	*A Step from Heaven*	14–16	Winner of the Printz Award for Excellence in Young Adult Literature in 2002, this novel chronicles the life of Young Yu, who at the age of four boards a plane from Korea to California.

Author	Title	Age Range	Brief Synopsis
Nelson, M.	*A Wreath for Emmett Till*	14–16	Emmett Till's story is told through a series of sonnets.
Philbrick, R.	*Freak the Mighty*	9–12	This classic novel about opposites who become friends has been taught in many middle school classrooms.
Pratchett, T.	*Wee Free Men*	12–14	A fantasy adventure where the nine-year-old protagonist, Tiffany, is destined to be a witch.
Roberts, G., and Klibanoff, H.	*The Race Beat: The Press, the Civil Rights Struggle, and the Awakening of a Nation*	16–18	The story of the reporters and photographers, both black and white, and their tenacious reporting about the civil rights movement.
Roth, P.	*The Plot Against America*	16–18	An alternate look at a great American hero, Charles Lindbergh, in which the author demonstrates how bigotry and fear can shape politics.
Sacco, J.	*Safe Area Gorazde: War in Eastern Bosnia, 1992–1995*	16–18	A graphic novel that chronicles the Bosnian war.
Salisbury, G.	*Eyes of the Emperor*	14–16	Historical novel about Japanese American soldiers that takes place during World War II in Hawaii.

(continued)

(Continued)

Author	Title	Age Range	Brief Synopsis
Stead, R.	*When You Reach Me*	9–12	A Newbery Award winner that tells the poignant story of Miranda as she navigates a world turned upside down by family events.
Strickland, C.	*The Annotated Mona Lisa*	16–18	This book provides a basic knowledge of art through photographs with annotations.
Satrapi, M.	*Persepolis: The Story of a Childhood*	14–16	This well-known autobiographical graphic novel tells the author's story of growing up in Iran before and after the 1979 revolution.
Smith, J.	*Bone*	12–14	This graphic novel fantasy is the first of thirteen volumes. The Bone cousins are on a quest in a valley that reminds many readers of a more humorous and comic version of *The Lord of the Rings*.
Soto, G.	*Buried Onions*	14–16	Young Eddie tries to stay out of trouble and gang life.
Spiegelman, A.	*The Complete Maus: A Survivor's Tale*	16–18	This famous graphic novel tells the author's story of his struggle to come to terms with his parents' brutal past at Auschwitz.

Author	Title	Age Range	Brief Synopsis
Tan, A.	*The Joy Luck Club*	16–18	A well-known novel that tells the stories of four Chinese American families as they establish their lives in America.
Tang, G.	*American Born Chinese*	9–12	A popular graphic novel that tells the story of a young boy who was not comfortable with his vulture or himself.
Thompson, C.	*Blankets*	16–18	This autobiographical novel chronicles the experiences of a young man during his first love.
Williams, D.	*Bitterly Divided: The South's Inner Civil War*	16–18	The Civil War is often characterized as "a rich man's war and a poor man's fight." This novel looks at the divisions of social class and political division in the South.
Ung, L.	*First They Killed My Father: A Daughter of Cambodia Remembers*	16–18	The autobiographical story of a woman who is a fugitive of the brutal Pol Pot regime.
Urrea, L. A.	*The Devil's Highway*	16–18	Every year thousands of undocumented immigrants venture across the dangerous desert that surrounds the U.S.-Mexican border. Many die during the journey. Urrea tells the story of illegal immigration with statistics, poetry, and stories.

(continued)

(Continued)

Author	Title	Age Range	Brief Synopsis
Zelazny, F.	*The Great Book of Amber*	16–18	The ten-book Amber Chronicles are collected in this one volume. The stories are about Corwin and then his son, Merlin, and their life on Earth and in Amber. This series is regarded as one of the best fantasy collections.
Zusak, M.	*The Book Thief*	16–18	In this story narrated by Death, Liesel and her family choose to lie and steal to protect a Jewish refugee.

Looking for more books? The Assembly on Literature for Adolescents is an independent assembly of the National Council of Teachers of English (NCTE). Founded in November 1973, ALAN is made up of teachers and their students, authors, librarians, publishers, teacher educators, and others who are particularly interested in young adult literature. ALAN, which is self-governing, holds its annual meeting during NCTE's annual convention in November and publishes the *ALAN Review.* Its Web site (www.alan-ya.org) features authors and titles for adolescent readers. The books are reviewed monthly.

RESOURCES *for* TEACHERS

ENGLISH TEACHER PROFESSIONAL RESOURCES

National Council of Teachers of English, www.ncte.org. Our professional organization maintains this Web site that offers countless professional resources.

International Reading Association, www.reading.org. This professional organization's Web site is filled with resources to support adolescent readers.

Read, Write, Think, www.readwritethink.org. The National Council of Teachers of English and International Reading Association's cosponsored Web site features lessons, units, and professional resources for literacy educators.

WRITING INSTRUCTION

National Writing Project, www.nwp.org. The National Writing Project is a network of educators supporting writing instruction at all levels.

Atwell, N. (1998). *In the middle: New understandings about writing, reading, and learning.* Portsmouth, NH: Boynton/Cook. The seminal how-to book for a writer's workshop in middle school.

Atwell, N. (2002). *Lessons that change writers.* Portsmouth, NH: Heinemann. The binder and accompanying book contain mini-lesson materials for writing instruction.

Berne, J. (2008). *The writing-rich high school classroom: Engaging students in the writing workshop.* New York: Guilford Press. A valuable resource for establishing a writer's workshop in the high school classroom.

DiPrince, D., & Thurston, C. M. (2006). *Unjournaling: Daily writing exercises that are NOT personal, NOT introspective, NOT boring.* Fort Collins, CO: Cottonwood Press. Useful for getting students into the habit of writing.

Fletcher, R. (2007). *Boy writers: Reclaiming their voices.* Portland, ME: Stenhouse. Addresses the specific needs of boys in the writing classroom.

Fulwiler, T. (1987). *The journal book.* Portsmouth, NH: Boynton/Cook. Provides teaching strategies for journaling in the classroom.

Passman, R., & McKnight, K. (2007). *Teaching writing in the inclusive classroom: Strategies and skills for all students, grades 6–12.* San Francisco: Jossey-Bass. Specifically addressing the needs of both regular education and students with special needs in the inclusive classroom, the authors provide over fifty writing activities that create individualized writing experiences.

Weaver, C. (1996). *Teaching grammar in context.* Portsmouth, NH: Boynton/Cook. One of the most important works to develop strategies for teaching grammar within the context of writing rather than in isolation. See Weaver's other books on teaching grammar, *Lessons to Share on Teaching Grammar in Context* and *The Grammar Plan Book: A Guide to Smart Teaching.*

LITERATURE INSTRUCTION

All About Adult Literacy, www.adlit.org. A literacy resource for parents and educators of children in grades 4 through 12.

The New Literature Network, www.online-literature.com. Particularly useful for creating readers' theater scripts.

Shakespeare in Education, http://shakespeare.palomar.edu/educational.htm. Contains links to sites designed to teach Shakespeare over the Internet and in the classroom, as well as sites that contain educational material related to the teaching of Shakespeare.

Web English Teacher, www.webenglishteacher.com/litmain.html. Provides links to literature, e-texts, and lesson plans related to specific authors.

Appleman, D. *Critical encounters in high school English: Teaching literary theory to adolescents* (2nd ed.). New York: Teachers College Press. Provides discussion and strategies for teaching adolescents about literary theory.

Daniels, H. (2002). *Literature circles.* Portland, ME: Stenhouse. The seminal work that provided teachers with the information and strategies to put literature circles in the classroom.

Daniels, H., & Steinke, N. (2004). *Mini lessons for literature circles.* Portsmouth, NH: Heinemann. Contains many mini-lessons for literature circles that encourage adolescent students to become active and independent readers.

McKnight, K., & Berlage, B. (2008). *Teaching the literature classics in the inclusive classroom, grades 6–12*. San Francisco: Jossey-Bass. Contains strategies for all levels of readers when teaching the literature classics in the middle school or high school classroom.

Rosenblatt, L. (1996). *Literature as exploration* (5th ed.). New York: Modern Language Association. Every English teacher needs to read this text by the foundational theorist for reader response, Louise Rosenblatt.

Wilhelm, J. (2007). *"You gotta BE the book": Teaching engaged and reflective reading with adolescents* (2nd ed.). New York: Teachers College Press. In this must-read for English teachers, Jeff Wilhelm provides reminders that reading is productive, playful, and personally meaningful.

SUPPORTING ADOLESCENT READERS

Beers, K. (2002). *When kids can't read: What teachers can do: A guide for teachers 6–12*. Portsmouth, NH: Heinemann. Beers discovered when she began her teaching career as a middle school language arts teacher that some of the students could decode the words on the page but could not comprehend the text. This book is invaluable for teachers who want to help and support students as they develop reading comprehension skills.

Tovani, C. (2000). *I read it but I don't get it*. Portland, ME: Stenhouse. An accomplished teacher writes about meeting the reading needs at all levels in her adolescent students.

Wilhelm, J. (2002). *Action strategies for deepening comprehension*. New York: Scholastic. Provides motivating strategies at all stages of the reading process.

TEACHING ENGLISH LANGUAGE LEARNERS

Fisher, D., Rothenberg, C., & Frey, N. (2007). *Language learners in the English classroom*. Urbana, IL: National Council of Teachers of English. Provides strategies to support English language learners in a mainstreamed English classroom.

Kess, J. (2008). *The ESL/ELL teacher's book of lists*. San Francisco: Jossey-Bass. Huge book filled with helpful resources for English language learners.

VOCABULARY

Blachowicz, C., & Fisher, P. (2009). *Teaching vocabulary in all classrooms* (4th ed.). Needham Heights, MA: Allyn and Bacon. A comprehensive text that defines and illustrates the best strategies for teaching vocabulary.

Fisher, D., & Frey, N. (2008). *Word wise and content rich, grades 7–12: Five essential steps to teaching academic vocabulary*. Portsmouth, NH: Heinemann. Articulates strategies for teaching vocabulary at the middle and high school levels.

PROFESSIONAL JOURNALS

National Council of Teachers of English, *English Journal.* Primarily for high school teachers.

National Council of Teachers of English, *Voices in the Middle.* Primarily for middle school teachers.

International Reading Association, *Journal of Adolescent and Adult Literacy.*

Illinois Association of Teachers of English, *English Bulletin.*

References

CHAPTER ONE

Kuehn, M. W. (1992). *Notes plus.* Urbana, IL: National Council of Teachers of English.

McKnight, K. S., & Scruggs, M. (2008). *The Second City guide to improv in the classroom: Using improvisation to teach skills and boost learning.* San Francisco: Jossey-Bass.

Passman, R., & McKnight, K. S. (2007). *Teaching writing in the inclusive classroom: Strategies and skills for all students.* San Francisco: Jossey-Bass.

Wong, H., & Wong, R. (2009). *The first days of school: How to be an effective teacher* (4th ed.). Mountain View, CA: Harry K. Wong Publications.

CHAPTER TWO

Ames, R. A. (1990). Motivation and effective teaching. In B. F. Jones & L. Idol (Eds.), *Dimensions of thinking and cognitive instruction.* Mahwah, NJ: Erlbaum.

Burke, J. (2008). *Teacher's essential guide series: Classroom management.* New York: Scholastic.

Chapman, C., & King, R. (2003). *Differentiated assessment strategies: One tool doesn't fit all.* Thousand Oaks, CA: Corwin Press.

Gardner, H. (2005). *Multiple intelligences: New horizons in theory and practice.* New York: Basic Books.

Glasser, W. (1986). *Control theory in the classroom.* New York: Harper.

Kronenburg, C. (1992). *A positive approach to discipline* (unpublished manuscript). Bloomington, MN.

Lightfoot, P. (2006). *Student portfolios: A learning tool.* Charleston, SC: BookSurge Publishing.

New Teacher's Handbook (p. 25). (1988). New York: Impact II.

Paulsen, L., Paulsen, P., & Mayer, C. (1990). *What makes a portfolio a portfolio?* (prepublication draft).

Sprick, R. S. (2008). *Discipline in the secondary classroom: A positive approach to behavior management* (2nd ed.). San Francisco: Jossey-Bass.

Wayson, W. (1981). *Handbook for developing schools with good discipline.* Bloomington, IN: Phi Delta Kappa Commission on Discipline.

Wormelli, R. (2006). *Fair isn't always equal.* Portland, ME: Stenhouse.

CHAPTER THREE

Beers, K. (2002). *When kids can't read: What teachers can do: A guide for teachers 6–12.* Portsmouth, NH: Heinemann.

Chalmers, L. (1992). *Modifying curriculum for the special needs student in the regular classroom* (pp. 1–5). Moorhead, MN: Practical Press.

Fountas, I., & Pinnell, G. S. (2008). *Guiding readers and writers: Teaching comprehension, genre, and content literacy.* Portsmouth, NH: Heinemann.

Haaer, D., Klingner, J., & Aceves, T. (2010). *How to teach English language learners: Effective strategies from outstanding educators.* San Francisco: Jossey-Bass.

Kress, J. (2008). *The ESL/ELL teacher's book of lists* (2nd ed.). San Francisco: Jossey-Bass.

Lavoie, R. D. (1989). *Understanding learning disabilities: How difficult can this be?* (video). Greenwich, CT: Eagle Hill School Outreach.

Wilhelm, J. D. (2001). *Improving comprehension with think-aloud strategies: Modeling what good readers do.* New York: Scholastic.

Wilhelm, J. D. (2004). *Reading is seeing.* New York: Scholastic.

CHAPTER FOUR

Gillies, R. (2007). *Cooperative learning: Integrating theory and practice.* Thousand Oaks, CA: Sage.

Jacobs, G. (2002). *Teacher's sourcebook for cooperative learning: Practical techniques, basic principles, and frequently asked questions.* Thousand Oaks, CA: Corwin Press.

Johnson, D., Johnson, R., & Holubec, E. (1991). *Cooperation in the classroom.* Edina, MN: Interaction Book.

Marzano, R. (2001). *A handbook for classroom instruction that works.* Alexandria, VA: Association for Curriculum and Supervision.

CHAPTER FIVE

Adler, M., & Rougle, E. (2005). *Building literacy through classroom discussion.* New York: Scholastic.

Atwell, N. (1998). *In the middle: New understandings about reading, writing, and learning.* Portsmouth, NH: Boynton/Cook.

Beach, R. A. (2006). *Teaching literature to adolescents.* Mahwah, NJ: Erlbaum.

Borax, J. (1992). *"Brian's totally awesome vacation journal." Starting from scratch: A writing manual.* St. Paul, MN: Dialogue Assessment Project of the St. Paul Public Schools.

Brewster, M. (1988, October). Rooming with characters. *English Journal.*

Caddy, J. (1989). *I-referenced responses to writing* (unpublished manuscript). St. Paul, MN: COMPAS.

Daniels, H., & Zemelman, S. (1984). *A writing project: Training teachers of composition from kindergarten to college.* Portsmouth, NH: Heinemann Books.

Dittberner-Jax, N. (1992). Responding to writing: Special concerns. *Starting from scratch: A writing manual* (p. 51). St. Paul, MN: Dialogue Assessment Project of the St. Paul Public Schools.

Dunning, S., & Stafford, W. (1992). *Getting the knack.* Urbana, IL: NCTE.

England, D. (1986). Teaching writing process and determining grades. *Quarterly of the National Writing Project and Center for the Study of Writing.*

Gardner, H. (2005). *Multiple intelligences: New horizons in theory and practice.* New York: Basic Books.

Gere, A. R. (2005). *Writing on demand: Best practices and strategies for success.* Portsmouth, NH: Heinemann.

The NWEA direct assessment prompt collection. (1989). Salem, OR: Northwest Evaluation Association.

Passman, R., & McKnight, K. (2007). *Teaching writing in the inclusive classroom: Strategies and skills for all students.* San Francisco: Jossey-Bass.

CHAPTER SIX

Atwell, N. (1998). *In the middle: New understandings about reading, writing, and learning.* Portsmouth: NH: Boynton/Cook.

Daniels, H., & Steineke, N. (2003). *Mini lessons for literature circles.* Portsmouth, NH: Heinemann.

Gilbar, S. (Ed.). (1989). *The open door: When writers first learned to read.* Boston: David R. Godine.

Gorman, M. (2003). *Getting graphic! Using graphic novels to promote literacy with preteens and teens.* Santa Barbara, CA: Linworth Publishing.

Gunderlach, P. (1993). *Notes plus.* Urbana, IL: NCTE.

Israel, E. (1993, March). Showing mastery through performance. *English Journal.*

Judy, S. N., & Judy, S. J. (1983). *The English teacher's handbook: Ideas and resources for teaching English* (p. 111). Glenview, IL: Scott, Foresman and Company.

Paprocki, J. (1993, March). Poet-tees. *Notes plus* (p. 7). Urbana, IL: NCTE.

Rosenblatt, L. (1995). *Literature as exploration* (5th ed.). New York: Modern Language Association.

CHAPTER SEVEN

Beers, K., Probst, R. E., & Rief, L. (Eds.). (2007). *Adolescent literacy: Turning promise into practice.* Portsmouth, NH: Heinemann.

Gurian, M. (2002). *Boys and girls learn differently: A guide for teachers and parents.* San Francisco: Jossey-Bass.

Gurian, M. (2008). *Strategies for teaching boys and girls: Secondary level: A workbook for educators.* San Francisco: Jossey-Bass.

Hayes-Jacobs, H. (2006). *Active literacy across the curriculum: Strategies for reading, writing, speaking, and listening.* Larchmont, NY: Eye on Education.

Johnson, D., Johnson, R., & Holubec, E. (1991). *Cooperation in the classroom.* Edina, MN: Interaction Book Company.

Kozacik, M. (1989). Doodles and directions. *Substitute teachers' lesson plans, National Council of Teachers of English,* 5–6.

McKnight, K. S., & Scruggs, M. (2008). *The Second City guide to improv in the classroom: Using improvisation to teach skills and boost learning.* San Francisco: Jossey-Bass.

Mills, R. (2009). *NorthStar: Listening and speaking, level 3* (3rd ed.). Upper Saddle River, NJ: Pearson Education.

Urban, M. (1989, December). Video biographies: Reading, researching and recording. *English Journal.*

CHAPTER EIGHT

Considine, D. (2002, October). Putting the ME in MEdia literacy. *Middle Ground: The Magazine of Middle Level Education,* 15–21.

Gee, J. (2003). *What video games have to teach us about learning and literacy.* New York: Palgrave Macmillan.

McKnight, K. S., & Berlage, D. (2008). *Teaching the classics in the inclusive classroom.* San Francisco: Jossey-Bass.

National Council of Teachers of English (NCTE). (2008). Position statement. www.ncte.org/positions/statements/21stcentframework.

Navarro, M. (2005, October 23). Parents fret that dialing up interferes with growing up. *New York Times,* pp. 9, 10.

CHAPTER NINE

Grant, K., & Ray, J. (2009). *Home, school, and community collaboration: Culturally responsive family involvement.* Thousand Oaks, CA: Sage Publications.

National Council of Teachers of English. (2002). *More lesson plans for substitute teachers: Classroom-tested activities from the National Council of Teachers of English.* Urbana, IL: National Council of Teachers of English.

Index